PRAISE FOR

MILES FROM NOWH

"Real people in real places—Dayton Duncan celebrates an authentic American West where the power of story illuminates the power of homeland." —Terry Tempestt Williams

"A gifted observer and a terrific idea have come together in a real love match. . . . An insightful and entertaining book, troubling and funny and consistently illuminating."
—Elliott West, *Montana: The Magazine of Western History*

"A meticulously researched, wonderfully entertaining portrait of an America that most of us spy only from the window of a jet."
—*The Seattle Times*

"Through colorful prose and a conversational tone, Duncan vividly brings to life a territory of America unexplored by most people. He weaves in historical anecdotes about Western heroes and villains of the old frontier days. And he tells the stories of modern pioneers— and lets them tell their accounts—in a refreshingly non-judgmental way." —*The Christian Science Monitor*

"This beautiful, warm, inviting book demonstrates Dayton Duncan's superb understanding of the great gulf (in our nation and in our imagination) between 'here' and 'there,' 'then' and 'now.' It is a remarkable, at times unusually moving, story about all of us, as lonely and as dusty as the roads he has traveled, as dense and as familiar as the lives he expertly examined. The best compliment I can give is that Dayton Duncan *loves* his country."
—Ken Burns

"Sharply observed, literate travel writing that drives home just how big—and big-souled—this country really is."
—*Kirkus Reviews*

"Duncan is an engaging traveling companion . . . [as] he blends his contemporary encounters with historical anecdotes, some of them familiar and some of them quite fresh and absorbing . . . [He] writes about the land with a skill and warmth that brings its people alive."
—*The Kansas City Star*

"Duncan's eye for the right detail and his judicious use of statistics and historical facts make *Miles from Nowhere* well worth reading."
—*Outside Magazine*

PENGUIN BOOKS

MILES FROM NOWHERE

Born and raised in a small town in Iowa, Dayton Duncan earned a B.A. degree from the University of Pennsylvania. He has been a reporter, humor columnist, editorial writer, chief of staff to a governor, and press secretary for presidential campaigns. His books include *Out West: American Journey Along the Lewis and Clark Trail* and *Grass Roots: One Year in the Life of the New Hampshire Presidential Primary*. After living three years in Kansas while working on this book, he and his family returned to their home in Walpole, New Hampshire.

DAYTON DUNCAN

PENGUIN BOOKS

MILES FROM NOWHERE

In Search of the
American Frontier

PENGUIN BOOKS
Published by the Penguin Group
Penguin Books USA Inc., 375 Hudson Street,
New York, New York 10014, U.S.A.
Penguin Books Ltd, 27 Wrights Lane, London W8 5TZ, England
Penguin Books Australia Ltd, Ringwood, Victoria, Australia
Penguin Books Canada Ltd, 10 Alcorn Avenue, Toronto,
Ontario, Canada M4V 3B2
Penguin Books (N.Z.) Ltd, 182–190 Wairau Road, Auckland 10, New Zealand

Penguin Books Ltd, Registered Offices:
Harmondsworth, Middlesex, England

First published in the United States of America
by Viking Penguin, a division of Penguin Books USA Inc., 1993
Published in Penguin Books 1994

10 9 8 7 6 5 4 3 2 1

Photograph of Alex Joseph and his wives reproduced courtesy of Tom Smart.
All other photographs taken by the author.

THE LIBRARY OF CONGRESS HAS CATALOGUED THE HARDCOVER AS FOLLOWS:
Duncan, Dayton.
Miles from nowhere: in search of the American frontier/Dayton Duncan.
p. cm.
Includes bibliographical references and index.
ISBN 0-670-83195-6 (hc.)
ISBN 0 14 01.3122 1 (pbk.)
1. West (U.S.)—Description and travel—1981– . 2. Frontier and
pioneer life—West (U.S.)   3. West (U.S.)—Guidebooks.   4. West
(U.S.)—Social life and customs.   I. Title.
F595.3.D86   1993
917.804′33—dc20   92–5600

Printed in the United States of America
Set in New Aster
Designed by Kate Nichols
Map by Virginia Norey

To my pioneer family,
Dianne, Emmy,
and Will

Si-chom-pa Ka-gon (Old Woman of the Sea) came out of the sea with a sack filled with something and securely tied. Then she went to the home of the Shin-au-av brothers. . . . She delivered to them the sack and told them to carry it to the middle of the world and open it. . . . Shin-au-av-pa-vits (the elder) gave the sack to Shin-au-av-Skaits (the younger) and told him to do as Si-chom-pa Ka-gon had directed, and especially enjoined upon him that he must not open the sack lest some calamity should befall him.

As he proceeded, his curiosity overcame him and he untied the sack, when out sprang hosts of people who passed out on the plain shouting and running toward the mountain.

Then Tov-wots suddenly appeared being very angry. "Why . . . have you done this? I wanted these people to live in that good land to the east and here, foolish boy, you have let them out in a desert."

A Southern Paiute legend
collected and translated by
John Wesley Powell

The Contemporary Frontier

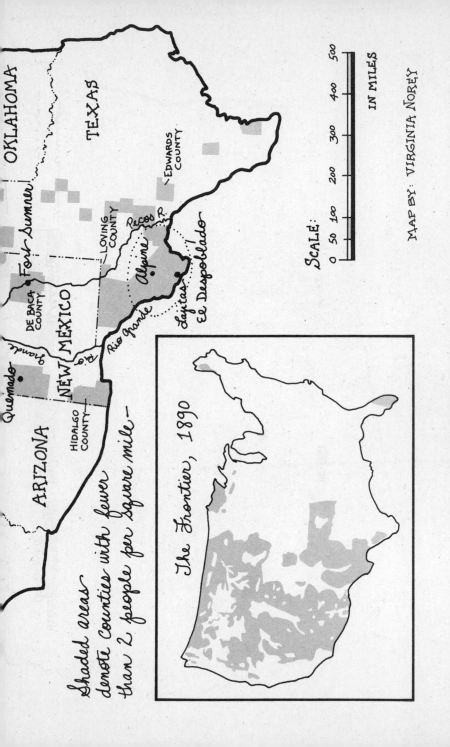

Shaded areas
denote counties with fewer
than 2 people per square mile—

The Frontier, 1890

OKLAHOMA

TEXAS

EDWARDS COUNTY

Fort Sumner

LOVING COUNTY

Pecos R.

Alpine

DE BACA COUNTY

Rio Grande

Lajitas
El Despoblado

NEW MEXICO

Rio Grande

Quemado

ARIZONA

HIDALGO COUNTY

SCALE:

0 50 100 200 300 400 500

IN MILES

MAP BY: VIRGINIA NOREY

ACKNOWLEDGMENTS

I wish to thank the following people for their contributions in making this book possible:

A. M. Rosenthal, who first suggested the topic to me in 1988.

Calvin Beale, at the U.S. Department of Agriculture's Economic Research Service, the guru of students of rural America, who generously shared information and statistics with me and guided me to some good stories.

Ernest Hebert, Charles Gusewelle, Bob Trebilcock, Jim Ronda, and Jim Robbins, who read initial drafts and offered advice for improvements.

Chuck Verrill, my agent, who worked beyond the call of duty on this project.

David Stanford and Roger Devine of Viking Penguin, who polished the rough edges off the manuscript.

All the people living miles from nowhere—too many to name—who opened up their homes and their lives to me.

American Demographics for help with the map.

Peter and Kate Goelz, good friends who encouraged us to move west of the Missouri River while I worked on this book and who looked after my family during my long absences on the road.

Dianne Kearns Duncan, my wife and frontline editor, and our daughter, Emmy, two Yankee ladies from New England who uprooted themselves and moved to Kansas with me for this book; and our son, Will, Kansas-born, who is the enduring legacy of this project.

Fairway, Kansas
August 1991

CONTENTS

INTRODUCTION: TRAVELS IN A CONESTOGA

THERE IS A PART OF AMERICA THAT EXISTS MILES from nowhere. People live there, but not many. So few, and sprinkled so thinly over such vast territory, that even by standards of the covered wagon days this land would still be considered unsettled. It lies within the boundaries of the Lower 48, yet in many respects it is a different country. Counties the size of states might have no doctor. A "town" that appears as a dot and a name on the map might turn out to be even less—an empty, abandoned building. Or it might consist of a post office, a gas station, a small grocery store, and a one-family residence—all under one roof. Out there, a minister might drive all Sunday to preach at four different services, and see a total of thirty parishioners. The neighborhood bar might be 75 miles away. A schoolhouse might be made from logs, have one room and one teacher, and serve only a handful of students. Several of them might arrive for classes on horseback.

Spend months traveling across this territory and you'll be stopped more often by cattle drives than stoplights. During long stretches, your digital radio will race automatically through the numbers, hissing as it searches endlessly and in vain for a signal strong enough to lock onto. Road signs with messages like NO SERVICES NEXT 90 MILES will lose their shock value, you'll see so many of them. Distances between one ranch and another, let alone between one town and the next, will stretch your conceptions of the term "neighbor." As you hurtle down a road at night, yard lights at ranch houses and the occasional twinkling cluster of lights from a small town will punctuate the total darkness only infrequently, haphazardly. You'll think you've reached the galaxy's outer limits and are about to enter deep space.

It has been called many names: the Empty Quarter, the Margins, the Yonlands, America's Outback, the Lands Nobody Wanted, and the Last, the Remnant, or the Surviving Frontier. For more than a hundred years, people whose sole goal was to scurry across as quickly as possible have referred to it as godforsaken, as in "*Who* would want to live in that godforsaken . . . ?" Others call it a forgotten region, but in truth it has never been well known and you can't forget something you never knew. It has just been ignored. Even "virtually uninhabited," the term most often applied to it, is a dismissive phrase defining the place not by what it is or by what it has, but by what it seems to lack: people.

But it *is* inhabited. Someone does live there. And those people are the answer to the question "Who would want to live here?" If you take the time to stop and ask, and if you phrase the question less boorishly, they'll tell you why. Stay long enough and they'll tell you other things. They'll probably recite the poem, in one of its many versions, that their pioneer parents or grandparents tacked to the wall, a few short lines distilling their history and meant to be understood as part lament, part defiant boast, and part cosmic joke:

50 miles from water
40 miles from wood
30 miles from nowhere
And I gone there for good

They'll tell you about the hardship and struggle it often requires to survive in this place, but they'll tell you about the joys as well—about feeling secure enough to leave their homes, their cars and sometimes even their businesses unlocked when they're gone; about a sense of community strong enough that moments of personal success or grief, like high school graduations or funerals, become shared experiences that heighten the sense of triumph or diffuse the sorrow; about a feeling of freedom that they say springs from what in earlier times was called "elbow room"; about the daily pleasures of witnessing nature essentially unalloyed by the intrusions of man, like a gentle summer morning when the fresh dew on the grass almost invites you to join the deer grazing on the field outside your back door, or the awesome silence of a desert night, or even the stark and humbling beauty of a winter storm you know will keep you homebound for days.

They'll tell you the life they lead is different, perhaps not as different as in the old days of the frontier, but certainly unlike life in most of America in the late twentieth century. And they'll tell you the rest of the country doesn't understand them, always condescends to them, and never consults them when decisions are made about what should happen to the land they occupy.

Before you leave they'll also tell you the special name *they've* given to this place. They call it home.

ONE HUNDRED YEARS AGO A YOUNG, RELATIVELY UN- known history professor from Wisconsin pronounced America's frontier closed.

Frederick Jackson Turner believed that what distinguished the United States from other nations had been its settlement experience. In an address to historians gathered at the World's Columbian Exposition in Chicago in 1893, Turner contended that America's frontier was unlike others in history: it was not a static, fortified line separating one densely populated country from another, but an ever-moving zone, the "meeting point between savagery and civilization." With each advance of settlement westward from the Atlantic coast, as pioneers confronted the primitive conditions of the frontier, a growing nation had been compelled to adapt, build, and reinvent its institutions. "American social development," he said, "has been continually beginning over again on the frontier."

For individuals, Turner believed the frontier was also the "line of most rapid and effective Americanization." From people of varied backgrounds and homelands, the recurrent frontier process had molded a singular "composite nationality," which he described as inquisitive and acquisitive, pragmatic and inventive, restless and energetic, exuberant and boisterous, but most of all fiercely independent—an individualism, born of the frontier environment, that fostered freedom and democracy and was in turn fostered by them.

At the time, Turner's frontier thesis was a novel interpretation, countering the prevailing theories of historians who focused either on the East Coast, where most of them lived, or on tracing the "germs" of America's democratic institutions to the Teutonic tribal councils of the Black Forest. (*Germanic Origins of New England Towns* by Herbert Baxter Adams, the leader of the American Historical Association in the early 1890s, neatly combined both preoccupations under one cover.) By the turn of the century, however, Turner had successfully redirected his profession's gaze westward. He emerged as the nation's preeminent historian. Many parts of his theory have since been challenged and roundly disproved, especially the notion that the frontier was a democratizing influence on the nation. His idea that 1890 marked the closing of the frontier and the end of an era, now at the center of a larger academic and public debate over the nation's heritage, has nevertheless remained the conventional perspective of America's development.

Turner had relied on the census of 1890 to transform his theories—which he had been developing for several years—into the frontier's eulogy. Previous censuses had depicted a frontier line that from the time of the first federal census in 1790 had marched steadily westward every ten years. By the latter part of the 1800s, the government estimated, this line was proceeding toward the Pacific Ocean at a clip of seventy to seventy-five feet a day.

The frontier line was based on population density. Explaining the government's methodology in 1882, census geographer Henry Gannett wrote that "an arbitrary line must be drawn somewhere beyond which the country must be considered as unsettled, although it may not be absolutely without inhabitants. Such a line may be properly taken as to exclude regions having less than two inhabitants to a square mile. All the country outside this line may fairly be considered as unsettled territory, peopled, if at all, by a few scattering hunters, prospectors, and cattle herders."

In the official parlance of those days, if the "petty population" of an unsettled area grew enough to place it on the settled side of the frontier line, the region was "redeemed from wilderness and brought into the service of man." No one at the time doubted that every square mile of the United States would eventually be settled. It was just a matter of time, some even thought foreordained. Redemption was the nation's manifest destiny.

But when Robert Porter, the superintendent of the centennial census in 1890, looked at his bureau's most recent population-density maps to prepare his report, he confronted a problem his predecessors had never faced in telling the nation how much farther west the frontier line had moved. The nation's settlement pattern was no longer cooperating.

The maps were color-coded to display different densities of population. Unsettled areas with fewer than two people per square mile were white; settled areas were various shades of sepia pink. The rising tide of population that had swelled in so orderly a fashion, upon reaching the most arid parts of the West, had evaporated into discrete pools. Many of the newly settled areas were represented by distinct enclaves rather than extensions from the frontier line of 1880. The western half of Porter's new map looked as if someone had splashed drops of pink ink on the page. A neat and tidy description of the American frontier's location would be impossible.

Rather than struggle with this dilemma, Porter declared victory and retreated: "Up to and including 1880 the country had a frontier of settlement, but at present the unsettled area has been so broken into by isolated bodies of settlement that there can hardly be said to be a frontier line. In the discussion of its extent, its westward movement, etc., it can not, therefore, any longer have a place in the census reports."

It's worth noting that Porter's comment, tacked onto the end of a census bulletin in 1891, did not say the frontier had closed, died, or disappeared. It said the previous conception of a single frontier *line* was now outdated and the Census Bureau simply wasn't going to bother with it anymore. The statement could easily have moldered in the dust of statistical and demographic arcana had it not been for Turner, who came across the bulletin a year later, slipped it into his files, and in 1893 resurrected it from obscurity to add a dash of topical eventfulness to his theories.

Turner's address, "The Significance of the Frontier in American History," opened by quoting the census bulletin. Then the young historian added his own opinion of what it really meant. "This brief official statement," he intoned, "marks the closing of a great historic movement."

The speech would become required reading for generations of history students. Accordingly, Porter's words were elevated into the best-known, most momentous two sentences ever written by a Census bureaucrat. With or without the government's consent, its official seal of approval had been forever stamped on the closing of the frontier.

"And now," Turner concluded, "four centuries from the discovery of America, at the end of a hundred years of life under the Constitution, the frontier has gone, and with its going has closed the first period of American history."

A CENTURY LATER, THE CENSUS OF 1990 COUNTED nearly 250 million people living in the United States, a four-fold increase from the 62 million residents in 1890. The nation's overall population density, at 17.8 people per square mile then, is now 70.5 people per square mile. In an age of interstates and jetliners, suburban sprawls and shopping malls, computer chips and satellite dishes, the notion of an American frontier has receded even further from the nation's consciousness, seemingly surviving primarily in romanticized Westerns or their reruns, themselves a generation out of fashion.

Alaska—huge, remote, straddling the Arctic Circle, with roughly one inhabitant per square mile—might occasionally be cited as a place where a frontier still exists. But a frontier within the Lower 48 states? No, those days supposedly ended long ago.

And yet, by the same, arbitrary criterion the Census Bureau once used to define the frontier and pinpoint its location, such a frontier survives. In 1990, on the centennial of the "closing of the frontier," the census found 132 counties within fifteen western states in the Lower 48 that still had fewer than two people per square mile.*

Considered together, those 132 counties comprise 13 percent of the nation's contiguous landmass—401,781 square miles, an area a little larger than everything east of the Mississippi River and north of the Mason-Dixon line. Inhabiting this expanse are 488,796 people, a population about the size of Pittsburgh's. The number of homeless Americans in the rest of the nation is greater by half than the number of people with homes in the contemporary frontier.

If Robert Porter were momentarily brought back to life and shown a current population-density map with areas under two people per square mile displayed again in white and the rest in pink, his first reaction would be that not much has changed since 1890. The map's "unsettled" area would be only marginally smaller than it was a century ago.

Even more strikingly, this contemporary frontier appears in essentially the same location as it did on Porter's map: the deserts of Utah and Nevada and southeastern Oregon; the arid southwestern corner of Texas; Nebraska's Sand Hills; scattered areas of Colorado, New Mexico, and Wyoming; the Death Valley region of California; Idaho's mountainous River of No Return area; and clusters on the Great Plains of Montana, the two Dakotas, Kansas, and the panhandles of Texas and Oklahoma.

A cursory look at economic statistics would also tell him that, just as Henry Gannett once said, it is still predominantly "peopled, if at all, by a few scattering hunters, prospectors, and cattle herders."

Magically transported across a hundred years for this glimpse, Porter might star in a movie named not *Back to the Future* but *Forward to the Past.*

---

* Alaska has been more than adequately chronicled in recent years as a "last frontier" and is not within the purview of this book. In 1890, my benchmark for comparison, it was not even yet an organized territory; the state still does not have counties, but seventeen of its twenty-five jurisdictions have fewer than two persons per square mile. The same applies to a small sliver of Yellowstone National Park in Montana, a jurisdictional anomaly which the Census Bureau enumerates separately. With those additions, the United States has 150 counties or county equivalents below the old Census Bureau standard of "settled."

As the nineteenth century ended, cities with populations over 250,000 could be counted on two hands. Twice as many Americans lived in rural settings as in towns of more than 2,500 residents. And yet areas with densities under two people per square mile were already considered below the threshold of "civilization." What, then, are we to make of such sparsity on the eve of the twenty-first century, when 78 percent of the nation lives an urban existence?

Fewer than two people per square mile. It seems not just an abstraction, but an incomprehensible abstraction in modern times. It is Los Angeles County, the nation's most populous, with 8,000 people instead of 8,863,164; Chicago's Cook County with 1,900 residents rather than 5.1 million; all five boroughs of New York City with 600 inhabitants. It is 15,648 people spread across the state of Massachusetts. It is 6 million people in all of the Lower 48 states—the population of Indiana spread from Atlantic to Pacific, Mexican border to Canadian.

But America's contemporary frontier is not an abstraction. It's real. You don't have to cross any borders to find it, explore it, meet its people.

It is immense and widely dispersed, however, so the journey there will take some time. You'll have to travel by land: commercial airlines fly to where people are, not to where they aren't. But the contemporary frontier can be reached. Far from the interstates and the cities they connect, far from the land of franchises and strip development and tract houses, even beyond the small but regularly spaced farm communities and their row crops is where a land-hungry nation nibbled but lost its normal appetite. Out there is the frontier, miles from nowhere.

I TRAVELED ACROSS THE CONTEMPORARY FRONTIER in a GMC Suburban, a huge beast of a vehicle that looks like a station wagon on steroids. Most states consider it a truck. It was five years old, already had 75,000 miles on its odometer, and was pocked with rust spots when I bought it, but it had the features I thought I would need: enough space inside to hold my supplies and allow me to stretch out at night if there was no place else to sleep; high clearance and four-wheel drive for rough back roads and bad weather and treacherous terrain; and an oversized fuel tank that would allow me to cover 500 miles between filling stations despite poor gas mileage. A late-twentieth-century adaptation of the prairie schooner. I called it the *Conestoga*.

It came with some extras I originally thought superfluous but which I grew to appreciate over a year's travels. Power windows let me air out my living quarters with the flick of a few switches while on the move, or batten down the hatches when I was on the downwind side and about to meet another vehicle along some gravel road. I didn't use the air conditioning much, but it came in handy on hot desert stretches when the other alternatives were suffocating from heat or suffocating from dust. I even surprised myself and ended up using the cruise control. Although my itinerary was the virtual opposite of most modern travelers—I was hurrying across more populated places to get to the less populated ones—many of the more than 30,000 miles I logged were on straight highways that would have invited a driver, lost in thought as I often am behind a steering wheel, into unsafe speeds. The cruise control kept me legal.

The *Conestoga* also had a good sound system. Its radio scanned on its own for a signal, a feature that probably saved me from either a bad back or an accident from hunching constantly over a dial in search of the one station available in the more remote spots. A tape deck filled in when even one station wasn't available, which was often.

By some quirk of the atmosphere on a winter night in eastern Montana, when mine seemed to be the only vehicle on the road in the continent and the white lights on the horizon never got any closer because they were stars defining the curvature of the earth, the radio pulled in some station from Los Angeles. It was broadcasting a traffic report for the evening rush hour: the freeways apparently were all clogged. The contrast between my situation and those of my fellow travelers, gridlocked in America's most populous county, struck me as absurdly funny, a joke I could share only with the Buddha-like face of the full moon lifting over the prairie behind me. I also couldn't help but feel smug and superior—probably the same way those Angelenos on the jammed freeway would have reacted to a radio report that out in Powder River County, where I was, the closest McDonald's is a hundred miles away.

In western Nebraska one late-spring afternoon, I was about to turn southwest, toward a sky roiling with menacing clouds. A quick scan picked up a local station interrupting its broadcast, the audio portion of ABC's network television news, with a tornado sighting. Adequately warned, I headed southeast instead, toward Kansas and home, and kept from being transported to Oz.

Along the Rio Grande in west Texas I listened to a lot of Mexican stations whose deejays seemed to shout across the studio at a microphone with its echo chamber switch on. Near some Indian reservations, I heard news reports in native languages—mesmerizing strings of indecipherable words punctuated by a brief "George Bush" or "Saddam Hussein" or "Bureau of Indian Affairs." Market reports from the feedlots and commodity exchanges, broadcast repeatedly on Anglo stations, were in my language but equally unintelligible. Some stations in rural areas featured regular reviews of movie videos, reflecting the fact that their last movie theater had closed a long time ago. Mostly, I listened to a lot of country-western music.

The four-wheel drive wasn't necessary very often, but when it was, it was *very* necessary. In Lake County, Oregon, my map showed a road leading through the Lost Forest, a stand of ponderosa pines and large junipers growing inexplicably amidst sand dunes in an area that receives half the rainfall such species normally require. Both the dunes and the trees seemed out of place in this location, as if God were holding them in reserve for a future seacoast. The road in was good enough, but it quickly degenerated into a trail, which then split into several paths without any signs saying which one led out the other side. Rather than retrace my route, I picked one path and went forward—at a top speed of about five miles an hour. An hour and a half later I was lost and stuck in a drift, up to my axles in sand so fine that if you dropped a dime you'd cough from the dust it would raise. The closest town was 30 miles away; the sun was setting. The four-wheel drive and a lot of gentle rocking back and forth finally got me through.

Other times I needed the extra traction because of the weather. I ran into a couple of blizzards on the northern Plains and a freak ice storm in early spring on the panhandles of Oklahoma and Texas; I was able to keep moving, although toward what I wasn't sure, given the visibility. A "scenic shortcut" I took on someone's recommendation, from Yellow Pine to Stanley, Idaho, the morning after a six-inch snowfall in October, turned out to be four hours of unpaved, unplowed mountain roads—up and down across the gabled roof of the continent.

No one in his right mind would have been on those roads in those conditions. I had to back down a mountainside to accommodate two huge trucks on their way to the gold mines near Yellow Pine, encountered eleven other vehicles (mostly elk hunters) and a mail truck, and had a near collision with a Toyota pickup on a steep slope. It was driven by a man who had been repairing a reservoir dam deep in the forests for the last five months and was in a hurry to get out before the snows locked him in for the winter. With chains and rocks, we kept his truck from slipping over the precipice as he edged around the *Conestoga*. When we were done and ready to proceed our separate ways, he caught sight of my Kansas plates and shook his head. On another such shortcut, weaving between the eerie salmon-colored buttes of the Valley of the Gods in San Juan County, Utah, the rock road I was following crossed two streams. Normally, they're dry and easy to ford. On the day I was there, they were flowing with the muddy runoff from a rainstorm on the higher elevations. My only way out was through the water and the mud. Without the four-wheel drive, in any of those situations inconvenience would have been the least of my worries. Actual survival might have become an issue.

The sparsely settled counties of the contemporary frontier are found in places of climatic extremes. I drove through cold and winds so fierce that the *Conestoga*'s heater couldn't keep up with them, and through heat so intense the air conditioner was useless. Even in nice weather, signs along the road indicated nature's danger: in Wyoming and eastern Colorado I saw iron gates that can be swung across major highways to close them during winter storms and high winds; in southwest Texas, where the minor highways dip into the dry riverbeds instead of bridging them, there are flood-gauge poles with markings up to seven feet high; in Alpine County, California, near the ridge of the Sierra Nevadas, sticks rise at least eight feet above the road shoulder so that snowplows will know where the sides of the pavement are in midwinter. Dust storms in Texas and eastern Oregon forced me to drive with my headlights on at midday.

I had one breakdown, a blowout on a rough road on a desolate mesa in southeastern Utah. During the hour it took to unload a spare and put it on, only one car went by—a tourist from Australia who stopped for directions. A hubcap bounced off in a small town in Meagher County, Montana. I hadn't noticed it, but a local man tracked me down at a café to return it to me. On U.S. Highway 50 across central Nevada, a 250-mile stretch of two-lane, punctuated by only two towns and billed as the "Loneliest Highway in America," it was my turn to help. A pickup/camper had its hood up and a sheet with "Please" written on it flapping in the wind over the back door. The truck was owned by a retired couple from Reno and its wheel bearings had burned out. They were on their way to Illinois to pick up their RV, which someone had stolen a year earlier before being caught when he tried to trade it in on a Corvette. "It wasn't much—just our life savings," said the wife. They asked me to report their situation to the nearest police station, which I did, 35 miles farther down the road. That same day, the radio reported that a section of Highway 50 next to a practice bombing range had been closed to traffic while authorities checked whether a bomb on the pavement was a live round or a dud.

Across the many miles of my journey, I saw only three hitchhikers, all along the interstates I rarely traveled. But I did see a lot of wildlife on or near the roadside: enough deer, antelope, elk, coyotes, eagles, and hawks to stop counting; a few roadrunners and javelinas (peccaries); one fox, one bobcat, one rattlesnake, and one tarantula so gargantuan it would have wrecked my front-end alignment if I'd hit it. In the Sand Hills of Nebraska it seemed like there was a box turtle on the pavement every other mile. That none of them had been squashed was, I decided, a reflection of both the sparsity of traffic and the polite consideration of the few drivers I met, all of whom waved to me as we passed.

Road-killed critters were relatively uncommon throughout my trip—deer mostly, but occasional dogs, sheep, calves, birds, and indistinguishable lumps of fur and flesh being picked at by crows. One exception was in Glasscock County, Texas, a parched landscape where only cholla cactus and mesquite seem to thrive. I counted twelve deer, one eagle, and one sheep dead in the ditch along a 30-mile stretch of highway. The carnage seemed to begin and end at the county lines. In some of the places I visited, the cars and pickups had metal grille guards mounted on their front bumpers to protect the headlights and front end from deer jumping into their path at night. A goat rancher in the hill country of Edwards County, Texas, told me he had once hit five deer driving home from a rodeo about 70 miles away, "but I had a good grille guard so it didn't slow me down none."

As things turned out, I used the *Conestoga* as my hotel on wheels only a handful of times. One reason was the weather. The back end of a car gets mighty uncomfortable on a subzero night; in summer, it was sweltering, not to mention the thick accretion of dust that settled over everything. Another reason was hospitality. In many places—particularly those where no motels were available—people often offered me a cot in the bunkhouse, a bed in a guest room, or a floor upon which to unroll my bag. But the main reason was the comparatively cheap motels and hotels I found: about twenty dollars a night on average. I manufactured other reasonable justifications. The motel owner often served as a good initial contact in a small community; a phone in a room was helpful in lining up the next day's interviews or in providing someone a number where they could reach me; a table and a light made it easier to compile the notes I had babbled into my tape recorder during the day. In truth, however, it was the prospect of a warm bed at night and a hot shower in the morning at prices I could afford that lured me back most evenings. The *Conestoga* became my overnight lodging of last resort, and I used it less often than I had anticipated.

There was more variety among the establishments I patronized than you might expect in such sparsely settled regions. On a particularly frigid night in Broadus, Montana, the motel owner advised me that I'd have to turn on the electric baseboard heater in the room and it would "take a while" to warm things up. I sat on the floor, as close as I could get to the heater, wearing my parka and gloves for two hours before daring to undress and jump under the icy sheets. Halfway through the night I woke up drenched in sweat, turned down the thermostat, and went back to bed, only to wake up a few hours later freezing again. On the other hand, in both Big Timber, Montana, and in Marathon, Texas, old hotels had been painstakingly restored and turned into fancy bed-and-breakfasts, with restaurants serving fine food. The one in Big Timber even had saunas on the second floor, as well as the greatest selection of exquisite pies I've ever come across in a lifetime of pie expeditions. At a motel in Loa, Utah, the office was the family's living room—a teenager registered me while talking to her boyfriend on the phone—and a sign in the front yard said they also sold nightcrawlers.

In some towns in Texas and the Southwest, motels frequently proclaimed themselves as "American owned and operated." This turned out to be a coded message: that the competition was owned and operated by someone who had recently immigrated from another country, usually India or Pakistan, and therefore presumably would be unacceptable. I always took it as a signal to search out the immigrant-owned motel and stay there—they were always just as clean, often cheaper, and run by people who rightfully considered themselves to be as American as their neighbors. One such motel, in Inyo County, California, was constructed from barracks that had been part of the Manzanar internment camp for Japanese-Americans during World War II.

Sometimes choosing a place to stay involved no choice at all: there was only one available. West of Death Valley I paid fifty dollars at a motel without a telephone (not just in the room but in the whole establishment), without a television set, and, at least on the morning I woke up, without hot water in the shower. Coffee and orange juice cost three bucks; gasoline was more than two dollars a gallon. If the service had been surly instead of friendly, I would have thought I was in New York City.

My most memorable night in the *Conestoga* was next to the Anasazi ruins at the Hovenweep National Monument in Utah. I had been on a string of bad luck for several days, ever since losing my favorite pocket knife. I had fallen during a hike and banged up a leg pretty badly; had been stood up by a couple of people who had promised to meet me for interviews; and then had the flat tire on my way to Hovenweep, which is a Ute Indian word for "deserted valley." Alan Whalon, the monument's superintendent, filled me in about the Anasazi, whose culture reached its peak with their cliff dwellings and stone towers on the Colorado Plateau about seven hundred years ago, before those early people mysteriously abandoned their settlements and essentially disappeared. Fearing and respecting the spirits left behind, the Navajos in the area generally steer clear of the ruins, he said, but a lot of white people create a problem by illegally ransacking them for relics. He told a few spooky anecdotes and then advised me to drive the next day to the nearest tire shop—about 50 miles away—for a new tire. A flat spare, he said, is a "cosmic weakness" inviting more trouble. (I didn't dare tell him my lost knife had already exposed me.) "Murphy *lives* out there," he said, gesturing to the dark void of the desert outside his door and directing me to my campsite on the edge of a canyon filled with old cliff dwellings. Late that night, a fierce wind suddenly picked up across the mesa. It wailed and whistled through the ruins, bent the junipers prostrate, and rocked the *Conestoga* with its gusts. Bursts of white lightning, too distant for thunder, illuminated the landscape as if some angry god were flashing snapshots of a crime scene. I didn't sleep much. At dawn I headed directly for the tire store and got there before it opened.

Early on in my travels, I discovered another, unintended advantage to my choice of vehicle. Garfield County, Montana, my first stop, set the pattern. Its one car dealership, the Pioneer Garage, is a Chevy franchise. "We probably have more Suburbans per capita than any other county in America," one resident told me. "Ford people have to go to Forsyth," in another county. After a year of visiting the other most sparsely settled counties, I would expand that boast beyond Garfield County. Their name to the contrary, Suburbans seemed to be the unofficial Official Vehicle of the Contemporary Frontier. Intangibly, the *Conestoga* helped me fit in with my surroundings. It made me a little less of a stranger. It also provided this assurance: if some "cosmic weakness" caused a serious accident, there might not be a hospital nearby for me but at least my companion wouldn't have to be towed a hundred miles into the next county for repairs.

BESIDES HAVING A LOT OF SUBURBANS WITHOUT ANY suburbia (or urbia), the counties I went to revealed other patterns.

Which is not to say that each county with fewer than two inhabitants per square mile is a carbon copy of the others. As with the motel and hotel accommodations I experienced, there was an unexpected diversity among the counties. Some of them encompass pristine wildernesses, jaw-dropping scenery, last refuges from the ceaseless grasping of mankind to lay a heavy hand on the land; others have been not just touched but scarred forever. The nation's cleanest air has been measured in the contemporary frontier; also the highest incidence of airborne particulates and the highest levels of radioactive fallout. There are sand formations made by the Creator over the millennia, and some created in a decade by plow-happy farmers; the hemisphere's largest manmade forest, and some open pits that once were mountains. The highest elevation in the contiguous states is in one of these counties;

so is the lowest. Some of the West's largest reserves of unspoiled, untapped fresh water, as well as places where the water is either gone or ruined. The country's hottest and driest spots, also occasionally its coldest. I visited some counties that are essentially vertical and all forest, some that are horizontal and treeless, and some that combine it all. I stood in alpine glades near the snow-melt birthplaces of major rivers like the Rio Grande, the Missouri, the Salmon, the North Platte, and the Green; and in blistering deserts where rivers disappear after choking to death on sand and rock and salt. Going to the places with the fewest people took me to the counties with the most beef cows, the most ewes, the most goats, the most cropland in use, and the most cropland idled under a federal subsidy program. I saw houses owned by some of the nation's wealthiest people, who travel in and out by private jet; and I saw mud-walled homes without electricity or running water whose impoverished owners still rely on one horsepower to get around. So there was plenty of variety.

But certain characteristics, issues, and themes kept reappearing. Although they showed up in different manifestations and with different emphasis, many basic elements were the same.

Of the 132 counties in the contiguous states with fewer than two people per square mile, all but one lie in the broad western belt of land between the 98th meridian and the Sierra Nevada and Cascade mountain ranges. (Kenedy County, Texas, the sole exception, has the 98th meridian virtually as its western border.) This is the land of little rain. Average annual precipitation in most of the region is less than 20 inches, less than 10 inches in some parts. By comparison, the Midwest receives 20 to 40 inches of rainfall a year and most of the East gets 40 to 60 inches; the sodden northern Pacific coast, where the mountains capture the moisture from the ocean's prevailing winds before casting a long "rain shadow" across the deserts to the east, gets more than 60 inches. The few spots in the semiarid and arid West that experience more reliable and sufficient precipitation are the spots where it does the least good for traditional settlement patterns: on the highest elevations and steepest slopes of the Rockies and other mountains.

This dry reality had several repercussions as white settlers moved westward and tried to impose their civilization on the indigenous ones they replaced. Agricultural methods that had been developed farther east failed outright in the West and had to be adjusted. Dryland farms grew their crops in alternate years and therefore needed at least twice the acreage for the same production levels. Irrigation permitted some traditional farming, but at greater cost and only in relatively thin belts along rivers or over aquifers. Raising livestock emerged as the predominant agricultural activity, but in very different proportions of animal-to-acre than back where the rain was plentiful and the grass was thicker and greener. Other economic endeavors—mining and lumbering and trapping, and later, oil drilling and tourism—tended either to cluster people in enclaves or sprinkle them lightly across the land.

Even the cities that grew up in the West, where enough water could be found to sustain them, represented an adaptation to the climate and terrain. They were fewer in number and surrounded by less densely settled areas than their counterparts in other parts of the nation. As they continued to grow, the extra water they required came at the expense of the surrounding areas. The result has been variously called an oasis, archipelago, or hydraulic society: a concentration of people in large settlements that suck up the water and residents around them. Counterintuitively, this pattern has turned the dry West into America's proportionately most urbanized region, surrounded by its least populated land.

The counties comprising the contemporary frontier are scattered throughout this territory of the West. In a region characterized by dryness, rough terrain, harsh weather swings, formidable mountains, or long distances between urban areas, these counties are usually the driest, roughest, harshest, most inaccessibly mountainous, or farthest from the cities. For those reasons, they were often the places initially passed over during the century-long, sea-to-sea settlement boom that lasted from the nation's founding until and beyond Turner's declaration of the frontier's "closing." For the same reasons, they remain today the Lower 48's most sparsely settled areas. A few are gaining population; most are losing, or barely maintaining their minimal level.

People in these regions have always had to adapt to weather and terrain, but the counties of the contemporary frontier have made a further adaptation—to their unique paucity of people. Health care, education, religion, politics, law and order, transportation, communication, sense of community, sense of self, even the act of finding a mate—virtually every human institution and activity demonstrates the impact of few people and long miles. The very sparsity of people makes life different.

In fact, life in these counties is more distinct from that in the urban West than the urban West's is from the rest of the country's. A greater gulf exists between life in, say, Montana's Garfield County and Billings, the nearest city, than between life in Billings and other cities its size, like Utica, New York, or Tallahassee, Florida. And there is even a distinct difference between conditions in Garfield County and those in the rural counties of, say, eastern North Dakota or central Kansas where the population density is still an uncrowded 10 people per square mile. Rural Iowa teems with people by comparison.

Because the counties of the contemporary frontier were often among the last to experience white settlement, their connection to their frontier past is shorter and stronger. The pioneer experience is not a remote history lesson to a good number of their inhabitants. And in physical appearance these counties conform to the popular image of what the old West looked like, partly because so many television series and movies, from "The Lone Ranger" to *Dances With Wolves*, were filmed there.

But the old frontier and its modern version, I would learn, are not the same. Time and the advance of technology have changed these remote places—changed why people live there, how they live there, even how they die there.

Traveling on the centennial of the census that marked the "end of the frontier," I was interested in those changes, as much in the historical differences and connections to the past as I was in learning about present-day life. The timing also made it appropriate to consider larger issues. *Did* the frontier "close" a hundred years ago? Besides the past and present of these places, what about their future? What will happen and who will decide what will happen? A century ago, the question was, When will these counties grow enough in population to be considered "civilized" and "redeemed from wilderness and brought into the service of man"? Today, the questions might be, Why didn't they grow with the rest of the nation? Will the sparsely settled counties, most of them losing population, keep on having fewer and fewer people until they are redeemed *into* wilderness?

IN THE SAND HILLS OF NEBRASKA A RANCHER TOLD
me a story that exemplifies how vast the chasm is between the lives of
most modern Americans and those of residents of the contemporary
frontier.

The Sand Hills comprise one of America's most singular and con-
tradictory landscapes. Huge dunes, some of them 400 feet high and
20 miles long, spread across nearly 20,000 square miles of northern
Nebraska—the largest sand dune area in the Western Hemisphere.
This sand sea, however, has been more or less stabilized over thousands
of years by a natural grass cover. Imagine the drifting dunes of "Law-
rence of Arabia" with a coarse beard of prairie grasses, and you can
begin to see it in your mind. The Sand Hills also happen to lie atop
the immense Ogallala aquifer, close enough to its surface, in fact, that
many of the interdunal valleys are lush wetlands.

Plains Indian tribes once contested for the region as a summer
buffalo hunting ground. White people pretty much skirted around it
as much as possible. Most took one look at the trackless, treeless, sandy
hills, assumed things were even sandier and drier in the interior, and
moved on somewhere else. In the late 1870s, however, cowboys pursuing cattle that a blizzard had driven deep into the Sand Hills were
astonished to discover large herds that had been surviving there for
years—mavericks that had fattened and prospered on their own,
thanks to the region's grasses and watering holes. As one sign still
proclaims outside the town of Arthur, Nebraska, this seemed to be
"God's Cow Country."

Between 1900 and 1920, when the government offered enlarged
homestead parcels on the assumption that with the proper incentives
the hills could be farmed, the region's population briefly doubled. It
topped out just above two people per square mile in 1920 before col-
lapsing in the face of the drought of the 1930s and the realization that,
whether He had cattle or buffalo in mind, perhaps God *had* meant this
place to be grazed but not farmed. The population of the Sand Hills
is now about the same as it was in 1890, roughly one person per square
mile.

It became my favorite part of the contemporary frontier, and during a year's travels I used any excuse I could concoct to return so I could experience it in every season. Something about the terrain and its paradoxes of sand and marsh, of cactus and cottontails, of dramatic starkness and soothing gentleness, always seemed to grip and hold me in its spell. There was something about the people, too.

John Streiff, for example. He was seventy-seven when I met him, hunched and pained from Parkinson's disease but still wiry enough to drive his old pickup around and over the grassy dunes to show me his ranch in McPherson County. He shifted without using the clutch. Grinned like a teenager with every hump that momentarily lifted us into weightlessness. At the top of the largest dune he stopped and we got out to look around.

Our view extended for 25 miles. In every direction the sea of sand and grass swelled and rolled uninterrupted to the distant horizon that encircled us. Besides his own, there was only one other house in the vista, and it was vacant. John pointed to a small clump of trees in the middle distance. He had planted them as a snow break years ago. The government offered financial incentives for ranchers to plant trees—for wildlife habitat, erosion control, wind and snow breaks—but he had never asked for payments. What trees he planted he did because *he* thought it would improve things, and therefore the effort was worth his time and money. One year he had planted 2,000 trees. Only five survived. The next year, he planted again. And so on.

He called any government subsidy "agricultural food stamps" and wouldn't have anything to do with them, lumped them in with the experts from the state college whose advice he found silly and the modern farmers who in the 1970s had moved into parts of the Sand Hills, plowed up the fragile grass cover, irrigated with water pumped from the Ogallala aquifer, and tried to make a quick profit in corn, an enterprise John considered with contempt for its profligate short-sightedness. Most of the irrigators had gone bust, in their wake leaving exposed sand to drift onto their neighbors' pastures.

To truly understand this land, John believed, you have to spend enough time in it to come to terms with its limits and its demands. There is no shortcut, no substitute. You have to put in your time. You learn by being there and letting the land teach you what is required. Living in the Sand Hills is not interchangeable with living anywhere else. Like the hills themselves, the mode of survival is unique to the place.

An August wind huffed across the dunes from the southwest. We marked its progress toward us—an odd sensation, watching a wind before you feel it or hear it. It riffled the surface of a blue lake, bent the green marsh grasses, tossled the leafy tops of John's hand-planted trees, and swept over the tawny prairie grasses. When it reached a hillside covered with wild sunflowers, they turned their golden heads in unison, like an audience at a silent stock car race. Then it passed through us at our lookout, too warm to offer relief from the heat, in too much of a hurry to linger. Nearby, a soapweed yucca cactus rattled like a snake's tail from the breeze. Then the wind was gone. We watched it move to the far horizon. At the farthest rim of our vision, it waved good-bye by kicking up a few puffs of sand on a dune's crest.

As if this communion with the wind and land had been the whole point of bringing me there, John climbed back into his pickup, started the engine, and waited for me to get in. On the drive back to his house, he told me about some other outsiders he had once shown around.

After his wife died, John had started corresponding with relatives of hers in Maryland. Often he would simply describe how he spent his time: cutting hay on a natural meadow that covered 1,000 acres; devoting an entire day checking on windmills and traveling for miles between them without seeing another person; placing old tires on the ground near telephone poles and fence posts to prevent the exposed sand from enlarging into a "blowout"; carrying a couple of matches in his pocket in case a prairie fire threatened to engulf him and he needed to burn a protective circle around himself to escape being consumed by the flames; having the mail delayed for five weeks because a blizzard's drifts blocked all the roads; and other aspects of life in a place twice the size of Maryland yet with a population of about 20,000 people.

The relatives finally decided to come out for a visit. After they had been in the Sand Hills for a day, seen it with their own eyes, and watched John at work, he sat them down in his living room that night and asked, "Well, what did you expect?"

"John," the husband replied. "We expected to find the world's biggest liar. But from now on, we'll believe anything you say."

CHAPTER 1

BIG DRY

THE NAMES THAT WHITE SETTLERS GAVE TO THE
places they encountered as they moved west across America tell quite
a bit about both the namers and the named. Set aside for a moment
those names from someone's European homeland or American hometown, names like Norfolk and Portsmouth, New England and New
Orleans and New Mexico, or Portland, Oregon, named by Maine natives
when the Bostonians who accompanied them lost a coin toss; and
those honoring kings, statesmen, and explorers, names like Georgia
and the Carolinas, Lincoln and Washington, Lake Champlain and Lew-
iston and Clarkston; or those the settlers arrogantly appropriated from
the Native Americans as they simultaneously appropriated the Indians'
lands, from Narragansett to Yakima, Shawnee to Cheyenne.

Focus instead on the place names that reflect either the settlers' expectations or their first impressions of the landscape. Among the counties with fewer than two people per square mile, some patterns emerge.

The devil and his lair get more than their due: Devils Ink Stand, Devils Chair, and Devils Bowl, North Dakota; Devils Tower, Wyoming; Devils Garden and the Dirty Devil River, Utah; Hell's Half-Acre in Texas; Hell's Backbone in Utah; a part of North Dakota once described as "Hell with the fires put out"; and more Hell Creeks than you can count.

Intimations of danger and mortality: Skeleton Canyon, New Mexico; Casket Mountain, Texas; and Death Valley, California, itself filled with names like Funeral Peak, Dante's View, Furnace Creek, Dry Bone Canyon, Rim of Hell, the Devils Cornfield and even Devils Golf Course. Despair: the Confusion Range in Utah; Crazy Woman Creek in Wyoming; Montana's Crazy Mountains. The Badlands of both North and South Dakota encompass some of those states' most sparsely settled counties; the Craters of the Moon are in an Idaho county with fewer than two people per square mile.

Even water, the source of life, often carries an ominous name: the Dismal River of Nebraska; the Bad River of South Dakota; Dry Fork, Utah; Rocksprings, Texas; Alkali Lake, Oregon; the Big Sandy and Little Sandy in Wyoming; Sand Creek in Colorado; the Powder River of Wyoming and Montana; Idaho's River of No Return.

Vainglory has been humbled: Metropolis, Nevada, apparently once a thriving community, now is a sage-covered plain pocked with cellar holes; Centropolis, Nebraska, exists only in a county history book. Sprinkled across the Sand Hills of Nebraska are places like Lilac, Audacious, Harmony, Oasis, Conquest—all of them once post offices, all of them now defunct. Capitol City, which once dreamed of being Colorado's seat of government, sits near the Continental Divide on a mountain road that closes during the winter; of the two houses there now, neither of them original, one is a bed-and-breakfast without a telephone.

Hopeful, peaceful names like Providence or Concord are not to be found. Cherry County, Nebraska, and its county seat, Valentine, are named for army officers, not for the fragrant fruit tree or love letters. Alamo, Nevada, recalls a bloody last stand. Wagontire, Oregon, and

Wheeless, Oklahoma, conjure up images of breakdowns on the pioneer trail.

Consider Garfield County, in eastern Montana, first stop on my journey through the contemporary frontier. It is laced with creeks—pronounced "cricks" in these parts—but because of the semiarid climate, those creeks are most often merely corrugated interruptions in the tawny prairie rather than babbling waterways, evidence of promises withheld rather than fulfilled. Their names, by themselves, vividly condense the county's terrain, climate, and history.

The two biggest are Big Dry Creek and Little Dry Creek, comment enough, perhaps, on the annual rainfall, although Sand Creek and Snow Creek round out the picture. Lodge Pole Creek, Tepee Creek, Indian Creek, and Squaw Creek refer to the region's original, displaced inhabitants, the Sioux and Assiniboin. Antelope Creek, Little Porcupine Creek, Bear Creek, Wolf Creek, Sage Hen Creek, Calf Creek, and Skunk Arroyo tell of other denizens, some of them also now gone. There is a Cottonwood Creek, as there seemingly is in every western county, and a Woody Creek, Tree Creek, and Ash Creek. Lone Tree Creek gives a better summary of the predominant landscape; Smokey Butte Creek describes another portion. Hell Creek, Skeleton Creek, Lost Hill Coulee, and Widow Coulee imply tragic stories of hardship, forgotten now but once fresh in someone's memory.

Garfield County is where I met Margaret Stafford, on sloping land between the drainages of two creeks which, in turn, empty into the Missouri River. One is Seven Blackfoot Creek, so named, I was told, after seven Indians were hanged there for stealing horses. The other one is Devils Creek. Not too far away stood a post office. It's closed now. But at one time people in the area got mail delivered there, addressed to Trouble, Montana.

MARGARET STAFFORD, AGE EIGHTY-FOUR, LIVES BY herself without electricity or running water. A dirt road dead-ends at her front door, 21 miles from the closest pavement and 43 miles from Jordan, Montana, population 494, the nearest town. Miles City, another 84 miles away, is, with a population of 8,461, the closest settlement large enough to be officially considered "urban" (a population over

2,500). The nearest "metropolitan area" (more than 50,000 people) is Billings, 212 miles to the southwest, roughly the same space between New York City and Washington, D.C. Between Margaret's and Billings, however, are only three small towns.

Her place perches where the treeless undulations of eastern Montana prairie crumble into the chaos of steep, eroded badlands and twisting, pine-dotted coulees known as the Missouri River Breaks. It is rough land. The notion of trying to make a living off it wouldn't occur to most people. Even where the terrain is smooth and cooperative, the weather isn't. If rains arrive, which is seldom, they often accompany storms so violent that the government has dubbed a strip passing through Margaret's land "Lightning Alley." Winters are arctic. Summers broil and bake the soil. Rude, insolent winds, with nothing standing in their way, bully across the expanses. For good reasons, this area was one of the last ones homesteaded in the United States.

Margaret arrived from North Dakota in 1925. A brother had already filed for a 640-acre homestead and wanted her to do the same nearby. She was appalled at the conditions she found: blocks of wood for furniture, apple boxes for cupboards, a diet of beans and meat. She didn't like it at all. "You're fifty years behind out here," she told everyone. Reluctantly, never intending to remain once she had "proved up," earned title, and transferred it to her brother, she filed for her land. But a year later, she married. Using hand-hewn logs, she and her husband built a one-room dwelling, dug partly into a sidehill on her land. Repeated pleas to her husband that they move somewhere else were rebuffed. They lived in the one-room hut for twenty years, until she used an inheritance to add on two other rooms. In the 1970s the marriage broke up, half of the homestead parcel was sold, and Margaret's husband left. Years earlier, her brother had lost his land to debt and moved away.

On a winter day in late January, I visited her in the house she had built but never wanted, on the land she owned but had often cursed —the place she had called home for sixty-four years, the home she now wouldn't think of leaving. She served a lunch of Jell-O salad and brownies, cups of instant coffee heated on a kitchen stove she had purchased at auction in the 1960s, becoming its fourth owner. The stove, a Zenith, could use either bottled gas or wood for fuel—bottled gas in summer, so the small kitchen wouldn't become a sweatbox;

wood in the other seasons, when the stove doubled as a source of heat. Her son, who lives about a quarter of a mile away, supplies the wood, she said, "but I split all of it."

The wall clock and the radio in the kitchen were battery-powered; the lamps and a refrigerator in the small entryway ran on kerosene. A wash basin for the dishes rested on the counter, where other kitchens would have a sink and faucet. Margaret hauled her water from a nearby spring; her bathroom was an outdoor privy. "That's just more work," she said of modern conveniences. "You work harder cleaning up electrical equipment than living the old-style way." Her television set, which she got ten years earlier, operated off a six-volt battery and she said she watched about a half-hour a day. Her phone was installed in 1975. "I waited until I could get a private line," she confided. "I lived on one of those party lines in Dakota, and it caused *more* trouble."

She asked if I minded if she smoked and then, with gnarled hands mottled by liver-colored blotches, got out some paper and tobacco. "Those bought cigarettes would kill ya," she explained. "I roll my own."

After lunch we toured the rest of the house: the log-walled room in the back, once the entire dwelling, was now a bedroom; in between it and the kitchen was the living room. In one corner was a maple secretary that had been her father's, who had homesteaded in southwestern North Dakota and founded the town of Mott's first newspaper, *The Hettinger County Dynamo*. In a few places the secretary had black stains from the heat of a lamp's flame. Along another wall stood a Kimball pump organ. Long ago, Margaret had traded two Jersey heifers—wedding presents—for it. "I thought maybe Sonny might play," she said. He hadn't, but the organ had been carted around in the old days to dances and parties where someone else performed on it. She pumped the foot pedals a few times and pressed a couple of keys to show that the organ still worked. "What's one of these worth now?" she wondered.

Outside, Margaret gestured to some barns and sheds and stock fences, the remnants of a cattle ranch that operated until she sold the herd in 1985. "I helped build them all," she said, proudly, then she turned simultaneously melancholic and self-mocking. "Now everything's falling down. I can't live more than a hundred more years. I'm not going to fix it up for someone else."

She had been born on a homestead, her father's. Eighty-four years later, despite the dreams and desires of her youth, out of a combination of factors—the harsh breaks of life, but also by her own choice—she remained on a homestead, her own.

"I didn't want to stay in this country, but here I still am," she said. "Now I'm glad I'm back in this hole, long as I can navigate." Friends and her son bring her mail twice a week and groceries when she needs them. She journeys to Jordan about three times a year; the last time she had been there was in August. "Don't ask me to *stay* in that rotten little burg," she said. "Everybody knows everybody else's business. And what's going on with the rest of the world? You tell me. Well, that's why I stay out here."

The more I traveled around her remote Montana county and the other parts of the contemporary frontier, the more I came to regard Margaret as emblematic of its residents. Her conditions aren't exactly representative. Having first thought that people here were "fifty years behind their times," she now lives fifty years behind many of her neighbors. Conveniences like electricity, indoor plumbing, a kitchen faucet are available, she just doesn't want them. But her outlook is shared by the others I would meet. She harbored no illusions about life in this place—it could be hard, damned hard. A streak of fatalism was necessary to survive it. So, too, was a dose of humor and optimism. Margaret was also fiercely insistent that no one believe she felt trapped by circumstances. She envied no one. From what she knew of the rest of the country, she preferred staying exactly where she had made her home.

"It's quite a world," she said, shaking her head. "I've been a pioneer all my life."

The sun was shining. Several days earlier, after more than a month of subfreezing readings, Jordan had been the coldest spot in the United States: 45 degrees *below* zero. Within twenty-four hours, the temperature had swung to 44 degrees *above* zero—the kind of sudden weather reversal not unusual for the High Plains' manic-depressive climate. Now a north wind was once again stirring itself. Protected in the lee of her homestead, Margaret rested her stooped shoulders on a gate and basked in the warmth of the brief thaw. She knew from experience it wouldn't last long.

IN OCTOBER 1896, THREE YEARS AFTER FREDERICK Jackson Turner's speech on the closing of the frontier, a small wagon pulled up to the banks of Big Dry Creek. Arthur Jordan stepped down and pitched camp. Born in 1873 near Wolverhampton, England, Jordan had run away from home at age fourteen and, after several failed attempts as a stowaway from Liverpool, made passage to America. By sixteen he was in southeastern Montana working off and on as a stage driver, bullwhacker, cowboy, and trapper. Other cowboys called him "The English Kid." Now, in his early twenties, he was married and ready to put down roots.

With him were his wife, Hattie, and their daughter, Esther, who three weeks earlier had been born in a camp tent on the prairie. After supper, Hattie saw a large buffalo wolf 50 yards from their tent, which Arthur promptly shot and skinned for its pelt. A few days later, standing at the tent's opening, he shot an antelope. The first week of November, winter arrived in the form of a blizzard. The family was forced into their partially completed cabin, although it still had no chimney or stove. Thus the birth of what would become Jordan, Montana.

The Jordans were not the first whites in the area. With the slaughter of the southern buffalo herds complete in the 1870s and the extension of railroad service to Miles City in 1881, thousands of hunters and hide skinners had swarmed into eastern Montana. By 1884, the northern herd was gone. When a frantic William Hornaday, chief taxidermist for the U.S. National Museum, hurriedly set out in 1886 to gather specimens before the species was extinct, he was directed to the river breaks north of the Big Dry, where rumors said remnant bands still roamed. It took him two months to track down twenty-five buffalo for his collection. The American Museum of Natural History showed up the next year, scoured the region for three months, and left empty-handed.

As the buffalo were disappearing, cattle were showing up, trailed in from both Texas and the Pacific Northwest to fatten on the free grass before being shipped to market from Miles City. Big outfits ruled the prairies in the large corner between the Missouri and Musselshell rivers. Vigilante groups called the Stranglers—so named because their first hanging victim took a long time to die—enforced the cattlemen's law against the horse thieves and cattle rustlers who sought refuge in the maze of breaks along the two rivers. The brutal winter of 1886–87 decimated the free-ranging herds and ushered in the era of smaller stock ranches, many of them run by "squatters" and former cowhands like "The English Kid."

Jordan's solitary cabin soon became a way station for cowboys and hunters traveling between Miles City and the Missouri River. He began stocking tobacco, ammunition, and other supplies. At the turn of the century his place was designated as a post office, bearing his name and serving a dozen ranches dispersed across a hundred-mile radius. Jordan added another cottonwood log building and partitioned it into a store and post office.

When he and his family returned after visiting friends during the week of Christmas 1901, they were surprised to find three men operating a saloon in the post office. Rather than complain, Jordan, a practical man, gave them some extra logs for a separate building. Hattie was becoming overworked providing free meals to everyone who passed by, so Jordan convinced an old roundup cook nicknamed "the Darber" to open a restaurant in yet another log hut. "The Darber" called it quits within a year. Drunken cowboys got in the habit of shooting up the place after meals, and he lost his profits constantly replacing the broken dishes. The unflappable Jordan—"those big-hearted cowboys had to have their fun," he said, even after they did the same thing to his store and post office one day—persuaded the mail carrier to install his wife as the new proprietress; she enforced order by brandishing her broom. A fourth building, a livery stable, went up the same year. In 1902, after selling his store supplies to two businessmen who wanted to move in from Miles City, Jordan laid out a Main Street and staked lots for a proper town.

Arthur Jordan considered himself a frontiersman, not a twentieth-century town builder. He preferred running his trap lines and herding cattle to being a merchant and town father. Although well respected and law-abiding himself, he counted among his friends men who were attracted to the area because the nearest sheriff's office was more than a hundred miles away. A few were rustlers; one was killed trying to rob the bank in Harlem, Montana; another particularly notorious acquaintance, who dined with Jordan whenever he was passing through on the run, was an accomplice of the outlaw Kid Curry and reportedly died in a shoot-out in South America.

By Jordan's own account, written in a straightforward tone neither boastful nor shameful, in those early years the town that bore his name "was known as the most tough and vicious little town in the northwest." In addition to being postmaster, Jordan shouldered other, unofficial burdens. When someone died—murders, suicides, and drunken shoot-outs seemed almost commonplace—Jordan usually dug the grave, made the coffin, said the prayer, and put up a tombstone. The Big Dry region was still part of Dawson County, the nation's largest at the time, stretching from North Dakota to the Musselshell, and county officials in Glendive, the county seat 130 miles east of Jordan, viewed west Dawson with a combination of disgust, alarm, and indifference. They provided no money for a local jail—although the county attorney in Glendive once suggested that the best punishment for a convicted criminal would be to sentence him to *live* in Jordan for six months. So whenever a lawbreaker was arrested, Arthur and Hattie ended up keeping him in their home until he could be escorted elsewhere. After the official justice of the peace was scared off by some of the wilder boys, who put a noose around his neck and paraded him across the prairie, Jordan, a slightly built but apparently fearless man, filled in temporarily.

The winter of 1906–1907 was as disastrous as the one ten years earlier. Jordan lost half his cattle, sold the remainder, scouted around Canada for two years in a vain search for a place to start over, then returned and filed on a homestead east of town. Soon afterward, things began changing.

Two railroads surveyed potential routes through the region. Congress passed the Enlarged Homestead Act, raising the limit to 320 acres for nonirrigated western lands, followed by the Stock Raising Homestead Act, which permitted 640-acre filings. The outbreak of World War One increased both demand and prices for wheat. A string of unusually wet years encouraged the onrush of farmers to believe, as they were being told, that "rain follows the plow." More people moved in. Some of the wildlife moved out—the last Audubon's bighorn sheep sighted in the United States was seen in the region in 1916. The boom was on.

In 1919, Garfield County was organized from the western half of

Dawson County. The town of Jordan, located in the center, won a pitched election battle to become county seat against three other towns that had sprouted on the prairies. A dance hall built in 1914 was converted into the courthouse.

The census of 1920 registered 5,368 residents in the new county. A railroad promotional brochure titled "Garfield County in the Pacific Northwest, Garfield County in the New Corn Belt" invited more settlers, although no tracks had actually been laid. Jordan billed itself as the "natural metropolis" of this new Eden, with "the resources to make it one of the most active and important commercial centers in eastern Montana." The sky was the limit, and in this part of the country, the sky is very big.

Arthur Jordan, in the meantime, had grown uneasy with it all. He had already relocated again, to the county's northern edge where Hell Creek empties into the Missouri—just a little east of where Margaret Stafford would homestead a few years later. He tried to continue ranching, but an outbreak of blackleg fever killed his calves and drove him out of the business for good and into a series of moves around the county. He provided for his family by trapping wolves for the government, by floating lumber down the Missouri to fuel the new housing boom, by cutting cedar posts for ranchers, and by selling mink, muskrat, and weasel pelts. He built yet another cabin at the mouth of Hell Creek and began plans to improve a large island in the river by squatting on it, but someone else claimed title. The family moved again.

During this time, on a visit to the new "natural metropolis," Jordan ran into his old friend Robert Leavitt, another early settler who had first entered the region in the 1890s trailing a herd of cattle. Leavitt was a white man from the South, but due to his thick accent and the cowboy penchant for giving everyone a nickname, he had always been known as "Nigger Bob." He had helped Jordan lay out the town in 1902 and now ran one of its saloons. ("What's the use of paying out money to dig a well when you can get a drink of anything for fifteen cents at Nigger Bobs?" a local paper wrote in 1908.)

Leavitt was an affable man who gave free Bibles to every child in town and always carried a faded photograph of his mother in his breast pocket, but on this day he seemed uncharacteristically despondent. Jordan asked him why. "Nigger Bob" complained that he missed the old days, when he could leave his saloon on occasion and join a roundup. "These new people that have come into the country," he added, "look at me as if I were some caged animal in a zoo." A few months later, he sold his saloon and went to Miles City, where he lay down for a nap in a vacant lot one afternoon and died with his arms folded across his breast.

In 1922, nearing the age of fifty, Arthur Jordan decided that he, too, had had enough. He hitched a team to his wagon, loaded up his wife, his two young boys, and his trusty camp tent, and headed for the mountains.

IF HE'D STAYED AROUND A LITTLE LONGER, JORDAN would not have felt so hemmed in. Garfield County's population in 1920, only slightly more than one person per square mile, was the highest concentration of humanity it would ever witness. Drier weather, lower prices, harder times—that is, a return to the norm on the Great Plains—began driving people out in the 1920s. The drought and depression of the 1930s turned the retreat into a rout. By 1940 the county was home to only 2,641 souls, less than half its peak twenty years earlier. Every census afterward posted a small decline. Covering 4,491 square miles, Garfield County is the size of Connecticut. The current population is 1,589, a density of 0.35 people per square mile. Jordan, with about a third of the county's residents, is its sole surviving town.

The plains in this part of Montana are neither flat nor rolling. They swell, like an ocean making the transition between choppy and becalmed. Jordan lies in a trough between two swells. From any distance, you wouldn't be aware that the town exists. Near Big Dry Creek large cottonwoods grow, and there are a few multistory buildings, but most of the town, like the rest of the prairie vegetation, hugs close to the ground.

Jordan's Main Street, one of its two paved streets, includes a two-block-long business district lined on both sides with false-front buildings: one grocery store, one bank, one title company, one flower shop, one hair salon, one drug store, one dry goods store, one funeral parlor, one crafts shop, one saddlery, one lawyer's office, one car dealership, one combination barber shop and state liquor store, and two bars. Several of the businesses are open only part-time. Three buildings stand vacant. Along the highway that intersects Main Street are three gas stations, one motel, one hotel, the county courthouse that once was a dance hall, and, a mile south of the town center where the county's two paved highways meet, Jordan's one restaurant. The town itself has one municipal employee.

At first glance, theology appears to be the only enterprise bucking this reductionist trend: Jordan has seven churches. Even religion, however, is not immune. "Jordan's gotten down to the irreducible minimum," said the Reverend Harvey Senecal, sixty-three, in his study at the Community Presbyterian Church. Senecal, a big man with a deep voice, had moved to Jordan a year earlier from a small town in Kansas. "This church was willing to take me, despite my age," he explained. "It had gone one and a half years without a minister." He defined the community as a "semi-frontier" with a survivor mentality, forged by the fresh memory of the hardships of the pioneers who arrived and then persevered while most of their compatriots abandoned the region. "These are sons and grandsons who literally starved their way through, hard-bitten ranchers who suffered, really suffered to stay here," he said. "They're proud of that."

On Sunday the week before, an assistant to the regional bishop of the Evangelical Lutheran Church of America had been in Jordan to install the Reverend Senecal as pastor of the Lutheran church a block and a half away. Jordan churches had temporarily shared ministers before—an ex-priest, married to an ex-nun, had once conducted services for two Protestant congregations; the Seventh-Day Adventist preacher had recently filled the Presbyterians' minister gap. A formal contract officially and permanently recognizing the same minister for two denominations, however, was something new. (The contract provided that when Senecal retired, a Lutheran minister would be hired and shared.)

Sharing a minister allowed the two congregations to afford a full-time preacher and yet preserve their separateness. "We had to do something or the two churches would have gone under," according to a Presbyterian elder. "I told them: 'We're all going to the same place anyway. It's not like we've got brands on us that say Presbyterian and Lutheran.' "

Every Sunday, Senecal conducts a Lutheran service—"I do it by the book; I'm an ultra-Lutheran in that respect," he said—and then walks back to his home church for a Presbyterian service. He designs a single sermon to fit both congregations. At the Presbyterian service I attended, where about fifty people half filled the small church, the program called for the singing of Hymn 262, "Come to the Savior Now." When the time came, a murmur of confusion spread through the flock. A woman rose to say that "Come to the Savior Now" wasn't the name of Hymn 262 in their hymnal. The Reverend Senecal, momentarily flustered, corrected his mistake: "Come to the Savior Now" was number 262 in the *Lutheran* hymnal; the congregation then stood to sing number 262 in theirs, "Thy Life Was Given for Me." An announcement at the end of service invited people to a "singspiration" at the Catholic church that evening.

Other evidence of the effects of low population density, of how different life can be in a place where the miles are longer and the people fewer, can be found at every turn. Garfield County is a case study of the contemporary frontier, rural America stripped down to its "irreducible minimum." Only essential services survive, and in numbers proportional to their local importance. In Garfield County, for instance, the solitary lawyer is outnumbered two-to-one by professional coyote trappers. The norm for the contemporary frontier is usually just one of everything. Sometimes, however, it doesn't even have one: like fifty-seven other sparsely settled counties, Garfield County, as large as some states, exists without a practicing doctor.

Dr. B. C. Farrand arrived in Jordan in 1925, enticed by a local recruiting team offering an incentive of $125 and the promise that a hospital would be built. For fifty years he was the county's sole practitioner. As promised, a hospital was built in 1928, but until Jordan got electrical service in the 1940s, Dr. Farrand's X-ray machine operated off its own diesel generator. (Electricity was not extended to rural Garfield County until 1951; five years later telephone service arrived in the countryside.) Roads being the exception rather than the rule at the time, the doctor traversed prairie trails to get to his ranch patients, often accepting wood, coal, cattle, and horses in barter for his services. Sometimes getting to and from one patient consumed an entire day. In the 1940s he and the local druggist purchased a single-engine airplane, equipped with skis for winter, to reach remote sites in less time. A newer hospital went up in 1952, but the doctor himself had already become the real medical institution in the county. Even today, people speak of him with reverence.

Following Dr. Farrand's retirement in 1975, the county's luck in attracting and keeping a replacement ran out. More incentives were offered: free flying lessons, cosigned loans for new cars, housing assistance, prepaid liability insurance, and guaranteed salaries plus a percentage of receipts. Some prospects showed up, seemed interested, and then brought in their wives, who took one look around the seemingly endless prairie and the tiny town so far from anyplace else and refused to let their husbands sign a contract. Over a decade, about ten doctors did sign, but none stayed for long—four years was the longest stint. "They'd walk all over us, bleed us dry, and leave," a local nurse remembered of the parade of doctors. Rapid turnover wasn't the only concern. One doctor had a drinking problem, a few were undergoing drug rehabilitation, another was a foreigner with a tenuous command of English and a short temper, and another was removed within a few weeks for incompetence.

Although his wife stayed near a ski resort in western Montana, disdaining to live in Jordan, the doctor who practiced for four years was generally well-liked by everyone. Then one night he suddenly walked into the Hell Creek Bar wearing a dress, high heels, nylon stockings, and a woman's wig. Hell Creek Bar is considered the wilder of Jordan's two bars. Its walls are lined with the heads of antelope and deer shot by its owners and patrons. The mood inside, depending on the time of day and mixture of residents standing at the bar rail, can range from sullen to boisterous. There are occasional fights on weekends. A sign behind the cash register says: "This is not Burger King. You do *not* get it your way. You get it my way or you don't get the Son of a Bitch! Have a nice day." Another advises: "Shirt and Shoes Required. Bras and Panties Optional." In other words, it's not the kind of place a man in drag would normally be expected to enter and then get out in one piece. The reaction to the doctor's unexpected appearance can be considered a measure of the community's appreciation for his years of service: it wasn't so much anger, laughter, or shock, it was more a feeling of sorrow—for him personally and for the fact that they were losing another doctor.

In the mid-1980s, Garfield County's medical services bottomed out.

Without a resident doctor for two years, and faced with increasingly stringent regulations, rising costs, and chronic accreditation problems, the hospital was closed and converted to a nursing home. People resigned themselves to devoting a day's time getting to and from routine care—in effect, the reverse of the situation when, sixty years earlier, Dr. Farrand once spent a day getting to and from a patient. The volunteer ambulance service, a source of county pride, became an even more crucial lifeline in emergencies.

Local leaders regrouped and pioneered an effort that has been recognized as a possible model for other sparsely settled regions. A bill was pushed through the Montana legislature reducing regulatory restrictions in isolated communities and authorizing medical assistance facilities (MAFs)—scaled-down hospitals providing emergency treatment and a few rooms for tightly prescribed short-term inpatient services. Jordan was designated as one of the pilot projects. A physician assistant was recruited, and another bill was passed to give PAs greater autonomy in dispensing health care.

"We're a stopgap," said Daniel Muniak, the physician assistant. "I hate to say that, because it implies lesser quality of treatment. I provide run-of-the-mill, humdrum medical care. Practicality is the name of the game. It's not second-class medicine, just limited. We don't need hospital surgery in Jordan." Having practiced in Alaska, rural Washington, and a town on an Indian reservation in South Dakota, he was attracted to Garfield County, he said, because "I like remoteness."

When I visited him in his office in the basement of the former hospital, the MAF was not yet in operation. He was seeing about 150 patients a month, half his projected goal. Building a practice was slow going. Over the years, in-county medical care had acquired a Groucho Marx image: many residents wouldn't entirely trust anyone willing to practice in Jordan; they kept driving to Miles City or Billings to see a doctor, or they simply refrained from routine medical care.

Garfield County has one high school. The seventy-nine students in its four grades are drawn from what Steve Cascaden, its principal, claimed was the nation's largest school district (an eastern equivalent would be a high school in Hartford, Connecticut, serving the whole state). Because some of the students live as far as 70 miles from Jordan on roads of uncertain passage during winter and spring, a third of the high school's population normally spends weeknights in a nearby dormitory. It is Montana's only remaining public-school dormitory and one of two in the contiguous states. (The other is in Harney County, Oregon, another county with fewer than two people per square mile.) More than any other institution, the high school creates a social cohesion out of a diffused populace and makes neighbors out of families that might live a hundred miles from one another.

"This is where everything goes on," Cascaden said. "This is what gives the community its focus." Graduations for a senior class of twenty students typically draw audiences of seven hundred people. (Funerals are another community-wide ceremony. All the stores in town generally close, and some services have been held in the high school gymnasium to accommodate the crowds.) In a county without a movie theater, the high school also provides one of the principal means of entertainment. During my two weeks in Garfield County, the local Mustangs played four basketball games, against towns 66, 75, 116, and 121 miles away. Nearly five hundred people attended the home games, and the Hell Creek Bar and Rancher's Bar were jammed afterward; angle-parked pickup trucks crowded Main Street. On the night of an away game, Jordan seemed a ghost town. With no local radio station, there are no broadcasts, but the morning after each game virtually everyone seemed conversant with play-by-play details: people had either attended the game themselves or had already heard about it from someone who did. "Drinkin', goin' to church, goin' to ball games—that's about all there is to do," said one school official.

For many of the high school students, entering their freshman year is a profound culture shock, even though the school has fewer than a hundred students. Their years in kindergarten through eighth grade were spent in one of thirteen one-room schools scattered around the countryside, each with an average of seven students, less than one per grade. The largest country school has twenty-eight pupils, the smallest has two.

One such school is the Ross School, a small log-and-chink structure built in 1930 on the side of a hill near the Musselshell River, about 70 miles from Jordan and 20 miles from the nearest paved road. At the time of my visit, it had six students, all boys, drawn from four ranch families in an eight-mile radius. Four of the boys were in four different grades; the two others were kindergarteners who attended two days a week. One set of brothers represented the third generation of their

family to attend the school. When their father was a pupil, before a
remodeling in 1958, the building still had a sod roof. With the exception
of the new roof and, more conspicuously, a satellite dish in the yard,
the Ross School appears on the outside as it did sixty years ago. The
inside, a single room about 15 by 20 feet, is also a mixture of old and
new: a stove in one corner and a well-used wooden teacher's desk, but
also a television set, microwave oven, and an Apple computer. A
clothesline was stretched across the front of the room. Several weeks
earlier, on the night the school produced its Christmas play, the line
had held the curtain; the temperature that evening had been 50 degrees
below zero, but fifteen people had attended. Now, with a snowstorm
in progress outside, the boys' winter jackets and jumpsuits hung from
the line, steaming from the stove's heat.

Lisa Peterson, the young teacher, had each of the four grade-school
boys' assignments for the day marked on pieces of paper in the work-
books on their desks when they arrived. Once they got started, she
moved slowly from desk to desk, giving individual instruction to each
boy. A file basket on her desk had four tiers, one for each pupil to put
his completed work. This being a kindergarten day, she devoted much
of her morning to the two youngest students. At one point, the fourth-
grader stood by the stove, quietly reading an illustrated children's book,
The Little Mouse on the Prairie, to the kindergarteners at his feet, while
Lisa helped the second-grader with his math; the sixth-grader was
working quietly at the computer, and the fifth-grader busied himself
with his social studies assignment. At recess they all went sliding on
the hill and then divided into equal camps to play army with snowballs.

This was Lisa's first teaching job. She had been recruited and hired
one week before the school year began, a circumstance not uncommon
among the more remote schools, where low starting pay ($12,000 a
year) and isolation ("teacherages," usually small trailers next to the
schools, are provided) combine to make attracting new teachers a
constant difficulty. She had been raised on a Montana ranch and was
no stranger to rural life in the West. Nonetheless, her new job confronted her with challenges from the beginning.

On her first drive to the school, Lisa's Chevrolet Citation had gotten
stuck in the mud and she spent the night in her car. When she finally
arrived the next day, she found a bird's nest and a family of rats in
her trailer. There was no water for three days. After her first weekend,

which she spent in Jordan, her car had a flat tire on the way back to school. "God was telling me not to come here," she said of this initi-ation. She traded in her car for a pickup with four-wheel drive; a cat, given to her by a local ranch wife, soon took care of the rats. Her television didn't work for three weeks, so she spent many nights alone in the tiny trailer reading everything she could get her hands on. The solitary remoteness was the hardest part of her job, she said: "You hear a lot of strange noises at night." She bought a gun and learned how to use it.

Among the network of country-school teachers that develops at occasional county-wide meetings and on weekends in town, certain tales from the past make the rounds each year. Some are scary and cautionary, others are more lighthearted. The message of them all is that surviving at a one-room school in these parts requires skills beyond those learned in the teaching colleges. Several years earlier, a salesman who had visited one of the secluded schools made a late-night return visit to the teacherage; his advances were ultimately rebuffed by the teacher shooting him in the leg. During a snowstorm one winter, a teacher and a friend were caught on a back road; the friend got out to find help on foot, became lost in the blizzard, and died from ex-posure. Two years before Lisa Peterson's tenure, the Ross School had achieved national attention when Paul Harvey's radio program re-ported that a rattlesnake, living under a corner of the building, kept interrupting classes with its rattling. The Three R's at the Ross School, Harvey said, were "readin', 'rithmetic, and rattlesnakes." At the end of the same term, impassable spring roads had forced the teacher to leave by horseback.

Sagas of prolonged but successful rat battles waged by young women in teacherages left unoccupied each summer are so common-place that they are recounted as an almost unremarkable rite of passage. On the other hand, a favorite anecdote is of a country teacher—a man, and as such a rarity—who discovered mice in his teacherage his first night and left the next day.

But the story I kept running into the most, not just in Garfield County but throughout the contemporary frontier, is that of school teachers marrying local ranchers. It would be impossible to verify, but my overwhelming impression is that these sparsely settled counties have the nation's highest percentage of people descended from school teachers. Everywhere I went I met women, in their late seventies to early twenties, who had come to their regions as first-time teachers, who had often decided they'd stay just a year because of the isolation they encountered, but who had then met a young man from the area and ended up a ranch wife. This phenomenon represents a seamless connection to the past.

The old frontier was predominantly male. During the mining booms of the mid-1800s, for instance, Colorado and Nevada's white populations were 90 percent male. In 1890, when the nation as a whole was split 51 percent male and 49 percent female, women in Montana were still outnumbered two-to-one, and the other western states with frontier regions had what census officials called an "excess" of males of 20 percent or more. Besides meeting the educational needs of frontier children, the influx of school teachers provided an unintended consequence: a ready supply of unmarried women. "The West wasn't won by a cowboy with a six-gun," an old rancher in Utah told me, standing next to his teacher-wife. "It was won by a cowboy with a school marm."

In the contemporary frontier, teachers fulfill similar multiple roles, although with a somewhat different twist. While sparsely settled counties are no longer so overwhelmingly male, they also are no longer places experiencing, or even anticipating, many new residents. Their population trends are generally either downward or stagnant. That is, more people move out than move in. Within communities struggling just to maintain themselves at the irreducible minimum, new teachers are one of the few sources of new blood. Additionally, in these primarily agricultural economies, school systems are often the second-largest employer; a spouse's teaching salary can make the difference in a family's financial solvency and therefore its survival in the area.

Garfield County doesn't preserve its system of thirteen small rural school districts (it once had more than a hundred) as either a local job program or a dating service. Nor are the one-room schools the county's philosophical statement in the academic debate over the relative educational merits of small class sizes or the back-to-basics movement. The school officials and parents I talked to were well aware of both the advantages and disadvantages: more individualized instruction on the one hand, a minimum curriculum on the other. Even the high school has no art or foreign language programs; an eight-man football team was recently reinstituted only after the kids promised the school board they would pay for their own equipment and get donations for the team bus and its gas. Country kids lucky enough to have the same excellent teacher for their first nine school years emerge with a solid educational foundation, but if the teacher is deficient in a particular subject, say science, they suffer from it.

Like so many other customs and institutions in the contemporary frontier, the schools function the way they do out of necessity, driven by the exigencies of few people and much land. The one-room schools persist because their alternatives are so impractical: busing to create bigger schools would be too unreliable and take too much time each day; putting grade-schoolers in dorms far from home would be unthinkable; and installing a mother and her children in a house in town for the school year while dad stays on the ranch is an option only some families can afford. In these regions you face reality stoically, without complaint (at least to outsiders), and where you can, you make virtue out of necessity. Students from the country schools, many people said, often do the best at the high school, just as many of the high school graduates fare well in the outside world when they ultimately leave, as so many do.

Sitting in the Rancher's Bar after one of the basketball games, two country-school teachers told me of their experiences. Sheila Baker, thirty-nine, is from the Flint, Michigan, area and had been a substitute teacher in Detroit before coming to Garfield County nine years earlier. She had been hired over the phone two weeks before school started. Since then she has taught at three different rural schools and was currently teaching nine pupils in six grades. The school building is a double-wide mobile home with two bathrooms and a built-on porch library. "It's a palace," the other said enviously. "She even has a dishwasher." Getting used to the silence at night had been Sheila's hardest adjustment. She said her friends at home "think I'm crazy to drive eighty-five miles to a Kmart." At one of the schools where she had taught, a kindergartener arrived twice a week in a small airplane flown by the child's father; it would land on the dirt road and taxi into the school's driveway.

Charlotte Moran, a twenty-six-year-old from a small town in western Montana, had sought out a rural school for her first job because she thought it would offer more variety and challenge and because her mother had once taught at one. Her first two years had been at a remote school with just one student; now she was teaching at a different one-room school, with three students in three grades.

Unlike Lisa Peterson, who hoped to find a job the next year where the schools were larger and the living conditions less isolated, these two teachers said they were content where they were. "In the suburbs and cities there's no courtesy. Everybody's shove-shove, push-push," said Sheila. "It's laid-back here. Nobody's in a big hurry." Some day she will probably have to relocate to a bigger district, for better pay and retirement benefits, she said, "but I hate to think about it." Charlotte merely said she planned to stay indefinitely. Later she excused herself and joined a young man at the bar—a local, her friend said, intimating that a marriage might be in the offing. History was repeating itself.

A PIONEER'S LOG CABIN SITS IN THE MIDDLE OF JOR-dan; behind it, an aluminum trailer house; behind the trailer, a steel tower with a satellite dish receiving television signals for the town's cable company. History is compressed that way here. The frontier past still lives, not just in relics and faded photographs but in the active memories of those who actually experienced it. You can meet people who knew Arthur Jordan and "Nigger Bob," old folks who as children arrived with their parents in the first wave of white settlers to file homestead claims and scratch a dwelling out of the side of a creek bank, even baby boomers for whom "The Mickey Mouse Club" and "Bonanza" were not part of growing up because their families didn't have electricity and, therefore, television.

In 1910, when Carl Harbaugh was eight years old, he and his mother and five siblings walked from Miles City nearly a hundred miles to the homestead his father had claimed. It took them four days. The first four years on the land, the eight-member family lived in a dugout, an earthen cave 14 by 16 feet. His mother draped cheesecloth under the ceiling to keep the dirt from dropping on the supper table. Excited by promotional pamphlets showing roof-high corn and plenty of free land, his father started a farm, but by the early 1920s, when dry weather had revealed the cruel agricultural truth, Harbaugh's father joined the

exodus of homesteaders out of Garfield County and bought some irrigated land near the Yellowstone River. Harbaugh and a younger
brother, however, remained.

Besides their homes and often their furniture, the retreating homesteaders also left their workhorses, which roamed in such destructive
numbers that the county paid people to gather them and get rid of
them. Preferring broncs to plows anyway, the Harbaugh brothers went
into the business. Some of the horses were sold for the dog-meat market, others were shipped to the Midwest for use on farms with more
reliable rainfall; the best were saved, bred, and trained for cavalry
mounts. During the 1930s, a three-year plague of grasshoppers darkened the skies, plastered the sides of houses, and stripped the range.
Harbaugh's house burned down in the drought and his family temporarily moved back into the ancestral dugout. He paid his taxes by
hunting coyotes and by selling buffalo skulls and horns for nine dollars
a ton—the same sort of things Arthur Jordan had done in hard times
a generation earlier.

Margie Harbaugh, Carl's wife, had arrived during the boom in 1916;
she was six years old and had two younger siblings. Her widowed father
was looking for a new start: relatives at home were pressuring him to
disperse his motherless children among them, something that had
happened to him when his own mother died, something which he was
determined not to repeat. A businessman, not a farmer, he had scouted
the newly opened Jordan region, had been told a railroad was soon
coming to the growing town and decided this was the opportunity he
was looking for. Margie's family traveled with a group from Antler,
North Dakota, crossing roadless prairie in a Maxwell touring car and
camping on the banks of the Missouri River until the winter ice was
thick enough for them to cross. Within four years, most of the Antler
group had given up and left.

"It took a lot of nerve to stay sometimes," Carl said. Two of their
sons have moved away, seeking better job opportunities. A third, their
oldest, operates a sheep and cattle ranch on thirty sections (about
20,000 acres) of land encompassing not only the original place but
those of many other homesteaders whose roots never stuck.

There are others who remained. Gerrit Wille was three years old
when his family left Holland for Montana with an uncle and another
family. "They didn't have any specific plans," he told me at the senior

citizen center in Jordan. "They didn't know anything about this country, they were seeking their fortune. They just came because the land was free." By European standards, three hundred and twenty acres seemed like a kingdom for the taking.

Wille remembered their wagon pulling up to Butte Creek, where they expected to find a new house waiting for them. Instead they saw a tarpaper shack with no windows, no door, no water, and no food. One of the young brides fainted. They slept on a bed of hay the first night and woke up infested with ticks. "Land of Milk and Honey," one of the men muttered, and they went to work. Wille's family became merchants in the small town of Brusett, where their store, now vacant, is about all that remains.

"It's not a place you'd say, 'I'm glad I'm here,' " Wille said, "but it grows on you." He handed me his business card, which listed his occupation as "retired." At the bottom, it said, "When I have the urge to work I lie down until it passes over. No Business, No Worries, No Money, No Prospects." He and his wife, a former school teacher, had five children, none of them still in the county.

As if in honor of Jordan's English-born founder, Garfield County's population, small though it is, has a certain international flavor. I met first- and second-generation Americans of Dutch, Russian, Irish, Scotch, German, French Basque, and Norwegian extraction. Except for different starting points, however, their stories all followed a similar outline: the hopeful arrival, the hard times, the neighbors' departures, more hard times, the children's departures. Despite those basic elements, their narratives were not portrayed as unremittingly sad or sentimental. Quite the contrary, people often chuckled about the hardships they had endured: wolves and rattlesnakes, plagues and drought, poverty and struggle, the electricity that was late in coming and the railroad that never did—all were part of a grand adventure, at least in retrospect. Their lives had intermingled two of the nation's most powerful folk epics, the immigrants' success and the settling of the West, perhaps for the last time. They saw themselves as living embodiments of America's promise.

A sense of toughness and flinty pride emerged from their stories. Where so many others had failed, they had met the challenge and prevailed. That more people had left than stayed was not just an inevitable recognition of the land and climate and local economy's human carrying capacity, it was a rigorous accounting that separated those who had the tenacity to make it from those who didn't. Feeling little sympathy for the people the land had repelled, the survivors sought none for themselves. Whatever scars they wore were battle medallions of life.

Norman Olson, a small, wiry man who arrived at age ten with his Norwegian father and uncle in 1920, still owned the wooden beam from the plow he walked behind to break the virgin sod seventy years ago. His uncle had owned a bank, hotel, and homestead, and then lost them all during the great out-migration that rocked the county. Foreclosure also took his parents' home and land. But Norman, still ranching and farming at age eighty, had eventually bought it back and now owned it, he made a point of telling me, free and clear. "You've got to decide whether you're going to stick it out," he said, "and then get to it."

The people who left, of course, are not around to tell their stories. Particularly on the Great Plains during the nation's last settlement surge, many homesteaders filed claims with no intention of remaining very long. Some were part of a more or less permanently poor and rootless class of Americans which, from the time Daniel Boone crossed the Cumberland Gap long before any homestead act, had gone from one patch of free land to another across the country. Some, who had retained their farms in the Midwest but ventured into the Plains as absentee landlords hoping to make quick profits in the wheat boom, simply didn't bother coming out to plant a crop when things went bust. Some were employees of the huge cattle outfits, which because of the homestead acts needed title to the range they already claimed and which underwrote cowboy-homesteaders with the understanding that the land would revert to the company; a portion of these claims even turned out to be filed fraudulently, by people whose names were taken from some distant town's rolls or who didn't even exist. Others, like Margaret Stafford, were relatives of homesteaders who came simply to help their kin expand their holdings. Still others planned only to satisfy the minimum residency and improvement requirements to "prove up," sell their land (hopefully at boom prices), and leave with their profits. If the boom had already turned sour by that time, some took a mortgage on their new title and disappeared, leaving devalued land in the hands of the bank, which normally turned it over for taxes to the county, which in turn auctioned it at minimum prices to a neighbor who could afford it.

The national imperative, expressed both psychically and legislatively, called for settlement and the disposal of public lands. In practice, the process was messier than our myths recall, and it often fell far short of Thomas Jefferson's vision of creating a nation of yeoman farmers. In such an environment, a sudden population spike followed by a quick decline was inevitable. Rather than tragic individual failures, at least some of the departures represented the successful fulfillment of somebody's strategy.

Whatever the intentions—and a large, but unclearly defined percentage of homesteaders, perhaps deluded by railroad and governmental promises of rich soils and adequate moisture, arrived with hopes of settling permanently—320 or even 640 free acres simply weren't enough to sustain a family in a place where dry skies mock the upturned sod and the planted seed. Throughout rural America, regardless of region, the inexorable byproduct of increased productivity per farmer has been fewer farmers and larger farms. On the Great Plains this national trend was further accentuated by the stark fact that rainfall is usually sparse and always unreliable.

With an average annual precipitation of about 12 inches, Garfield County witnessed a particularly quick winnowing. The county had 1,530 farms with an average size of 571 acres in 1920. Twenty years later, those numbers switched: 587 farms, each averaging 1,511 acres. Now there are 297 farms averaging 6,947 acres. One night I overheard one rancher talking to another in the Hell Creek Bar. "They say you need ten thousand acres these days to survive," he said. "I think it's closer to twenty thousand."

A few of the farms, in the better soil areas, are devoted exclusively to dryland cash crops like spring and winter wheat, but more than 90 percent of the county is rangeland. A typical, diversified livestock operation might have 300 cows and an equal number of sheep, several hundred acres for feed crops, and, if possible, some wheat acreage. "You have to be pretty versatile or you can't make it," said John Trumbo, who raises cattle, sheep, wheat, barley, oats, and hay, in addition to running a rustic guest ranch that offers guided elk, antelope, and deer hunts and fishing expeditions. Between calving, lambing, shearing, rounding up, branding, shipping, and winter feeding for two species, and between planting, tending, and harvesting four crops, not to mention catering to hunters and fishermen, there is no slack period at Trumbo's Hell Creek ranch. Except for the tourist component, his ranch is similar to many others I visited.

On average, it takes about 30 acres of Garfield County rangeland to support one head of cattle (or six sheep), although in some areas that carrying capacity drops to more than 100 acres per head. Such pastoral mathematics drive the sparsity of population in the county— and in most of the other parts of the contemporary frontier. Where climate, terrain, or their combination make traditional row-crop farming impossible and even small-grain field crops only partially practical, and yet where the main source of income nonetheless springs from what the land can support, people quickly become overwhelmingly outnumbered by acres and grazing animals. Over the seventy-year life of the county, the numbers of acres under cultivation and cattle and sheep on the range have oscillated wildly, reflecting changes in market conditions and weather patterns. All the while, the population kept shrinking. In Garfield County's case, the current proportions are now 1,809 acres, 46 sheep, and 32 cattle per person.

No one foresees the trend reversing. When drought, depression, and their sidekick, foreclosure, made their cyclical ride across the Plains during the agricultural crisis of the 1980s, more people were swept from the land. To stay competitive, the survivors increased their acreages. Some people began questioning whether an irreducible minimum actually exists. Perhaps, they suggested, the land is inexorably headed for virtual depopulation.

At the family level, these mathematics expose a profound difference from the old frontier. The end of homesteading essentially concluded the era of farming as a potential entry-level occupation. The only ones who can go into it these days are people who either inherited their land or made enough money in some other enterprise to buy their way in (often to ranch more as a hobby than to make a living). A farm unit that has to expand simply to continue sustaining one family means that the family can pass on its operation to only one heir. On some ranches, none of the kids want to go into the business; it provides too low a return on the labor and investment. But on those with more than one child who desire to follow in their parents' footsteps, economic reality performs triage on such dreams: just one can remain, and in many cases the others can't even stay in their home region since there are so few other job opportunities.

A bitter irony is at work here. Many of the ranchers I met were descendants of immigrants who came to the new land because they were not first-born sons and therefore were out of luck where primogeniture was either the law or the custom. Modern agricultural economics is enforcing a loose version of the same system, unrelated to order of birth but with the same end result. In this respect, life on the range in the contemporary frontier now mirrors the grazing industry upon which it's based. It has become a replacement-level society. Mothers seem destined to keep on giving birth, only to watch most of their offspring being culled out and shipped off to places where there are more people.

ONE NIGHT IN FEBRUARY 1981, TWO MEN TRIED TO rob Jordan's drugstore. One was captured immediately, surrendering after a warning blast from the sheriff's shotgun punched holes through a metal file cabinet and the back wall. The accomplice, who had been posted as a lookout in front of the Hell Creek Bar, jumped into his 1968 Cadillac and took off. Following a brief chase that ended up back in town, he leapt from his car and fled on foot. A thirty-man posse, composed of fire department volunteers and bar patrons, eventually surrounded and captured him in an abandoned building. That same evening, a local man had broken his leg during a fight in the bar, requiring an ambulance. An out-of-town trucker, who was stopping to get his coffee thermos filled, arrived at the Hell Creek Bar just as the ambulance showed up and as the bartender and several others were returning with their pistols and rifles. The last time he had been in Jordan, he told the local paper, a wife had been shot by her husband. The trucker said, "I believe I'll find a new way to get to Great Falls."

Needless to say, the incident got a lot of media attention outside Jordan. (In Bozeman, the *Daily Chronicle* ran the story under the John Wayne headline, "Reach, Pilgrim.") So did a picture four years later of the same sheriff, wearing a cowboy hat and six-gun, patrolling the town streets on horseback after he had lost his driver's license from a drunk-driving arrest in Billings. Both events burnished Garfield County's image as a place where the "Wild West" still exists.

The truth is considerably tamer. Nick Murnion, the county attorney and sole local lawyer, said the last serious gunplay in Garfield County was in 1984, the product of a love triangle. The most recent shooting death, resulting in a conviction of negligent homicide in 1979, was the first in about forty years. Sheriff Ed Dobler, a retired navy warrant officer from New York who replaced his more colorful and controversial predecessor in 1985, doesn't own a horse and doesn't wear cowboy boots or a cowboy hat. Much of the two-man department's time in the late 1980s, he said, was spent presiding at foreclosure sales and investigating highway accidents and violations (331 in two and a half years). Trespassing hunters are an annual headache, he said. There hadn't been a felony arrest in more than a year.

Arthur Jordan wrote that at the turn of the century "every shady character that could not stand the spotlight of civilization drifted in and around the new town, always ready to have their fun or start trouble." Remoteness plus sparsity of population equaled lawlessness. Now, almost the opposite applies. Time and again, people told me that one of the best things about life in Garfield County is their feeling of safety. A two-man sheriff's force, expected to cover not only the vast countryside but the town, is evidence of their sense of personal security. People leave their houses unlocked and their keys in their cars' ignitions while they shop. They don't worry about small children being alone on the streets of town. Where dirt roads meet highways, ranch families often park their best cars miles from their homes without fear of vandalism or theft; their greater concern is ruining the cars on the ranch roads, which they travel in their older pickups. In their view, lawlessness and danger and fear are city dwellers.

Rustling is the crime that most closely links past and present. By all accounts, the county's age-old reputation as a hotbed for stealing livestock still pertains. All that's changed are the methods the rustler uses. The long distances between dwellings make it relatively easy for someone to pull up a horse trailer on a remote road, herd in ten sheep or a few calves, and drive off undetected. The last time anyone could remember a rustler being caught in the region was when his tractor-trailer, fully loaded with stolen animals, had an accident on its way toward the state line. Ranchers I talked to considered rustling an annoyance, but more or less in the same category as the weather: something you can't do much about.

Particularly along the breaks of the Musselshell River, the traditional refuge for outlaws in the late 1800s and early 1900s, people often suspect that many of their lost animals clandestinely become part of a neighbor's herd. "Most of the people who originally moved in here were cattle rustlers and horse thieves or were moving away from something," a Montana law enforcement official who grew up in southwestern Garfield County told me. "There's no trouble *finding* rustlers —just go from one ranch to another—but *proving* it is another matter."

Gladys Stanton, the local judge who doubles as the county coordinator for programs for the elderly and drives the agency's bus for senior citizens, showed me her favorite case from the court's old leather-bound docket book. Some ranchers had posted bail for a man accused of rustling; upon release he had stolen some of their animals and vanished, so they petitioned for a refund of their bail money. No doubt the Stranglers would have responded somewhat differently. Who knows what they would have thought about a sign on Gladys Stanton's office wall: "Take the law into your own hands—hug a judge today."

There are other vestiges of the old frontier, but, as with crime, they are modulated echoes of a bygone era. The Jordan Stage still brings the mail and supplies from Miles City. Although its name is unchanged, the Stage is now a one-ton GMC truck that arrives and departs daily rather than a once-a-week, team-drawn wagon. For an unofficial donation, residents can hitch a ride to Miles City in the evening or back to Jordan in the morning with Zane Kittelmann, the stage driver. (The only official public transportation in the county is Judge Stanton's senior citizen bus, which goes to Miles City twice a month and to Billings every other month.) Kittelmann logs a thousand miles a week on his rounds. Besides the nuanced pleasures of prairie sunsets and sunrises, the main scenic attraction on the lightly traveled highway is a lone cottonwood, where the Rock Springs post office once stood about halfway between the two towns, near which some prankster has erected a sign: "Rock Springs National Forest."

When I rode with him, Kittelmann's cargo from Miles City included several bags of mail; eighty cases of milk for Jordan's grocery store, café, and schools; dry cleaning for residents (the grocery store was the local drop-off point); laundered towels and linen for the nursing home, bars, and motel; automotive parts for the Jordan garage; and a new bed and refrigerator someone had ordered from Sears. On his way to the Jordan post office in the predawn, he also delivered mail to sixteen boxes along the highway—those postal patrons, whose address is "Jordan Stage, Miles City," are perhaps the only people in the United States who receive their mail before seven o'clock each morning. One rancher was sitting in his pickup at the end of his lane, waiting in the chilly darkness for his mail and *The Wall Street Journal.*

Reinhart Rath took over Jordan's barber shop in 1950, before the town had a municipal water system, so part of the business was providing baths to people for fifty cents. With the bath sideline now outdated, Rath augments his revenues—haircuts are six bucks—by running the county's state liquor store and being the local distributor for water distillers. Most of the water in the county is highly alkaline. Without distilling, "it'll give you the gutache and runs real bad," Rath said. When I visited, the Reverend Mr. Senecal's son, Rusty, was sitting in the barber's chair getting his hair cut against a backdrop of booze bottles. Arnaud Elissalde, known locally as Basquo, was passing the afternoon there as well. He had arrived in Garfield County forty years before from his native French Basque region to herd sheep. In those days, before the larger outfits fenced their huge ranges and made the job of shepherd locally obsolete, Basquo lived alone on the range, following his herd by day and playing solitaire at night in a tiny sheep wagon while he listened to "Fibber McGee and Molly" on the radio. He would come into town once a year to bank his salary. Now he has a small apartment above the fire station and lives off his investments.

STRANGERS TO GARFIELD COUNTY AND OTHER PARTS of the contemporary frontier often experience what can best be described as a double case of the bends. The first, a response to a landscape comparatively devoid of inhabitants, is an almost physical decompression: no people, no buildings, no traffic, so much sky. You find yourself taking deep gulps of air, unsure whether you're unwinding from the press of humanity or becoming uneasy from the palpable remoteness. Paradoxically, the second is a sense of societal claustrophobia. The communities you encounter may be the most geographically dispersed in the nation, but they often are also the most closely knit.

"Everyone knows everyone else's business, but they'll always help you when you're in trouble"—it was a constant refrain I heard, repeated virtually word for word so many times I came to consider it the opening stanza of the region's national anthem. As the phrase itself implies, there are two sides to this neighborliness. Anonymity is not an option. If the sparsely settled frontier was ever a refuge for Americans seeking permanent escape from society's embrace, it no longer offers such sanctuary. Hermit personalities would do better by taking an apartment in New York City and bolting their doors.

In my travels I met a number of ex-urbanites—a few, not a lot of them—who had deliberately and successfully made the transition from one extreme of population density to the other. They were vastly outnumbered by the tales I heard of newcomers from some city who had lasted only a year before beating a hasty retreat. The harsh climate, the unforgiving land, the reductionist agricultural economics, and the vast distances to anyplace else—the main ingredients that caused the region to be sparsely settled in the first place—have conspired over time with new elements to keep it that way.

One such element is the at-most-one-of-everything services, which natives accept as a fact of life but which some newcomers find too inconvenient to endure. "We're not quite as much a 'now' society as the rest of the world," said Janet Guptill, editor of the local paper. "You sometimes hear grumblings about no fresh produce or no fresh bread, but these are not life-or-death matters. You learn to live with it." Another element is the society itself: not at all unfriendly or unaccepting toward new residents; quite the contrary, so much the opposite that people accustomed to city or suburban life can find it smothering.

It is as if within the contemporary frontier an autoimmune system has evolved that rejects more transplants than it accepts. You realize quickly whether you fit in—with the physical surroundings or the community. "There's no secrets here," said one man who had moved to Garfield County seven years earlier. He liked it and its people very much, but added, "If they don't like you, you might as well move out."

Most of the residents, then, are either survivors of the first generation of homesteaders, their descendants, or people who grew up in similar locales. Many of them went through school together and are related to one another. The telephone, which Jana Olson, the county's public health nurse, called "the most important invention ever for this place," keeps them as intimately informed about each other as they would be if they all lived in one compact housing project. Ask a resident about someone else in the county and you'll get a detailed personal and family history, warts and all.

Because they grew up with one another, "they make friends once in their life," said Rick Hannon, the high school guidance counselor and principal at Jordan's elementary school. "They identify with Garfield County, not Montana, not the rest of the nation."

A psychological profile of the county, he said, would reveal on the one hand "self-sufficient expectations—if they feel bad or hurt, they feel responsible for taking care of it themselves—a Marlboro Man attitude that the West is rough and it's tough and it's hard, and you have to put up with it. There's an independence and a sense of your own mortality that you can't forget. You know the animosity that the land has against you; you know the finiteness of your own self. They *expect* adversity. What would they do without it? If ten years went by and there were no crops, they'd still be here. They're part of the soil now."

On the other hand, accompanying their own sense of individualism is a tolerance for another's. "You're not choosy about friends and neighbors, you're thankful that they're there," Hannon said. "They don't always resolve their differences, they learn to get along with them. They may need that neighbor."

Their highly developed sense of place, which makes the people of the contemporary frontier so secure on their home ground, also creates a heightened sensitivity to the way the rest of the world views them. Any perceived slight to their area is taken very personally. "We're not as isolated or backward as other people think" is their anthem's second stanza. "We *choose* to live here" is the third.

From its inception, Garfield County in particular has struggled with its image. A "Pocket Directory and Booster Guide" published by local businessmen in 1926, referring to Jordan as "The Progressive Town," said: "God sort of hid this beautiful little inland county seat city off up here in the northeast corner of Montana to reserve it for the best people. We're glad you found it and if you have any good neighbors like yourself at home tell 'em about us. We still have room for a few good people." Roughly twice as many businesses were listed in the one-page directory as exist in Jordan today. The irreducible minimum was not in the "progressive town's" forecast.

Four years later, Isaiah Bowman, president of the American Geographical Society, made a field trip to the area, gathering material for
a monograph he published in 1931. Titled "Jordan Country," Bowman's
article presented Garfield County as an example of the pioneer-like
conditions that still existed in much of the Great Plains. He noted the
sparse population, people living in sod and log homes, only one doctor
(Dr. Farrand), and a region without phone, telegraph, rail, or bus services. In a speech to Jordan's business community, Bowman disclosed
that their town was farther from a railroad than any other town in the
nation. The broken promise of a railroad through the county was, and
still is, a festering wound locally: the extra distance to a railhead, even
greater now than when Bowman visited, had increased the farmers'
and ranchers' production costs and thwarted the Jordan boosters'
dreams of a "natural metropolis." Nevertheless, they tried to make the
best of their distinction, hoping to beckon new settlers with a brochure
proclaiming Jordan as "the most isolated frontier town in the United
States."

In 1947, Chevrolet conducted a nationwide promotional search for
the oldest Chevy still in operation. Leslie Storey, a local farmer, won
with his 1918 truck. *Look* magazine ran a breezy photo feature about
the parade and celebration Jordan held when the manufacturer presented Storey with a new vehicle. Without explanation—perhaps it
was a modification of Bowman's statistic—the article carried the headline: "The Loneliest Town in the U.S. Wins a Contest." Forty-three years
later, people still complain about that characterization.

By the time Dr. Farrand retired in the mid-1970s and community
leaders produced a brochure to help lure a replacement, a more defiant
tone had crept into the county's voice to the world:

Since we don't have people standing at our elbows everyplace
we go, we don't have the usual problems of our urban brothers
and sisters. We can go out in the evening to fill our lungs full
of clean, fresh prairie air without worrying about being mugged,
raped or in some other way assaulted. There is no need for us
to hide and crouch behind locked doors.

We live a couple of hours drive from any sizable population
centers. This makes us just a little bit more independent and
just a little bit more self sufficient. We have learned to fend for

ourselves and enjoy the solitude which such isolation brings.

The last thing in the world we really want is an influx of people. We only want people to come and live in our community who are willing to recognize the beauty of the land and the beauty of the people. There is no room in our community for complainers, belly-achers or people who are dissatisfied with life. Many of us who were born here intend to live and die here. We do this out of choice.

Garfield County's feeling that more populated areas don't understand it extends to the state's power centers as much as to the rest of the nation. In 1980, when the Montana Highway Patrol overrode protests and cut out its local coverage along the county's highways, the Billings paper said Jordan had been considered the "Siberia" of state patrol assignments. "We either get the beginners, the retirees, or the ones in the dog house," Janet Guptill said when an officer was finally reassigned to the county in 1990. Cecil Weeding, the local state senator whose district encompasses Garfield County and parts of five others —an area of about 15,000 square miles, twice the size of New Jersey, with just 14,000 people—considers his main role in the state capitol to be working against bills and regulations, designed for the more heavily populated parts of Montana, that would add hardship to his area. "As far as I'm concerned, *this* is normal," Weeding said of his district. "Everyone else lives a screwed-up life."

"The outside world makes fun of Jordan," the Reverend Senecal said. Stopping for fuel on his way to start his pastorship in Jordan, for instance, he had been told by a gas station attendant that "there's nothing but jack rabbits" in Garfield County. Over time, Senecal said, the region has developed an "us-versus-the-world attitude."

That attitude hardened in 1987, when the outside world brusquely intruded again on the tiny population's sense of itself. The nonprofit Institute of the Rockies, based in Missoula, a university town in western Montana, proposed that all of Garfield County and the thinly settled portions of nine surrounding counties be turned into the Big Open Great Plains Wildlife Range. Fences would be taken down throughout 15,000 square miles. Domestic cattle and sheep would be replaced by their wilder predecessors: 75,000 buffalo, 40,000 elk, 40,000 antelope, 150,000 deer, and, eventually, those grazing animals' original predators such as the grizzly, the mountain lion, and the buffalo wolf (the last of which had been seen in the county in the 1930s). The local agricultural economy, which the proposal contended was both heavily dependent on federal subsidies and wantonly destructive to the environment, would be transformed. The Big Open would become "an international destination, a magnet for tourists, sportsmen, photographers, and outdoors enthusiasts" drawn to immense, free-roaming herds "unequaled by any other place on earth save possibly the Serengeti Plain of East Africa." One thousand new tourist-related jobs were projected; the human population might double; a landowner who switched his 10,000-acre ranch to wildlife might clear $48,000 a year from hunting permits alone.

More people, more jobs, more money. No one had spoken of Garfield County's future in those terms since the Great Northern and Soo lines had promised a railroad through Jordan nearly sixty years earlier. Once forecast as the upcoming "natural metropolis" of eastern Montana, Jordan might be the next Nairobi. "There are two things standing in the way," wrote Robert Scott, author of the Big Open proposal. "A herd of 150,000 cows and calves and a herd of 150,000 sheep and lambs located on 250 ranches."

Actually, there was a third thing standing in the way, one that Scott had overlooked: the people themselves. As the plan for the Big Open had been devised, no one had bothered to solicit the natives' opinions about switching to a safari economy. Jordan learned about the proposal when someone sent a *New York Times* article about it to the president of the local Chamber of Commerce.

The reaction ranged from dislike to outrage. Every suspicion they had harbored that outsiders viewed them with, at best, condescension was seemingly confirmed. Every lingering resentment they had felt about the urban areas exerting too much influence over their lives and land was stirred again. When the cities far downstream the Missouri River had complained about chronic flooding and unreliable river traffic in the 1930s, the Fort Peck Dam had been built, putting Garfield County's best river-bottom farmland under water; and the electricity from the dam's hydroelectric turbines had been shipped elsewhere. When environmentalists had pushed through national legislation in 1972 banning the use of the poison 1080 to control coyotes, local sheepmen felt victimized; one of them, the president of the Montana

Woolgrowers Association, had been forced out of business by the losses he blamed on increased predator populations. Now the prospect was being raised of reintroducing *wolves*, a predator about which virtually every old-timer had some personal horror story to tell.

As they started reading the Big Open proposal and the many articles about it in national publications, Garfield County residents fixed upon the passages referring to failed homestead policies, degraded range- land, and federal subsidies, and upon portrayals of their community as existing in some sort of backwards time warp. It was "The Loneliest Town" all over again, combined with what they saw as both a threat to and dismissal of their way of life. "What upset people was that someone from the outside came and said the people had wasted their lives here," remembered Scott Guptill, who runs the local paper with his mother. "People were really insulted."

Jordan's Chamber of Commerce arranged a private meeting at the local restaurant to hear about the plan firsthand. Construing it as implicit support of the Big Open, some ranchers crashed the meeting, angrily confronted Robert Scott and other institute members, and ac- cused the merchants of selling out the region. During a later meeting, in a community hall near Brusett, someone thought a parked car with unfamiliar license plates must be Scott's (it wasn't) and shot out the back window. Within the Big Open's boundaries, no one seemed to like the idea—not even the ranchers who for some time had been supplementing their declining farm incomes by selling hunting privi- leges on their land or renting vacant homestead cabins to hunters and fishermen.

The Chamber's members, feeling intense heat from guilt-by- association, published a letter distancing themselves from the pro- posal. By learning more about the Big Open, they explained, they were now in a better position to defeat it. "We live in a society that waxes sentimental at the idea of wildlife and wilderness," the letter said. "Even though very few would ever opt to go to such an area they can gain comfort in knowing that something has been saved for posterity. . . . We do not need some mystical concept to make this suddenly become a land of enchantment. It has that potential right now [with hunting, fishing, and open space]. Those from without would have us be a garden of Eden, never mind the blood, sweat and tears which have gone into creating a balance on this once and still hard land."

Scott and some others weighed in with letters of their own, seeking to pacify the uproar. No one, said one letter, was advocating removing people from their homes or taking away their land, just the livestock and fences; an alternative, more sustainable economy could be created with wildlife as the sole resource. Montanans, not insurance companies (which had been buying up farmland) or railroads or the federal government, would own the land and decide its fate, said another. Better to "produce a commodity that is in short supply [wild game] than one that is already oversupplied [beef and wheat]," said a third.

But the debate was already over. More groups—the county's conservation district, the state association of grazing districts—joined the opposition. Politicians, from state senator Weeding to the region's congressman, came out against the plan. Even the volunteer president of the Institute of the Rockies resigned out of fears the controversy might hurt his employer, the Montana Extension Service.

Three years later, at the time of my visit to Jordan, the Big Open was still a sore topic. "Deep down, a lot of people think it's probably inevitable, but they'll fight it to their dying breath," one Jordan merchant told me.

To the extent the proposal was still alive, however, it was only among those who had supported it in the first place: people from somewhere else. John Trumbo of the Hell Creek Guest Ranch offered this explanation: "It's like someone told us here in Garfield County that they were going to take part of New York State, where no one lived, and turn it into a moose preserve. Not knowing anything about the place, it'd probably sound like a good idea. But around here we don't need more wolves, we don't need more coyotes, we don't need a Big Open. Everybody's got an idea for us. We just want to be left alone."

NEAR THE END OF MY STAY IN GARFIELD COUNTY, A winter storm whipped in from the northwest. Most everybody hunkered down in their homes to ride it out. The snow didn't seem to be falling, it was speeding horizontally, as if, since there was nothing in its path, its destination was a snow drift somewhere on the East Coast. The main highways were closed for a few hours and stranded travelers, primarily truckers, gathered at QD's, Jordan's restaurant, to await word that they could get back in motion. Downtown Jordan was silent. Ferocious as it was, even the wind seemed mutely aghast at the whiteout it was causing. That night the gale weakened but persisted. No one was on the streets of town when I went for a short walk. There were more houses than when Arthur Jordan had first started building his cabin on the Big Dry in a winter storm near the turn of the century. But it was hard to shake the notion that this was the same storm, responding with the same fury at the audacity of someone trying to plant human roots where the wind whispers its command through clenched teeth: *Shhhhooo, Shhhhooo, Shhhhooo.* A blinking yellow traffic light, suspended over the intersection of Main Street and the highway, rocked violently in the squall, straining at its wires to be turned loose.

The next day the storm was gone. Everything was back to normal in Jordan. It was time for me to move on. I ate lunch at QD's. About forty other people were there. A waitress brought a cake with candles to one of the tables and began singing "Happy Birthday." Everyone joined in, and when we reached the point of "Dear ———," I was the only one who didn't automatically know the name. It seemed like a representative moment in this place where people live so far apart yet so close together.

I made a final stop at the Hell Creek Bar before leaving town and got a reminder of another dimension of the residents of the county. A rancher I had met a week earlier, one of the more outspoken opponents of the Big Open, pulled me aside to "make sure you understand a few things." The reason the area had been homesteaded so late in the nation's history, he said, was because "all the good land had already been taken—it's the worst land, and nobody else wanted it." His voice wasn't bitter, it was fierce, astringent as the whiskey on his breath.

What he didn't say, because he probably knew I already understood it, however, was this: worst land or not, he and his neighbors *did* want it, just as their parents had wanted it when no one else did and had remained when everyone else had departed in defeat. He, too, intended to remain. The Big Dry country had always been something of a last refuge—for the buffalo, the Audubon sheep, the wolves, and even Arthur Jordan and the horse thieves. Now it was his.

A YEAR LATER, I CHECKED IN ON GARFIELD COUNTY by telephone to catch up on the news. The lone cottonwood comprising the "Rock Springs National Forest" had been cut down by the highway department; a community hall had been erected in Jordan by volunteer labor. A new nursing home was being proposed to replace the one in the old hospital. The old hospital, in turn, was to become the new county courthouse—and preserve Garfield County's distinction as being perhaps the only county in the nation that never built a courthouse. Dan Muniak's medical practice had taken hold and was expanding with the opening of the medical assistance facility. A family from Dodge City, Kansas, who had purchased the Garfield Hotel and were just moving in during my visit, had lasted only a few months before moving out and selling the hotel to the local banker. Charlotte Moran, the young school teacher from western Montana, had married her local boyfriend. *Time* magazine had done a story about one of the county's rural schools. It was generally favorable, but people objected to Jordan being called "a hiccup of a town" and thought they detected some implicit ridicule when the story said the students had never heard of Milli Vanilli, the rock group. Wool and wheat prices were down, cattle prices up. There were rumors that someone, perhaps even the federal government, had secretly reintroduced wolves into the area; some people linked it to renewed outside interest in the Big Open. A balmy 70-degree day had been followed by a snowstorm.

For me, the biggest news was about Margaret Stafford. During the first week of January, on a subzero Saturday night when her woodstove was going full blast against the cold, the roof next to her stovepipe had caught on fire. Rather than telephoning for help, Margaret had climbed up onto the roof to try to put the fire out herself. Her son, looking outside when his dog started howling, saw smoke in the distance and rushed over; his wife called the neighbors. By the time they arrived, the house was gone. The outbuildings were saved by shoveling snow on them.

Her father's antique desk and the pump organ for which she had traded two heifers were burned to cinders, along with everything else Margaret owned, except the clothes on her back and a few personal papers. Friends encouraged her to move into Jordan, but she had refused. She hauled a small trailer onto her land and started over. Still homesteading after all these years.

CHAPTER 2

VIOLENCE

THE WESTERN FRONTIER OF THE LATTER HALF OF
the nineteenth century was a violent place. Without question, this point
has been as overstated as it was overromanticized in the last hundred
years. From Ned Buntline's dime novels about Buffalo Bill Cody fighting Indians in the 1870s to breathless newspaper reports about shoot-
outs between lawmen and bandits, contemporary accounts were no
less sensationalized than the Hollywood movies and television series
about the "Wild West" that became popular several generations later.
The accumulated body count on those pages and screens—of massa-
cred settlers or of dead Indians and cavalrymen slain in pitched battles,
of innocent people murdered by gunslingers or of outlaw gangs wiped
out by honest sheriffs—no doubt would exceed the total human population of the frontier in those times.

But this popularized view of the old frontier, grotesquely exaggerated as it became, was not a total fabrication. In many respects, the western frontier was a war zone. White culture waged war against the Indian tribes, for whom warfare against one another was already a centuries-old tradition, and it waged war against the very environment, as the buffalo and other nearly extinct native species mutely attest, not to mention the landscape that was mined, dammed, and denuded. The white people also often warred among themselves—for rangeland, for the scarce supply of water, for mining rights and homestead claims, for who would emerge with political and economic control, even sometimes for where a county seat would be located. The agents of order and law were frequently far away; in their absence, criminals and vigilantes brutely struggled for dominion. Heavily male and heavily armed (and often heavily inebriated), the population of the region in those days was markedly different from the rest of the nation when it came to matters of life and death.

Truth may be the first casualty of war. Certainly in the melodramatic tales and legends it engendered, in the embroidered specifics of its individual incidents, and in the glorified justifications offered as its rationale, the war to "win the West" was no exception. Just as certainly, as in any war, the bloodshed wasn't constant nor was everyone a combatant. Make no mistake, however. It was a war of conquest waged on more than one front, and many people died violently and suffered profoundly during its conduct.

The contemporary frontier occupies much of the same space as its predecessor. And many of the West's old conflicts—between cultures and over the use of its resources—still exist, although they are now fought out in courts and legislatures by hired lawyers and lobbyists rather than on the dusty streets or the prairies by hired guns or the cavalry. But if "wildness" is defined as ruthless lawlessness and imminent conflict, an atmosphere in which human violence, deliberate or random, may break out at any moment, then the sparsely settled counties of the modern West should be counted among the tamer places of the nation. This is the age of the fear of "the other"—the unknown person waiting to do you or your family harm and injury. In the contemporary frontier, where everybody knows everybody else, there is seldom any "other" to fear.

American cities have replaced the frontier in the wild department, both in fact and in the cliches of popular imagination. People looking nervously over their shoulders when they hear footsteps at night; peering from behind shuttered windows as shots echo on the streets outside; worrying about their children being caught in a random crossfire, their womenfolk being cruelly abused by marauders, or their homes and businesses being robbed by a lawless gang; demanding greater protection from their government; viewing issues of personal safety in terms of racial stereotypes, so that someone of another color is assumed to be an enemy until proven otherwise; banding together in citizen patrols because the officers of justice seem too slow to arrive and too ineffectual to enforce the peace. Those basic elements once comprised the image of the western frontier. But they have been transferred to the image of city life.

The entertainment industry reflects this change and now distorts the urban life to caricature, much as it did the old West. Dead bodies now pile up against a backdrop of skyscrapers and concrete instead of mountains and grama grass. The classic Western *Fort Apache* reappeared as *Fort Apache: The Bronx* with only a change of locale and attire.

Tell someone from a sparsely settled area that he's going to a big city for a visit and he'll react the way a proper Philadelphian would have a hundred years ago to an impending trip to some remote outpost in the West: with an undercurrent of uneasiness for his personal safety, if not sheer terror. In both instances, part of that reaction would be misplaced, the product of exaggeration and tall tales. But part of the fear, in both instances, would nonetheless be a rational response to real dangers.

IN THE CONTEMPORARY FRONTIER THE OLD WEST'S most celebrated bloody moments are still remembered. My travels were like a tour of some vast Museum of Death and Conflict. Reminders that the western frontier's reputation for violence was earned greeted me at every stop. Here's a sampling:

Billy the Kid was killed in De Baca County, New Mexico, and is buried there next to two of his pals, also brought down by Pat Garrett's gun. The Wyoming cattle barons and small ranchers culminated their range war in Johnson County only after U.S. troops arrived to stop further bloodshed. Alferd Packer survived a tough winter in the San Juan Mountains of Hinsdale County, Colorado, by eating five of his fellow mining prospectors. Virtually all of the hideouts of Butch Cassidy and his "Wild Bunch"—from the Hole in the Wall in Wyoming, to Brown's Hole on the Green River and the Robber's Roost in Utah, to a ranch near Alma, New Mexico—were in counties that still have fewer than two people per square mile. Cassidy's group robbed trains and banks in locations throughout the West, sparsely settled or not. They often spent their booty in bigger cities, but the remote places were their shelter. Before leaving for South America with his sidekick Harry Longabaugh, better known as the Sundance Kid, Cassidy conducted his final United States train robbery in Phillips County, Montana. Two years earlier, Black Jack Ketchum, another member of the gang, had held up a train and been captured in Union County, New Mexico. When they hanged him in Clayton, the county seat, the long drop jerked Black Jack's head off. Madison County, Montana, was the home of the Virginia City vigilantes, who didn't bother with formal trials and used shorter ropes.

Kiowa County, Colorado, was the site of the infamous Sand Creek massacre in 1864, in which a village of Cheyenne Indians, prominently flying an American flag and white flag as proof it wasn't "hostile," was nonetheless attacked by volunteer troops commanded by Col. John Chivington. Known in civilian life as the "Fighting Parson" because he often conducted Methodist services wearing revolvers, Chivington is said to have told his troops, "Kill and scalp all, big and little; nits make lice," before they charged the unsuspecting, peaceful village at dawn. White Antelope, one of the chiefs, was gunned down while he tried to show the attackers a peace medal President Lincoln had given him. His ears and nose were cut off, his scalp taken, and his scrotum removed for use as a tobacco pouch. Nearly 200 Indians were slaughtered, mostly women and children. Their scalps, some of them women's pubic hair, were displayed to an exuberant crowd at the Denver Opera House. A government commission investigated and Chivington was dishonored in much of the nation, although he remained a hero to many westerners and a Kiowa County town still bears his name.

But the principal result of Sand Creek was an eruption of further violence as embittered tribes sought vengeance up and down the Plains. Two years later, in Johnson County, Wyoming, scalps were taken from white men. Capt. William Fetterman and 80 soldiers were surrounded, killed, and mutilated by Sioux and Cheyenne warriors near Fort Phil Kearny. Shortly after the battle of the Little Bighorn in 1876, Buffalo Bill Cody, scouting for the cavalry in Sioux County, Nebraska, killed the Cheyenne chief Yellow Hair and took the "first scalp for Custer." Despite the chief's name, the scalp that Cody hacked from his head and sent back east to Mrs. Cody for safekeeping had black, not yellow, hair. Yellow Hair had gotten his name for scalping a blond white woman.

Black scouts stationed at Fort Clark in Kinney County, Texas, won Congressional Medals of Honor for bravery against the Apache, Comanche, and Kiowa, but were never fully accepted by the white neighbors they were protecting. While attending a New Year's Eve dance at the fort, one of the Medal of Honor recipients was shot at such close range that the blast set his clothes on fire.

Chief Joseph and his Nez Percé tribe began their 1,700-mile flight to freedom with battles in Idaho County, Idaho. They fought off a surprise attack at the Big Hole River in southwestern Montana's Beaverhead County and then, after another battle near the Bear Paw Mountains of Blaine County, 40 miles from the Canadian border, Chief Joseph handed over his rifle and said, "I will fight no more forever."

If a county I visited didn't have a historical connection to incidents from the West's truly wild past, it often was linked to the celluloid version. John Ford's movie *Stagecoach* created two icons in the popular view of the frontier: John Wayne, the film's star, and Monument Valley in San Juan County, Utah, its location, whose starkly outlined buttes are now more familiar to moviegoers than any other landscape. The opening sequence of "The Lone Ranger" television show was shot in Inyo County, California, as were episodes of other popular westerns like "Have Gun, Will Travel," "Wild Bill Hickok," "Gunsmoke," and "Rawhide." Kane County, Utah, was used for so many cowboy and Indian movies and television series that it called itself "Hollywood East." (Business dropped off after some locals burned the film star Robert Redford in effigy for his stand against a proposed coal mine and power plant.) Happy Shahan's Alamo Village, a reconstruction of the site of Texas's famous battle, was built in Kinney County for the movie *The Alamo* in 1959 and has been recycled for countless horse operas ever since. Scenes from "Lonesome Dove" were filmed there thirty years later. The buffalo hunt from *Dances With Wolves* was staged at a ranch in Stanley County, South Dakota.

Sometimes the locales weren't exactly fitted to the narrative—*Drums Along the Mohawk, In Old Oklahoma*, and *Green Grass of Wyoming*, each conjuring different terrains and climates, were all filmed in southern Utah—but the sparsely settled counties offer filmmakers two things that more than compensate: plenty of rainless days to keep production schedules on time, and lots of scenery devoid of the trappings of the twentieth century.

Safely removed by time and distance, violence can be good for business. Promotional brochures for eastern New Mexico feature Billy the Kid on the cover. Virginia City, Montana, is a quaintly restored mining town where two of the major attractions are the building where the vigilantes summarily hanged their suspects and Boot Hill, where they were buried. I saw Butch Cassidy and the Wild Bunch placemats, calendars, and cookbooks in several counties. Fast-draw shoot-outs entertain people at Alamo Village. Niobrara County, Wyoming, stages an outdoor pageant every summer called "The Legend of Rawhide," in which a wagon train is attacked by Indians and the highlight is a particularly realistic skinning and scalping of a settler. Stores in Lake City, Colorado, offer coffee mugs, pens, and dolls commemorating the cannibal Alferd Packer; T-shirts with pictures of Packer and the skeletons of his victims are for sale, with messages like "Dedicated to Serving His Fellow Man" or "Have a Friend for Dinner." A local photography studio runs an Alferd Packer look-alike contest during the busy summer tourist season; a play reenacts his trial; the Chamber of Commerce's annual Alferd Packer Dinner is a big draw. "We tell people not to ask where the meat came from," a businessman told me.

Whether it's for a tour of a historic site or a visit to the ersatz reconstructions, tourists from the city and suburbs come to parts of the contemporary frontier for a taste of its wild and violent past. They spend their money and return to their urban homes—where they have to disarm their security system upon entering, where their local television station and newspaper consider only the most heinous crimes unusual enough to report.

Meanwhile, back in the places with few people, the current state of frontier crime is reflected in police logs published in the weekly papers. Like this one from *The Lusk Herald* in Niobrara County, Wyoming:

> Jan. 18—Provided a courtesy ride; returned a driver's license to an individual; attempted to deliver a message; assisted an individual seek[ing] medical attention.
>
> Jan. 19— . . . all policemen attending the hazardous materials training in Lusk.
>
> Jan. 20— . . . received report of a truck blocking a driveway; delivered a message; received a report of vandalism at New Beginnings Christian Fellowship; two written warnings were issued for speeding and for failure to display license plates as required.
>
> Jan. 21—Investigated a report of suspicious circumstances involving phone calls; provided a courtesy ride; unlocked a car door; assisted the sheriff's department with photos; received a report of cows on the highway east of town.

SMALL TOWNS RELATIVELY FREE OF SERIOUS CRIME can be found, of course, in every region of the country. In that respect the West's contemporary frontier is not distinct. What makes it different, besides the wars of conquest and brutal lawlessness of its relatively recent past, is this: violent death is still one of its hallmarks.

While the dangers of outlaw gangs, vigilantes, and Indian wars have passed, other threats to a long life remain. They include inhospitable weather, long distances from medical care, a way of life that exalts risk-taking and independence so that people are simultaneously more likely to get into life-threatening situations and yet less likely to seek help when they need it, a casual view of the carrying and use of guns, and a high concentration of occupations like mining, logging, oil-drilling, ranching, and farming that often put people in harm's way. (Mining and agriculture, for instance, have death rates from trauma that are nearly ten times higher than trade, services, and manufacturing—occupations more common to urban areas.) Suicide rates in the West as a whole are higher than in the rest of the nation; the highest rates are in its nonurban sections. Automobile accidents also take a deadly toll. As part of their everyday lives, residents of the contemporary frontier drive more miles (and usually at higher speeds) than their counterparts in other places. If an accident occurs in a sparsely settled area, it may not be immediately discovered; once it's discovered and reported, medical assistance is longer in arriving.

Counties with fewer than *six* people per square mile constitute what some experts call a "health-care frontier" with unique medical problems further exacerbated by the sparsity of services and the distances that impede emergency response. One study in Utah found that frontier residents have a mortality rate before age sixty-five a third higher than urban residents of the state. Another study, focusing on violent death among white and Hispanic young people (ages fifteen to twenty-four) from 1939 to 1979, described the West as more "dangerous" than other regions, again with the nonurban areas the most dangerous. In fact, in some of the rural counties the rate of violent death among young white and Hispanic males was higher than that of young black males in the nation's six most violent cities. In the urban ghettos the homicide rate was higher, but in the rural West the rate of other violent deaths (particularly suicides and automobile, work-related and other accidents) more than made up the difference.

I wasn't conducting a methodical study of mortality on my journey, but anecdotal evidence supporting the same conclusions accumulated with every small weekly paper I picked up in a sparsely settled county: Arthur County, Nebraska: three young men killed in two separate car accidents within one month. Johnson County, Wyoming: rancher dies after being thrown from a horse. Crook County, Wyoming: logger killed in accident. Harding County, South Dakota: fund-raiser held for farmer crippled by his overturned tractor. Niobrara County, Wyoming: man bitten by rabid coyote. Grant County, Oregon: one-car crash kills man, injures two. Sublette County, Wyoming: motorcyclist collides with moose. In Nebraska, Montana, New Mexico, South Dakota, Utah, and west Texas I met people who had lost relatives in crashes of small airplanes or helicopters; some were flying to check on cattle or sheep herds, one was hunting wolves, another was a doctor making his rounds by air.

News stories of suicides were more rare, but then again many small-town papers don't publish that as a cause of death, so I decided to dig a little deeper. John Day, Oregon, is the county seat of Grant County (population 7,853; 1.7 people per square mile), a mountainous area in the eastern part of the state. John Day, a member of the Astorians, who crossed the continent in 1811 to establish a fur-trading post on the Oregon coast, was attacked by Indians near the mouth of the Mau Hau River, a tributary of the Columbia, which soon became known as "John Day's River" in commemoration of his travails. A year later, on a return trip east, he became deranged and attempted suicide. Accurate details of when and how he eventually died are lost to history. The town bearing his name, it seemed to me, would be a good place to investigate the suicide issue.

Dan Kroy, the director of the local mental health center, pulled out a recent statewide study showing that Grant County has a disproportionate share of Oregon's suicides. (Other counties with fewer than two people per square mile have a similarly high rate.) Kroy's personal explanation was based on historical, biological, environmental, and economic conjecture.

"It took a special type of person to pack up a family and move west," he said. "*Something* got them on that wagon train, and it wasn't a cushy job that got them to say, 'I'll risk my life, my family, everything for a promise of something else.' One of those things might have been personality disorders that separated them from everyone else. A lot of them were nuts." By that, he said, he didn't mean they were all dangerous psychotics, but a high proportion of them may have had manic-depressive disorders of varying intensities, which often allow a person to live normally except for occasional bursts of energy and plunges into withdrawal.

"It's not necessarily a bad mental illness, just a personality trait," Kroy added, "and it's an inherited trait. It's also a perfect disorder for a rancher or logger—work, work, work, and then hide out." Boom and bust of the psyche. The logging industry was edging into its seasonal layoffs, and he was expecting an outbreak of trouble.

"This isn't an easy place to live," he said. Killing things, on the other hand, isn't that difficult for a population of ranchers, loggers, and hunters. It's what a lot of people do for their income and food.

Unlike in many other places—and unlike with John Day himself—suicides here aren't just threatened or attempted, they are achieved. The kill ratio is higher. "It's all gunshots. It's all lethal suicide. You don't talk to a therapist, you just go shoot yourself," he said. "Everybody has a gun and knows how it works. It's like hunting: it's no big deal, it's just death."

Kroy is the kind of man who enjoys speculating and doing it in hyperbolic language that both provokes and signals that he doesn't want to be taken overly seriously. Following a tour of duty in Vietnam, he had moved to Mexico, where he lived among expatriates who "either were 'wanted' in the United States and had to get away, or weren't wanted at all in the United States and had to get away." After moving to Africa for a while, he said, "the only reason I came back was for prime rib."

Whatever the causes behind them, he was hoping the new statistics would help his agency get a larger share of state mental health funds. "We have a higher percentage of depressed people in Grant County," he said, "but it's more difficult to treat people here. They're functioning real well. Unfortunately, they blow their brains out about three times more often."

AS IN THE PAST, THE AMERICAN FRONTIER IS STILL heavily armed. For instance:

I had lunch with the publisher of a newspaper in Saguache County, Colorado, who was wearing a .45 in a holster on his hip—a statement, he said, that he took the Second Amendment as seriously as the First. In Lajitas, Texas, on the Rio Grande, a sign at a restaurant door warned that carrying firearms at a place where alcohol is served constitutes a felony with a possible ten-year prison term. I thought it was interesting that someone found it necessary to post such a notice. Then I saw two men at another table, both wearing pistols. They looked like law officials out of uniform, but I didn't bother asking. Outside another café in west Texas was a sign that put a different spin on the issue: "Please unload gun and remove ski mask before entering."

At a weekend party I attended in Kane County, Utah, a combination of family reunion and celebration of the autumnal equinox, most of the men and teenage boys and some of the women were packing iron. Aroya, more of a ghost town than a settlement in windswept eastern Colorado, had a rundown house with a note posted on the front door advising, "We shoot every third salesman." I wasn't disappointed when no one answered my knock.

During jury selection for a trial in Virginia City, Montana, in the courthouse across the street from where the vigilantes once dispensed justice without such time-consuming details, a defense lawyer polled twenty-seven prospective jurors on their familiarity with firearms. Every one of them had used a gun at one time or another; twenty of them had fired a gun within the last year.

Seemingly every highway sign for a deer or elk crossing or with a cow on it to signify a stretch of open range was riddled with bullet holes; the only exceptions looked brand-new.

When I pulled up to the border crossing at Antelope Wells, New Mexico, population three, where a lonely American dirt road meets a lonely Mexican dirt road, the customs official and his wife were having pistol practice behind the port of entry building. The target was a human silhouette. "Here in Antelope Wells there hasn't been a larceny, a theft, a burglary, a rape, or a murder," said the customs man, Roger Morris. "Now up the road, maybe it's different." Of the twenty-two ports of entry on the Mexican border, Antelope Wells is the only one closed at nights. In the evening, Morris walks out the front door, shuffles across the dusty yard, and shuts a metal gate across the dirt road. Anyone wanting to cross the international border—legally—has to wait until morning. The closest motel (and gas station) is nearly a hundred miles away. Morris said he and his wife and teenage daughter spend their nights "sitting around as a family." They can receive one television station on their set; their hobbies are "shootin', huntin', campin', and talkin' about the Bible: this community is completely born again." Their daughter's high school is 75 miles to the northwest; her *bus stop* is 45 miles away. "We know we live a little different from the rest of America now, but we think the rest of the world is weird," he said. "We're not anti-people, we're just antisocial. We like people, as long as they're a hundred miles away." A car arrived, and he went out to inspect it. As I was leaving, he and his wife returned to their target practice.

Gun racks in the entryways of ranch houses I visited were as common as they were across the back windows of pickups—standard equipment. In downtown Paisley, Oregon, population 335, I walked past an empty pickup that had two high-powered rifles in its rack. The windows were open and the keys were in the ignition. In Buffalo, Wyoming, the local paper had a letter from a state senator explaining that, because of all the complaints he had received, he was withdrawing a proposed bill to make it illegal in Wyoming for anyone other than a law enforcement officer to carry a loaded gun into a school and to forbid convicted drug dealers from owning firearms. The bill had been drafted by the National Rifle Association, he explained, and "it was never my intention to start Wyoming down the path of restrictive firearms regulations." But some constituents had misconstrued it to say that it would outlaw carrying a loaded gun in a vehicle, so he was dropping the whole thing.

Bouncing across an endless range with a rancher in southwestern Montana, I lurched into the dashboard when the rancher suddenly stopped his pickup, grabbed the loaded rifle from behind his neck, and plugged a jackrabbit in the distance. A little later he braked again and shot a gopher from the front seat. "You probably think I'm a blood-thirsty bastard," he said as he drove on.

Some of the sparsely settled counties had even more firepower. Most of the nation's nuclear missile installations are located in the Great Plains—the greatest distance possible from an attack across the borders, assuming continued peace with Canada; in a region with a climate that keeps a missile's fuel and circuitry efficiently dry; and far enough from America's principal population centers that any enemy attempt to knock the missiles out would concentrate the initial destruction on the least number of people. While the air force bases that oversee them are near small cities (Cheyenne, Wyoming; Great Falls, Montana; Rapid City, South Dakota, and others), the missile silos themselves are often scattered discreetly along backcountry roads. You usually see them in somebody's wheat field or cattle and sheep range. Bare, two-acre plots ringed by steel fence, with four microwave surveillance sensors in each corner, an electricity pole with three transformers nearby, and a concrete slab in the center, they look like someone began work on a homesite before giving it up. I saw them all the time. Settlers in Montana's Judith Basin, Wheatland, and Chouteau counties no longer worry about depredations from Blackfeet Indians, but they are armed against any modern Red "hostiles" on prairies half a world away. Banner County, Nebraska, with 852 residents and 19 missile silos, probably has more megatons per person than any place on earth. It could battle Europe or China to a standstill. The tiny municipal airport of Philip, South Dakota, population 1,077, is protected by an ICBM sheathed in an underground concrete gun rack across the highway.

Matched against such an array of armaments, I traveled relatively naked. I only had my lucky pocket knife. But I never felt especially vulnerable, although the silent, awesomely cataclysmic implications of a missile silo always sent a little shudder up and down my spine. Times had changed. Statistically, I was more apt to meet my Maker behind the wheel instead of on the receiving end of a bullet (or, since my mount was my own, on the end of a hemp rope). My distinct impression is that all the carbines and shotguns and pistols I kept seeing out in the open are brandished more out of habit than need, that while the guns might have seemed absolutely necessary at one time for survival and self-protection, people carry them around now mostly because of cultural tradition. Perhaps the same could be said of the missiles. Nevertheless, when I lost my knife I replaced it quickly. For one thing, I missed its bottle opener.

MILES FROM NOWHERE, THE ENVIRONMENT ITSELF is potentially lethal. I got all sorts of unsolicited life-saving tips: how to avoid being bitten by a rattlesnake, how to anticipate a flash flood, how to navigate mountain roads in a snowstorm, where to take cover during a tornado, how to minimize the chances that a deer or elk might leap into my windshield, which water supplies were unsafe, how to respond to a chance meeting with a grizzly bear, what to do if the *Conestoga* broke down or ran out of gas in a spot that was dangerously hot or dangerously cold. "If it doesn't bite you or sting you, wait a little; it'll stab you." I heard that adage all across the arid regions, from southwest Texas to eastern Oregon.

To be sure, heavily populated areas can have violent encounters with Mother Nature, and when they occur, casualties mount fast. An earthquake in San Francisco, a hurricane in Charleston, South Carolina, a prolonged heat wave in Phoenix, or a twister near Wichita, Kansas, are grim reminders that forces exist against which mankind's technological defenses are puny. But in such places, the climate and terrain and wildlife don't constitute such a persistent threat to the unprepared and unwary.

Out where hardly anyone else is around, where the human-to-nature scale is transposed and the conceit of civilization can be stripped away with one quick shift of the wind, you're more aware of your own tenuousness. The thought crosses your mind: one reason so few people live here is that the environment is so darn unfriendly. You pay a little closer attention to the weather forecasts. You scan the sky for more than pretty sunsets. On the road, you watch the gas gauge; on foot, you watch where you step. You start remembering some of the tales you've read or heard.

On hot days in the desert, I remembered that a significant portion of the official visitor's guide welcoming people to Death Valley National Monument explains how to escape death and injury. A passage from Richard Lingenfelter's memorable history of the area, *Death Valley and the Amargosa: A Land of Illusion*, would rise in my memory. The process of dehydration—which has claimed two-thirds of the valley's victims —was described in detail:

> The first sensations of thirst begin with the loss of a little over a quart of water. By the time you have lost a gallon you begin to feel tired and apathetic. Most of the water lost comes from your blood, and as it thickens, your circulation becomes poor, your heart strains, your muscles fatigue, and your head aches. With further loss of water you become dizzy and begin to stumble; your breathing is labored and your speech is indistinct. By the time you have lost two gallons of water [which you can lose just by sitting in the shade all day on an average summer day in the valley] your tongue is swollen, you can hardly keep your balance, your muscles spasm, and you are becoming delirious. You are likely to discard your hat, clothes, and shoes, which only hastens your dehydration and suffering. With a loss of more than three gallons of water you will collapse, your tongue and skin shriveled and numb, your eyes shrunken, your vision dim, and your hearing almost gone. Bloody cracks will appear in your skin and you'll soon be dead.

Just thinking about this would make me pull over and down a can of pop or a quart of water from my cooler.

Hiking in the mountains, I recalled what the sheriff of Alpine

County, California (population 1,113; 1.5 people per square mile), had told me. Two years earlier, he said, the volunteer search and rescue squad in California's least populated county had performed the third-highest number of missions in the state.

Driving in the mountains, particularly on steep and winding descents when the *Conestoga*'s great bulk strained to be let loose, I would think about an anecdote I had read at a state park museum in Boulder, Utah. Not far away was the route of the Hole-in-the-Rock expedition. In the winter of 1879–80, a group of 240 Mormons from the established towns along the Wasatch range were dispatched by the church to settle the unpopulated southeastern corner of Utah. Much of the route was over bare rock, creased by eroded canyons and sudden escarpments. About halfway to their destination they reached the Colorado River and a drop of 1,800 feet over a three-quarter-mile distance. They blasted a path through a cliff with dynamite, and using ropes and chains lowered eighty-five wagons, their rear wheels locked, down the precipice. The entire trek was 125 miles. It took them fifty-five days. People now follow the first segment of the route for recreational outings; an annual Jeep rally is held along it. The clipping I saw in Boulder told of a group of Boy Scouts who started out on the trail in 1963. The brakes on their bus failed, and thirteen of them were killed in a crash.

Out on the Plains, whenever a snow squall started to obliterate the flat horizon from the sky and made it seem as if I were floating through a featureless world of white, the mesmerizing spell would be broken by the thought of another bus accident. In late March of 1931 a spring blizzard hit Kiowa County in eastern Colorado. School children in the tiny town of Towner were sent home early. A bus carrying twenty farm kids, inching its way across a back road in swirling snow that reduced visibility to zero, became stuck in a ditch. Its engine died. Outside the temperature plummeted. The children's lunches froze in their bags. They burned the bus seats and their books and rulers in a milk can in the aisle to try to keep warm. During the night, two children died. With the storm still raging the next morning, the driver set out on foot for help. He quickly became lost and froze to death. Back on the bus, the older children took charge. They gave their coats to the youngest kids and slapped their faces to keep them from nodding off into a fatal sleep. Snow blew in through a broken window and piled up inside. Thirty-six hours after being stranded, the bus was found by a search party of parents. Three more children, including the bus driver's daughter, had died from exposure.

THE MEMBRANE BETWEEN MEMORABLE ADVENTURE and tragedy is a thin one. In the contemporary frontier, danger often lurks just beneath the surface but doesn't always rise up to strike. In March of 1988, two school buses in Banner County, Nebraska, became stranded in another late-spring Plains blizzard. It could easily have been the Towner incident revisited. Luckily, both buses made it to farmhouses, where the students were socked in for three days while the storm howled across Nebraska's western panhandle. Electricity was knocked out, and in one of the houses, a widow's, the food supply began to run a little low, but no one really suffered. The phone lines were working, so the students' parents didn't endanger themselves with frantic searches; the kids were in the national news being interviewed from their holdout.

It was the second time in a year that Banner County (852 people, 1.1 per square mile) made big news. The previous fall, a 40-acre plot of marijuana had been discovered growing in the midst of a remote cornfield watered by a center pivot irrigation system. Thirty-four tons of marijuana, worth an estimated $136 million—a record haul in the state—was burned by authorities. (I came across several counties where the principal drug problem isn't drug use by locals, but drug runners trying to take advantage of the open spaces to transship their illicit products, destined for more populated places. The most extreme case is in southwest Texas, where the federal government has tethered some dirigibles to monitor air and land traffic along the Mexican border; other counties scattered around the West had tales of planes landing on the gravel roads and unloading drugs at waiting trucks.) How the marijuana crime was uncovered in Banner County speaks volumes about life on the contemporary frontier. Someone called the sheriff and mentioned that the farm gate always seemed to be locked and that there was a lot of night traffic on the gravel road. Both seemed suspiciously unusual enough to investigate. Butch Cassidy should have had such neighbors.

Banner County redefines the irreducible minimum. It has no gas station, no grocery store, no motel or hotel, no jail, no newspaper, no doctor, no lawyer. Its county seat and only settlement, Harrisburg (population about 100), is unincorporated. A town developer in the late 1800s donated the original courthouse and its site on the condition that the town be named for his hometown in Pennsylvania—a double win of sorts for him: besides picking the name, he also made money on the surrounding lots when nearby Centropolis, the other contender for county seat, couldn't match his sweetener and soon disappeared. In 1890, shortly after the county was organized, the census counted 2,435 residents. A hundred years later, with the population down nearly two-thirds, the county's commercial and retail establishments consist of a bank, two cafés (one also offered video rentals), some farmers who sell machinery, seed, and feed from their homes, and two hairdressers. (Hairdressers, like video rentals, are part of the irreducible minimum; I came across only one county without both.) There is one post office and one school in the county. A county historical museum covers one block in the center of Harrisburg and includes an old bank and filling station; you wouldn't know they are exhibits from the past except for the signs declaring them as such. Sheep were grazing on a corner lot across from the courthouse when I was in town.

Crime has never been a big problem in Banner County. There have been only two murders in its history, an average of one every fifty years. In 1895, a man tried to rob the bank but had trouble getting his pistol out, allowing the president time to escape and alert the community. When the bumbling bandit emerged—his booty was a bag of pennies—the publisher of the *Banner County News* wounded him in a shootout. He was captured, sentenced to ten years in prison, escaped, and, according to the county history book, ended up as a bank president himself somewhere in Wyoming. In the early 1900s, the county judge kept busy by performing marriages. Couples from all over western Nebraska and eastern Wyoming and Colorado flocked to Harrisburg, apparently because the judge didn't mind being called upon at any time of day or night, and he didn't report their names to any newspaper. In one seven-year period, he performed two thousand marriages, about one a day.

Sheriff Pat Mooney, looking for a better environment in which to raise his son, moved his family from the Imperial Valley of southern California to the rolling plains of Banner County in 1980. Since 1983 he has constituted the county's entire police force, one man covering

747 square miles. In 1989, the county court heard 901 cases: seven small claims, seven civil cases, seven probates, one felony (cocaine possession, discovered due to a traffic violation), and 866 traffic violations. Banner County has 650 miles of county-maintained gravel road and 60 miles of paved state highway within its borders—if it loses many more residents it will have a mile of road per person—but the highway is a popular route for people traveling between Interstate 80, about 30 miles to the south, and the city of Scottsbluff, about equally far to the north, and points beyond. They often don't adjust their speeds when they leave the interstate and end up with a ticket.

Once a year on the anniversary of the day the atomic bomb was dropped on Hiroshima, Sheriff Mooney monitors a protest at one of the 19 underground nuclear missile silos in his county. He's joined by security personnel from Warren Air Force Base in Cheyenne, Wyoming, about 70 miles away. Each missile in the county has two or three warheads, and each warhead is 15 to 25 times more powerful than the first atomic bomb, making Banner County's military might somewhere between 570 and 1,425 times that of the United States when it forced Japan to its knees in 1945. A hundred people usually show up for the demonstration, and if someone tries to climb the fence surrounding the silo the protester is stopped, questioned, and then released but not officially arrested. Authorities would just as soon not draw any extra public attention to the arsenal.

The missile installations create additional traffic in Banner County. Besides the unmanned silos, there are two launch control centers. According to a local farmer who has one on his land, each center has six officers, twelve enlisted men, and a cook. Personnel carriers rumble down the roads every time there's a shift change, and ground crews patrol the area constantly. Occasionally, a cow will rub up against a security fence at an unmanned silo or a farmer's machinery will hit it, touching off an electronic alarm and dispatching armed crews over the roads and by helicopter; tumbleweeds propelled by particularly brisk winds have also been known to scramble alerts. Every once in awhile a heavily guarded convoy appears on the roads with a missile replacement. One time a truck carrying a missile slipped off a back road and the guards dug machine-gun pits around it until it could be extricated. Sheriff Mooney said his only problem with the installations is that the young guards sometimes drive too fast patrolling the gravel roads. He's had to give a couple of them warnings, and once two of them collided on the crest of a hill.

In the old days of the western frontier, military protection was one of the first things settlers clamored to their government to provide and then constantly carped about once it arrived. Complaints that the protection wasn't adequate to the threat or that the military couldn't do things right date back to the first forts in Indian territory. Banner County didn't ask for its missile installations, it was selected because of its location and, some residents believe, because of its very sparse population. Nineteen nuclear missiles certainly mute the question of adequacy. Still, there are some complaints. "We don't worry about the missiles that are fired from here, or even the ones fired at them," one resident told me. "It's the ones that go up, then fall flat we worry about." Another farmer, who mentioned that landowners were given the choice of selling the sites at low prices or having them taken by condemnation, grumbled that the location and configuration of the two-acre installations made them a pain to plow around.

On the whole, however, no one I talked to in Banner County seemed overly concerned about living at Ground Zero or having who knows how many megatons of radioactive destruction poised under their soil. If the missile sites are ever abandoned, one farmer pointed out, they revert to the landowner—a hopeful thought, one you might expect from someone who begins each growing season with the notion, "*This* year we'll get enough rain," and often ends each season thinking, "Well, maybe *next* year."

IN APRIL 1892 AN ARMED FORCE OF ABOUT FIFTY MEN rode into Johnson County, Wyoming, with murder on their minds. Half of them were Texans who had been recruited for the mission by the promise of wages of five dollars a day, expenses, and a bonus of fifty dollars for each man they killed. The others were members or local hirelings of the Wyoming Stock Growers Association, a collection of wealthy cattle barons who had raised $100,000 for the expedition and had quietly used their powerful connections—with the railroad and state and federal officials—to minimize resistance to their invasion.

The cattlemen, many of them eastern-born and educated, had become increasingly irritated by conditions on the once-open range. Their dominance was waning, their easy profits declining. Rustling was on the rise. Small ranches were springing up, many of them owned by cowboys who, the association contended, could get in the business only by stealing cattle from the big outfits. Homesteaders interested in farming, not ranching, were erecting fences. To reassert their power, the cattlemen had tried numerous measures. They blacklisted any cowboy who owned cattle from working for them on the presumption that he must be a rustler. They rammed through the legislature a "maverick law" that declared any unbranded calf the property of the WSGA. They hired range detectives with the hopes that a few well-placed lynchings and shootings of suspected rustlers and troublesome small ranchers would send the others packing.

Instead, the result was increased resistance, particularly in Johnson County, at the time a huge and remote jurisdiction covering all of northeastern Wyoming where, the cattle barons claimed, the county courts kept letting rustlers free. Since the haughty plutocrats in Cheyenne considered them all low-life rustlers, even the county's honest small-time ranchers and homesteaders began defiantly calling themselves by that term. Their children played a game of white caps and rustlers. The white caps were the hated cattlemen, and none of the kids preferred impersonating them; in this game, the rustlers were the good guys and were expected to win. The WSGA plot was meant to teach Johnson County new rules to the game.

At the head of the invasion force rode Frank M. Canton, who had been a respected and efficient sheriff of Johnson County in the early 1880s before an offer of better money lured him into a job as the cattlemen's chief range detective. Tall, fearless, good with a gun and willing to use it, Canton was the sort of figure not all that unusual to the old West, where the roles of lawman and outlaw were occasionally as interchangeable as the skills that both required. Under his real name, Joseph Horner, he was wanted in his native Texas for bank robbery, rustling, and the killing of a U.S. cavalryman in a barroom brawl. Later in life he would serve again as a sheriff and deputy U.S. marshal—in Oklahoma and Arkansas, where he worked with "Hanging Judge" Isaac Charles Parker and was credited with helping eliminate the Doolin gang, and in Alaska during the Klondike gold rush. Since turning in his badge in Johnson County, he had been implicated in several cold-blooded murders and attempted murders, all believed to be at the behest of the cattle kings.

The regulators' invasion plan was straightforward. The telegraph line to Buffalo, the county seat, would be cut, severing all communication between the tiny town and the outside world. The town would be stormed and its leadership assassinated—the three county commissioners, the deputy sheriffs, and most of all the new sheriff, W. E. "Red" Angus, who Canton's employers believed had not been energetic enough in protecting their interests. During the resulting confusion, the force would hunt down and execute seventy men on a "dead list" that Canton and other detectives had compiled. Johnson County would be brought to heel.

It all seems unimaginable today, so nakedly arrogant and brutal. Even by nineteenth-century standards of the West, when a certain amount of vigilantism was tolerated as not only justified but necessary to enforce peace, and when conflicts over land, economic power, and many other things often resulted in bloodshed, the plan was chilling in its disregard for innocent lives and orderly justice. But because of their money and control of the state's newspapers and politicians, the cattlemen of the Cheyenne Club believed they could get away with it. They didn't, but then again they did.

With the telegraph lines successfully disconnected and Buffalo unaware of its presence, the force decided to take care of some of the men on the "dead list" at a ranch on the way into town. The attack on the ranch turned into an all-day siege. Nick Ray, a cowboy the vigilantes wanted, was shot from ambush as he emerged from his cabin early in the morning, but Nate Champion, another one on the list, held out inside the cabin until it was set ablaze in the evening. In between trading fire with the surrounding intruders, and tending his wounded and dying partner, whose body he had dragged back into the cabin, Champion calmly penciled a concise narrative of the battle into a pocket memorandum book:

> . . . Nick is shot, but not dead yet. He is awful sick. I must go and wait on him. It is now two hours since the first shot. Nick is alive; they are still shooting and are all around the house. Boys, there is bullets coming in like hail. Them fellows is in such shape I can't get at them. They are shooting from the stable

and river and back of the house. Nick is dead, he died about 9 o'clock. I see smoke down at the stable. I think they have fired it. I don't think they intend to let me get away this time.

. . . Boys, I feel pretty lonesome just now. I wish there was someone here with me so we could watch all sides at once. . . . There was a man in a buckboard and one on horseback just passed. They fired on them as they went by. I don't know if they killed them or not. . . . I shot at the men in the stable just now; don't know if I got any or not. I must go and look out again. It don't look as if there is much show of my getting away. I see twelve or fifteen men. . . . They are shooting at the house now. If I had a pair of glasses I believe I would know some of those men. They are coming back. I've got to look out.

Well, they have just got through shelling the house like hail. I heard them splitting wood. I guess they are going to fire the house to-night. I think I will make a break when night comes, if alive. Shooting again. I think they will fire the house this time. It's not night yet. The house is all fired. Goodbye, boys, if I never see you again. Nathan D. Champion.

His last entry complete, Champion bolted from the inferno and was quickly killed by four bullets. The regulators took his guns and pinned a note to his lifeless body, "Cattle thieves, beware." In his blood-soaked memorandum book was found what A. S. Mercer, the angry chronicler of the invasion, predicted "will be quoted in history as the utterance of a brave man throughout all time to come. No stronger expression of nerve and heroism has ever been recorded."

The side trip to kill Champion and Ray unglued the invasion strategy. The element of surprise had been lost. The two men Champion had seen being chased by the regulators made it to Buffalo and alerted the townspeople, who quickly mobilized to defend themselves. One merchant rode up and down the streets of town, calling people to arms and then opening his store doors to pass out guns and ammunition. Within an hour a hundred men were organized and deputized by Sheriff Angus; more kept streaming in as couriers spread word of the invasion across the county. Women gathered and began cooking meals for the swelling army of ranchers and farmers. Schools and churches were turned into barracks.

When it became clear that the raid was turning into a war, Canton's contingent detoured to a ranch of an association friend about 14 miles from Buffalo and soon found itself surrounded, outnumbered, and besieged. For two days the opposing forces exchanged shots, although no one was killed. The men from Johnson County decided to give the vigilantes a taste of the same medicine they had administered to Ray and Champion, whose bullet-ridden and charred remains had already been brought back to Buffalo for an emotional funeral. They constructed a moving breastwork, dubbed the Go-Devil, behind which they planned to approach the ranch, toss dynamite into its fortifications, and wipe out the invaders.

Here's where the cattlemen's well-oiled connections paid off. The telegraph lines were mysteriously reconnected, and the hired guns tapped out an SOS. Calling the unexpected turn of events an "insurrection," Wyoming's governor wired President Benjamin Harrison. With the prompting of the state's two senators, also on the cattlemen's side, Harrison ordered troops from nearby Fort McKinney to the regulators' rescue. Just as the Go-Devil was lumbering into action, the U.S. cavalry arrived. The vigilantes were taken into protective custody, eventually ushered out of the county and, after various legal maneuverings, released. Many of them, like Canton, went on to careers as reputable lawmen.

The only regulator who can be said to have paid a heavy price for the invasion was the Texas Kid, a young recruit of the cattlemen who had fired the first shot into Nick Ray. After returning to his home state, the Texas Kid got into an argument with his wife. She chastised him for being on the wrong side in Johnson County. He shot her to death and was hanged for the crime.

ARRIVING IN A NEW COUNTY, MY SEARCH FOR CONnections and differences between the old frontier and the new, between the contemporary frontier and the rest of the nation, often led me to the local sheriff. The stories each one told were helpful in understanding the shifting nature of crime and violence over a hundred years' time. So when I arrived in Johnson County (6,145 people, 1.5 per square mile), not surprisingly the first person I wanted to meet was the man holding the job once filled by both Frank Canton and Red Angus.

"We don't consider law enforcement to be 'frontier' here," said Sheriff Larry Kirkpatrick, who had been a deputy for six years before becoming sheriff in 1982. An IBM computer sat on his desk. "Even the old West is computerized," he said as he punched its keyboards several times to pull up statistics and reports to answer my questions. His officers, like himself, are graduates of the state's law enforcement academy and products of a screening process that would make it difficult for someone operating under an alias and wanted for bank robbery in another state to put on a badge.

In his fourteen years on the force, Kirkpatrick has worked on fourteen homicide cases, most of them bunched in the late 1970s and early 1980s, when an oil and uranium boom brought Johnson County both a burst of prosperity and a rougher edge reminiscent of its past. The most recent murder, the first in eight years, was in 1989. After a night of heavy drinking, two young men beat to death an aging Basque ranch hand on a remote road. Kirkpatrick's officers solved the case and tracked down one of the killers in Montana within three days; the two men were sentenced to life in prison. (This was a switch from a century earlier. On the one hand, Canton and his well-connected company had literally gotten away with murder in 1892. On the other hand, that same year a murderer named Charles Miller was hanged in Johnson County; at the public execution was a man to whom Miller had given a handwritten invitation in exchange for a dozen doughnuts.)

A more representative type of modern violent death had occurred the month before my visit. A car carrying three people went off a mountain road and rolled down a ravine. The accident wasn't discovered for seventeen hours, when some tourists stopped to take a picture of a deer and saw the wreckage. Two young men were dead, but a woman survived.

Johnson County's dramatic scenery is unchanged. On the west are the Bighorn Mountains, a seemingly misplaced spur of the Rockies, lofty and often brooding under a cloak of clouds their peaks have snared. The Bighorns arch out of the alkali plains that cover the rest of the county and whose choking dust storms were the curse of Montana-bound cattle drives. From a turnoff high in the Bighorns I looked out eastward thinking that if my eyes were sharp enough I might see the skyline of Chicago. Driving from border to border on the treeless plains, bisected by the Powder River, I tried to count the antelope but gave up after reaching a hundred. Buffalo (population 3,302), the only town of note, nestles between the two starkly different terrains. A billboard welcomes you to "Peaceful Buffalo," a helpful reassurance since it would not be hard to imagine someone still thinking that a few snips of wire could cut the town off from the rest of the world while dastardly deeds were perpetrated. A sign on the interstate east of town warns, "No Services, 68 Miles."

Also unchanged, though slightly diminished, is the rustling, Sheriff Kirkpatrick said, particularly with sheep. Despite advances in law enforcement technology—airplanes, rapid communications, a special school on livestock theft—catching a rustler is mostly a matter of luck, he said. "It's like break-ins of vacant cabins in the mountains—you just can't cover them. After midnight there's nobody on the roads, there's nobody to catch you." A recent case, in which a rancher was caught shearing his neighbors' bucks in his corral, had resulted in a conviction, but the judge declared a mistrial. In his closing argument, the county attorney had told the jury that "rustling is a serious problem in Johnson County" and the judge considered the statement prejudicial. No doubt, members of the Cheyenne Club rolled over in their graves.

There were other legacies of Frank Canton and Red Angus. The memory of Canton probably is the reason that Johnson County is one of the few Wyoming counties without any private range detectives, despite the rustling problem. And when I saw a bullet hole in Kirkpatrick's office window, my mind fastened on Angus, the sheriff slated for assassination. I kept eyeing it nervously while we talked. Before I left, I asked about it.

"Oh that," Kirkpatrick said. "I wondered if you'd notice." He walked over and peeled it off the glass. It was made of plastic, a sight gag he had put up as a joke.

IN THE FAR-FLUNG MUSEUM OF DEATH AND CON-flict, the principal Shrine to Violence is in De Baca County, New Mexico (population 2,252, one person per square mile), a windswept and barren stretch of short grass prairie in the eastern half of the state.

Fort Sumner, the county seat and only incorporated town, owes its existence to what has been called "America's first concentration camp."

In the early 1860s, after military campaigns defeated the Navajo and Mescalero Apache, the government wanted to find a spot suitably remote from any place that the white settlers and miners might covet in which to confine the tribes. The army found such a location at Bosque Redondo (round grove of trees) on the banks of the salty Pecos River. Here Fort Sumner was built to hold them. It was a failure from the outset.

Having burned the Navajos' hogans and crops, seized their livestock, and cut down their ancient fruit orchards in eastern Arizona, Kit Carson's troops led the tribe on the "Long Walk" to its new home on the other side of the New Mexico territory. It was late winter, and Navajos perished by the hundreds from exposure and starvation. Eighty-six hundred of them made it to the fort, joining five hundred Mescaleros and five hundred soldiers to form one of the highest concentrations of people in New Mexico at the time, four times the immediate area's current population. Weakened from the forced march, more Indians died from disease and harsh weather. Then near-starvation set in. They dug irrigation ditches and planted crops, which were ruined by a succession of floods, drought, and insects. Their herds of goats and sheep couldn't find enough grass to prosper and were easy prey to raiding Comanches and Kiowas. They ran low on food and clothing. Government rations arriving from supply points nearly a thousand miles away were often rancid from the long haul to the fort. The Mescalero Apaches finally broke free and fled to their mountain homes, but the Navajo remained and suffered. While the government wasn't deliberately trying to exterminate them—from $1 million to $2 million was being spent each year to support the fort, an astonishing figure for the Civil War and postwar period—their numbers dwindled.

By 1868, only 7,200 Navajos were left. Prompted more by a desire to stanch the exorbitant drain on the Treasury than by concern for the Indians' misery, the government finally abandoned the Bosque Redondo experiment, signed a new treaty with the Navajo assigning them lands in their native region, and sent them home. Lucien Maxwell, once the owner of the single biggest tract of land in the United States, a 2-million-acre land grant in northern New Mexico, bought the fort in 1871 and retired there. He turned the officers' quarters into his main house and resettled the land with several dozen Hispanic families. Fort

Sumner as a town was born, although the original site was abandoned for higher ground a few miles north, closer to the railroad, in the early 1900s. The fort itself vanished long ago.

Although it certainly qualifies, the Fort Sumner State Monument, a low-slung modern building dedicated to preserving the history of Bosque Redondo, is not the Shrine to Violence. Nearby, in the fort's old cemetery, is a marble tombstone, bound in shackles and enclosed by an iron cage to thwart the people who keep trying to steal it. This is the shrine. It's where Billy the Kid, America's most famous outlaw and unlikely folk hero, is buried.

Born Henry McCarty, he went by several names in his short life: Henry Antrim, Kid Antrim, William Bonney, and finally just "the Kid" until the dime novelists and tabloid writers added Billy to the term and turned him into a national legend often bearing only slight resemblance to the truth. He was short, thin, blue-eyed, buck-toothed, generally gregarious but capable of explosive violence; loved to dance and to read the *Police Gazette*, practice with guns, and flirt with Hispanic girls; didn't smoke or drink, but was good at poker and monte and fluent in Spanish; fell in as a teenager with a rough group of men who lived on the fringes of the law and who never considered him the leader of any gang; got embroiled in the Lincoln County War, which had many of the same elements of cattle, politics, and violence that marked the Johnson County Invasion, except that in New Mexico it was more of a bloody civil war, the lines were less clearly drawn, and considerably more people died; shot and killed four men for sure and took part in the killings of five or six more, a grisly enough tally but far short of the twenty-one attributed to him by sensationalists who liked the symmetry of one killing per year of his life; witnessed the violent deaths of many compatriots, including those of his two closest friends, Tom O'Folliard and Charles Bowdre, who in separate incidents were shot by Sheriff Pat Garrett; was himself captured by Garrett, tried and convicted for murder and sentenced to hang, but escaped from custody as his gallows were being constructed, killing two officers—half his confirmed count—on his way out; and then died on July 14, 1881, from a slug from Garrett's gun, after walking into the darkened bedroom of Lucien Maxwell's son, where the officers entrusted with guarding the Navajos at Fort Sumner had once slept. His last words were "*¿Quién es? ¿Quién es?*" Who is it? He never knew what, or who, hit him.

Within a year of his death in 1881, five Billy the Kid books appeared, including one written by Garrett, a proud man sensitive to any perceived slights to his honor, who didn't think his side of the story was being fairly portrayed. Garrett was alternately revered and reviled for his success in doing what he had been elected to do: rid the area of the Kid and his ilk. He could be gruff and overly officious, and often stepped on the wrong toes. In subsequent years he had trouble getting elected to anything in New Mexico. Teddy Roosevelt, an admirer, finally made him a customs collector in El Paso, but Garrett quickly got into political hot water with the locals and wasn't reappointed. In 1908 he was murdered, shot in the back of the head, apparently in a land dispute.

At last count, there were more than a hundred books and forty films about Billy—about five books and two movies for every year he lived —with no end of them in sight.

THE PHENOMENON OF BILLY THE KID'S FAME HAS been much analyzed, but never fully explained. Who can say why a relatively minor hoodlum would grab and hold the world's imagination for more than a century? Whatever the causes, one result is clear: he turned out to be worth more dead than alive. New Mexico's tourism department ranks him with the Santa Fe Trail in drawing power, at the top of the state's historical attractions. Fortuitously for the boosters, who refer to him as "America's most enduring legend," the Kid had exploits in all parts of New Mexico, allowing historical markers to form a Billy the Kid Trail for tourists to follow up and down the state. (Capitalizing on the memory of an outlaw killer might appear unseemly to some; for the sake of propriety, Pat Garrett's name is occasionally thrown in with the Kid's on the promotional brochures, but it takes second billing and is usually in smaller print.) Reproductions of a photograph of Billy—a tintype taken of him in Fort Sumner in 1880, standing jauntily with the barrel of his rifle in one hand and is other hand dangling beside his holstered revolver, his two front teeth slightly protruding through his lips—appear everywhere.

Nowhere is he more important economically than in De Baca County, where he brings in an estimated half-million dollars a year in tourist business. Fort Sumner sits on a U.S. highway that people from

Texas use as a shortcut driving to New Mexico's mountains. Given the flat and treeless terrain of the area, they'd be more likely to speed on through De Baca County if the legend wasn't there to hold them up.

Twenty-one thousand people a year stop at the Billy the Kid Museum in town. Among its many exhibits are the guns he used in his last escape (or at least *believed* to be the same guns, according to their display sign), locks of his hair (purchased from a local barber), his spurs (purchased from a pallbearer), an old jail door ("Billy Was Behind These Bars"), the door into Maxwell's bedroom (the shotgun holes are not related to his death), a curtain from the room, and a rock from Stinking Springs, where Garrett and his posse killed Bowdre and captured Billy.

South of town, adjacent to the Bosque Redondo historical park, is the Old Fort Sumner Museum, which sells Billy the Kid T-shirts, posters, envelopes, license plates, playing cards, hats, and about twenty books from the endless outlaw *oeuvre*. It doesn't have as many purportedly authentic Kid relics as its competitor in town, but then again it's got the real grave site and tombstone, while the other museum makes do with a replica. Both charge two bucks for admission. Visiting the grave is free.

Thirteen miles east of Fort Sumner is Bowlin's Big Red Indian store, much publicized on billboards lining the highway from both directions for its cold drinks, modern rest rooms, food, public phone, live rattlesnakes, World Famous Taos Moccasins, Indian jewelry and pottery, New Mexico souvenirs, and official headquarters of the Billy the Kid Outlaw Gang Inc.

Joe Bowlin is one of the pioneers of modern tourism in the Southwest. After World War II, he and an uncle and cousin set out to open a string of stores. They would start in a big city, say El Paso, and start driving west toward another big city, like Tucson. When they got to the point where someone might be getting hungry, need gas, or have to go to the bathroom, they would look for a building to buy. "We tried to do it with a kid in mind," he told me. Not *the Kid*, a kid. "Kids are gonna make you stop. They want to be an Indian or a cowboy, so we fashioned signs to attract kids." Headdresses, tom-toms, and toy guns were prominently featured. Eventually, they had seventeen stores. In De Baca County, not surprisingly, Bowlin commands the crucial eastern approaches to Billyland. Besides the Big Red Indian, he owns the museum by the grave, which is off the main highway but has big signs directing tourists there before they reach town and the competing museum.

Bowlin has been one of the main forces in seeing Billy the Kid in terms of economic development. "It's a product that you don't have to get funding for," he said. "It's here. It's a salable product. Your shoe factories and other industries that get a government grant come and go, but your history and your legends are here forever."

He's spent a lot of time and money developing and protecting that legend. In 1950, Billy's gravestone was stolen and remained lost for twenty-six years. As president of the local Chamber of Commerce, Bowlin received numerous tips on the gravestone's whereabouts. One he got in 1976 led him to Granbury, Texas, where the thief had it mounted next to a barbecue pit as a conversation piece. Bowlin returned it with great ceremony. The state tourism director put shackles on it; Pat Garrett's son was there; the national media recorded the event. Five years later, the headstone was gone again. More headlines. A truck driver, whose CB handle was "Billy the Kid," had taken it and hidden it under his bed in Los Angeles. The trucker's company agreed to build the iron cage that now guards the grave and its marker. Few in the media missed the chance at a story about an outlaw's gravestone behind bars.

The next threat came in 1986, when a book appeared about Brushy Bill Roberts, one of several men who have claimed to be the Kid, that Garrett had killed the wrong man. (No slouch at promotion himself, shortly before he died in 1950 Brushy Bill had petitioned the governor of New Mexico as Billy seeking a pardon, a request dismissed as a hoax. For one thing, Brushy Bill didn't even know enough Spanish to say "¿Quién es?") The book was written by a judge in Hico, Texas, about 90 miles southwest of Dallas, where Brushy Bill coincidentally was buried. Anyone at all familiar with Texans would immediately discern the potential consequences. Given the choice between visiting a Billy the Kid grave in their own state or one in New Mexico, they'd choose the former, more out of Texas pride than to save gas. You can almost hear those westbound cars accelerating on their way through De Baca County.

Reading newspaper accounts about the Brushy Bill claim, Bowlin got angered that they often didn't have a counterview from Fort Sumner. He and his wife, Maryln, sprang into action. They built a float depicting the *real* grave and entered it in parades in both states; they arranged for a debate with the Texas judge; they formed the Billy the Kid Outlaw Gang to "preserve, protect and promote Billy the Kid/Pat Garrett history in New Mexico."

Garrett is included in the trail, if not the group's name, because "we're not only backing up our history, we're defending Pat Garrett's name and honor," Bowlin told me. "If he let a man escape, that's a blot on him." Still, it was clear where his sympathies, as well as those of other people I talked to in the county, reside. The Kid was "just a product of his time," Bowlin said. "He wasn't a gangster, never held up a train or a stagecoach, never robbed a bank. He didn't kill anyone who didn't need killing. I wouldn't consider him an outlaw any more than anyone else in that era. I don't know where you'd put him in today's time. He wouldn't do drugs, so I don't know how he'd get into trouble. He wasn't a rogue. I don't even think he'd make a good hippie. He was a hardy little bugger, but he was well liked by everybody around here. I never heard anybody say they was afraid of Billy the Kid." As for Garrett, "he wasn't liked, he wasn't well liked in the first place."

By his own reckoning, Bowlin spent $15,000 disproving Brushy Bill's claim. He showed me a manila file five inches thick with documents, including a copy of the imposter's family Bible and a census report from 1900 that showed Brushy Bill's age as twenty, which would have made him not yet two years old when Garrett got his man. Brushy Bill "just wanted to be somebody," Bowlin concluded. "He once said he was Jesse James."

The wrangle had its benefits. "It probably woke us up" in De Baca County, Bowlin said. "Before, we took everything for granted." In three years, the Gang grew to more than a thousand members in forty-two states and seven foreign countries. President Ronald Reagan was made the two hundredth member. At a governor's day in Fort Sumner, New Mexico's chief executive joined the Gang and made his cabinet pay their membership dues on live television. ("The governor hates Billy —he calls him a little bastard—but he likes Pat Garrett," Bowlin confided.) The group hosts annual Billy the Kid–Pat Garrett Days in different towns and, with the assistance of the state's tourism bureau, has distributed 90,000 brochures promoting the Kid's trail. "Billy the Kid is an excellent marketing tool," a state official said when the trail was announced. "We're not out to glorify the Kid. We're simply giving people access to the information they've always wanted. It's just like putting up a highway sign." The Gang has been instrumental in finding more sites for the signs. Bowlin showed me the latest suggestion for a historical marker, from a member in England, who said he knew how to locate the place where the Kid ate his last Christmas dinner.

The day before I arrived, the Gang scored its greatest coup. Sam Donaldson and a television crew from the ABC show "Prime Time Live" had been in the area for a feature story on the Brushy Bill controversy. Members of the Gang dressed up in Western outfits and rode across the prairie for the cameras; local descendants of people who were in Fort Sumner the night of the killing were interviewed; a forensic expert conducted a computer analysis of photographs of Billy and Brushy Bill and declared them two different men. Bowlin estimated that 60 million people had seen the broadcast. "The fruits of our (the Gang's) labors paid off," he told the local paper. "There's not enough money in the world to buy that kind of publicity."

As it turns out, there had been another controversy about Billy that Bowlin didn't tell me about. I discovered it in some back copies of the *De Baca County News*. In early 1989, the owners of the Billy the Kid Museum in Fort Sumner sued the Bowlins. The suit claimed trade name infringement, unfair competition, and unfair trade practices, because the Bowlins had changed the name of the Old Fort Sumner Museum to *Billy the Kid's* Old Fort Sumner Museum and put up a big billboard pointing people south to find it. The plaintiffs said the new name was too similar to their museum's and could confuse and divert prospective customers. A month later, the Bowlins countersued the Billy the Kid Museum to drop Billy from its name. Both suits were filed with the county's district court clerk, who happened to be president of the Billy the Kid Outlaw Gang Inc.

It had all the makings of a good Western feud, involving as it did the standard ingredients of economics, politics (the village trustees were dragged into the dispute, and when the governor came to town, he made sure to visit both museums), and a gunman, albeit one that had been dead for a century. But conflicts are handled differently in the contemporary frontier, even though this one, like Billy's life, was settled out of court. No shots were fired. Nobody died. The Bowlins removed Billy the Kid from their museum's sign and added "the authentic grave site of Billy the Kid." Both lawsuits were dropped, and peace was restored before the end of the tourist season.

BEING IN THE PLACE WHERE THE SHRINE TO VIO-lence commemorates the sudden death of one of the Wild West's icons, I spent some time in De Baca County looking into its violent deaths in modern times. I talked with the sheriff and the coroner, walked through the town's graveyard, checked statistics in the courthouse, and perused back issues of the weekly paper. Here's some of what I found:

• There hadn't been a murder in fifteen years.
• A young man drove his car into a gully on an isolated state road north of town and wasn't found until the next day, dead.
• A church bus loaded with children got hit by a cattle truck east of Fort Sumner; nineteen kids were killed. About ten years later, the driver of the cattle truck apparently fell asleep and drove his car into an abandoned building in the near-ghost town of Yeso, just beyond the bus accident site. He was discovered the next day. No one knew how long he'd been dead.
• Several local people had been killed in small-plane crashes.
• A twelve-year-old boy driving a pickup rolled the vehicle, was pinned underneath it, and died.
• An older man had an accident on the road to Roswell and wasn't found for several hours, when a rancher saw him and called for help on a cellular phone. A Roswell ambulance, 60 miles from the site, was dispatched. He died later in the hospital.
• A passenger in a car that blew its front tire north of town was seriously injured and flown by helicopter to Albuquerque, about 150 miles away, where he died.
• Within the last year there had been two alcohol-related deaths. One man was found dead from alcohol poisoning. The other apparently had been drinking heavily, fell down in the street, crawled up next to a bar, and froze to death.
• Two men were killed when their truck, after waiting for an east-bound train, crossed the tracks and was hit by a westbound train. Several beer cans and empty beer cartons were found in the truck.
• Late one November night, when the temperature dropped to 21

degrees, a man went off the highway about 20 miles south of town. A school bus driver found him the next morning; he had been there nearly twelve hours by the time help arrived. He was alive, but never recovered from the injuries and died from them four years later.

• There had been two suicides in the previous year.

At first glance, they seem fairly mundane. Traffic fatalities mainly. But consider two things. By proportion of population, one death in a car wreck in De Baca County is equivalent to 400 in a county of a million people. Three or four traffic-related deaths in the Fort Sumner area (the average in previous years) is the same as 300,000 to 350,000 in the nation (versus an average of about 45,000). The other difference is that in more heavily settled areas, some of De Baca County's accident victims would have been found sooner, received treatment earlier, and probably would have been saved.

Sheriff Jim Bilberry, a lanky rancher turned lawman, age fifty, told me he had personally witnessed three men die, two in construction accidents and one when a horse fell and rolled on its rider. One of Bilberry's sons was killed at age fourteen, when a friend pointed a gun at him, thinking it had blanks in it, and fired a live round.

"It's considered a matter of pride in these parts to drink the most whiskey, be the toughest, drive the fastest, don't wear seat belts or hard hats, and ride the rankest horse," he said. Given the long distances and the lonely roads, "if you have an accident, it's Katey-bar-the-door."

Sheriff Bilberry had been in office a year and a half when we talked. He and his four deputies had been focusing their efforts on cracking down on speeders, drunk drivers, drug use, and teenagers drinking at parties. The long lists of traffic citations in the weekly paper, sometimes filling two columns, testified to their work. So did the fact, he said, that so far there hadn't been a traffic fatality in the county since he took office, during which time fatalities had increased in the rest of the state.

Bilberry was proud of his crackdown. But it was also getting him into deep political trouble. Tourist businesses were openly complaining that the county was getting the reputation of being a speed trap; Texas travelers were starting to use alternate routes to the mountains. Bilberry had also given citations for drunk driving and other traffic violations to a lot of county residents, some of them well connected. Losing your license is serious business in places where long drives are part of everyday life and public transportation is nonexistent; many violators had quietly tried to get Bilberry to quash his charges, but he refused. When the sheriff sought approval for an additional officer and patrol car, specifically for traffic duty, the county commissioners initially turned him down, even though the expense was covered by a grant and wouldn't cost the county any money. "It will make more people mad rather than cure the [speeding] problem," one commissioner had explained. Putting their money where their sentiments were, the commissioners had even once paid a speeding fine for an economic development official Bilberry had caught.

"My convictions on the law bein' the law run real deep," Bilberry said. "We've tried to conduct and enforce the law in a way that it makes no difference who you are, how much political influence you have, or how much money you have. It's new to people."

Not entirely new, really. Even though he was more sympathetic to the Kid than to Pat Garrett, one of the chroniclers of the saga wrote that when Garrett started after Billy and company, the people of the county made the "appalling discovery that the new sheriff intended to observe his oath of office." Garrett was a hard drinker, a heavy gambler, and a professed agnostic, while Bilberry is a teetotaling, born-again Christian; but they both shared a certain lack of diplomacy in carrying out their duties that many people found grating.

I was in the county early in an election year, and an opponent had already declared for sheriff. Most of the merchants I talked to seemed confident the "Bilberry problem" was going to be solved. "We don't want people to start detouring around De Baca County," a commissioner told me. "They drop a pretty good bit of money here." A motel owner said, "He's a good-hearted man, but he just got carried away. There's nothing we can do except elect a new sheriff."

When I called Bilberry a year later, he was back at his ranch. He had been voted out of office. Shortly before his term ended, two young men, who had stolen a car in Clovis and were headed toward Albuquerque to get rid of it, had rolled it in De Baca County and were killed. Bilberry said he hated to see his perfect record spoiled, "but if it had to happen, I guess this was the best way; they solved eighteen auto burglaries with it." He didn't think he'd ever run for sheriff again. The ranch was taking up all his time. A couple of days earlier, while helping him herd cattle along a road, his wife had been bitten by a rattlesnake.

"What did you do?" I asked.

"Drive like hell to the hospital," he said.

IN HIS EXCELLENT BIOGRAPHY *BILLY THE KID: A Short and Violent Life*, Robert M. Utley, a respected and prolific historian of the West, makes the case that "in the flesh and in legend, Billy the Kid embodies the frontier's affinity for violence. . . . Only in a quick reliance on violence did the frontier differ from the nation as a whole in the relentless quest for power and wealth, and then it was largely a difference of degree."

The difference of degree seems to have flip-flopped in a century. "Wilding" and gangs are now urban phenomena. In the West's contemporary frontier, the enduring legends of violence still fascinate us, in part because they are safely distant, in time as well as miles. It's harder to make heroes of outlaws or to romanticize wars and bloodshed when they're in your midst. New Mexico was once embarrassed by Billy the Kid and the cattle war that spawned him, fearing they would inhibit settlement and progress; today, they are considered major attractions.

Meanwhile, the enduring truth of the places miles from nowhere is that the environment—the weather, the land, the mundane facts of what you do for work and how far and fast you go to get there—is as potentially dangerous as it always was. Some of that is unchangeable. Recognizing that, in addition to reflecting the violent past they share, the residents of the sparse places confront life with a fatalism less common in the rest of urban/suburban America. Still, the myths and legends of the Wild West tug at them as much as on everyone else.

On my way out of De Baca County, I stopped again at the Big Red Indian. One corner of the store is devoted to the headquarters of the Billy the Kid Outlaw Gang Inc., with numerous displays about the group and its hero. In the same corner is the post office for the eastern half of the county. Next to the post office window was a stack of wanted posters. The top one had the picture of Donald Ray Wooley, Jr., who, while still in his early twenties, had been convicted and jailed for murder in Louisiana. He had escaped and was on the loose. Describing him as five feet eight inches tall, 135 pounds, slender, with brown hair, the poster said he "has stated he would not return to jail. Consider Wooley armed and dangerous." No reward was offered; no aliases or nicknames were listed. I kept my eye out for him while I traveled, but I don't think he and I were headed for the same places.

CHAPTER 3

ESCAPE

THE CONTEMPORARY FRONTIER'S MOST IMPROBABLE
community is in Saguache County (pronounced sa-WATCH, population
4,619; 1.5 people per square mile), where the snow-capped Sangre de
Cristo mountains rise abruptly and dramatically from the flat desert
floor of southern Colorado's San Luis Valley. Native Americans once
considered the area a sacred and spiritual place where members of
competing tribes could conduct vision quests in peace. Because of its
powers, they called it a "dream corridor." It still is. Dreams—big
dreams—seem part of the landscape. Not all of them come true.

At the turn of the century, a gold mine in the mountain foothills
created the town of Crestone, which grew to a population of several
thousand people before the miners discovered that the rich ore lay in
pockets instead of extensive veins. The resulting bust nearly sucked

the town down to oblivion. In the 1970s, with only a few dozen residents, Crestone was teetering on the brink of the final ignominy of any town, loss of its post office, when a development company bought the adjacent Baca ranch, a 160,000-acre Spanish land grant, and began work on a grandiose retirement village in one corner of it. A golf course, community buildings, an inn, a few "spec" houses, and enough roads and underground utilities for 10,000 people were installed. Midwesterners, flown in for free, were shown the spectacular scenery and encouraged to buy one of the 5,600 building lots. About a hundred homes went up before the bottom started to fall out. The cold winters, the isolation (the nearest town of any size is about 50 miles away in another county), and the lack of medical services dissuaded all but the hardiest retirees from sticking it out. The company lost an estimated $50 million.

After going through a series of owners, the Baca Grande development has shifted its focus. Acreages are now being sold, on the basis of videotapes and at twice their local value, to U.S. servicemen stationed in Guam, Hawaii, and the Philippines, who think a couple of hundred dollars down is a good deal for their own little piece of America. Like the Midwesterners before them, many soon lose the land they had never seen in person. They decide the taxes, development fees, and interest payments aren't worth the price of their dream; foreclosure is often the simplest way out. Of the 3,600 landowners, 160 have built homes. Nonetheless, locals still believe that Crestone-Baca is destined to become the biggest community in Saguache County.

More big dreams. A Japanese firm is hoping to make a killing by raising 1,500 head of buffalo and running a resort next to the Great Sand Dunes, the highest sand dunes in North America, south of the Baca. Two entrepreneurs have tapped a geothermal well and are raising alligators and exotic fish in the warm-water tanks. And an international investment company, led by some of the world's biggest corporate raiders, is proposing to spend half a billion dollars to pump fresh water, millions of gallons of it, from an underground aquifer beneath the Baca, pipe it uphill over mountain passes, and dump it into the headwaters of either the Arkansas or South Platte rivers to sell it to the burgeoning populations of Denver and Colorado Springs.

In the midst of all this, some of the 300 souls of Crestone-Baca are busily pursuing the biggest dream of all. Parts of the sprawling, failed retirement village are being turned into a "Refuge for World Truths," where the earth's spiritual rebirth can begin.

On one knob of the mountain foothills stands a Hindu ashram, a solar-heated temple to the Divine Mother. Ram Loti, formerly Deborah Wood, a soft-voiced woman dressed in blue cloth wrapped over one shoulder, briefly explained to me the teachings of Babaji, her spiritual master who died in India at age fourteen, concluding one of his incarnations. "Remember God at all times. Serve people." That, Babaji had said, was the essence of all religions. "One of the reasons we're here is to show people there are many paths," Ram Loti said. "It's whatever works for you. We're not into conversions."

Downslope from the ashram is the Spiritual Life Institute, home to nine Carmelite hermit-monks, among them Father Dave Denny, a young man with a close-cropped beard and translucent blue eyes that sparkle like shards of sky. Father Denny was raised as a Disciple of Christ (another monk I met had converted from Judaism), but had encountered the Roman Catholic order of Carmelites in college. "Lights went on in my head," he remembered. "They had an intellectualism, a sense of humor—they weren't a bunch of weirdos. I had been unaware of the mystic tradition of the Christian church. The church keeps that part hidden." At the Baca monastery—and at one deep in the woods of Nova Scotia—the Carmelite hermits, men and women, try to keep that mystic tradition alive through silence, solitude, and contemplation. The order moved to Saguache County from Sedona, Arizona, where a housing development had been built next door and forced the hermits to seek a more remote location. The institute offers rooms for people of any religion interested in a spiritual retreat—"no fuss" is the basic rule for guests—and maintains a spartan cabin high up the mountainside to which each monk makes periodic journeys to be alone. The mountain's name is Kit Carson Peak, but the monks prefer to call it Mount Carmel, in honor of the place in Palestine where the first Carmelites lived as hermits in the twelfth century. The mountain chain itself did not require renaming: Sangre de Cristo means "blood of Christ."

At the San Luis Valley Tibetan Project, Marianne Marstrand-Burkhar outlined the plans for a Buddhist monastery, shrine, retreat center, and farm to grow medicinal plants—"a place to preserve Tibetan culture, which was in danger of becoming extinct because of the

Chinese communist invasion of Tibet." When some Tibetan lamas visited to help select the site for the shrine, she said, they felt "physical energies" coming from the ground. They also referred to an eighth-century prophecy: "When the iron bird flies and horses have wheels, the Tibetans will be scattered across the world like ants, and the Teaching will come to the land of the Red Man." That land, Marianne believes, is among the piñon trees at the base of the Sangre de Cristos.

Other faiths are gathering at the refuge. A Zen Buddhist center, already providing training sessions and retreats, is planning a domed meditation hall. Sufis, mystic Muslims, hope to establish a retreat. Taoists have a proposal for a small community and farm. Rediscovery Four Corners offers summer youth programs in which kids live in tepees and learn American Indian ways of life. The Aspen Institute, which once operated a satellite think tank at the Baca, has turned over its buildings to Colorado College for a conference center. Shirley MacLaine, the actress and author of books about reincarnation, is negotiating to buy some land.

The bulletin board at the Bistro, the only restaurant, was plastered with notices and business cards: the Green Earth Organic Farm to conduct a discussion series; a Hymn to the Sun to be held on Saturday; a free introduction to the Buddhist Path; a massage therapist; the Harmony Ranch Bed and Breakfast ("An Oasis of Tranquility for Women"); and the county's only doctor, in the valley town of Moffat, who calls himself the "Country Doc" and offers acupuncture as part of his practice. *The Crestone Eagle*, a monthly newspaper, had ads for: a Reiki master offering a "unique and powerful hands-on healing technique"; *Yhantishor*, a novel that "contains so much transformational material that it must be read slowly and meditatively"; the Rolf system of structural integration from a "certified advanced Rolfer"; a sixty-minute tape cassette of an interview with medicine man Rolling Thunder on "prophesies, right livelihood and natural healing"; Design Harmonics, "environmentally sensitive building and landscape design"; and Amway.

Having bumped into prophecies and energy fields everywhere I stopped in Crestone-Baca, I was prepared when I finally met the person coordinating the Refuge for World Truths. Hanne Strong, a statuesque, Danish-born woman who radiates a combination of aristocratic sophistication and vivacious earthiness, could be described as a high-energy source in her own right. For an afternoon in her living room, she spoke nonstop on topics ranging from Indian pipe ceremonies to hopes of developing hardy plants that can survive an impending desertification of America. She said some of the earth's highest vibrational energies emanate from under the Baca's soil—higher than those at Stonehenge, Machu Picchu, or the Cathedral at Chartres. Native American and oriental shamans have felt them; a Swiss once measured them on something called a Bovis scale. "Sit at that table," Hanne said, pointing to her dining room, "and you'll be zapped by one and a half million positive earth energies." Then she laughed huskily. "You could reach enlightenment in one dinner."

Although she was implementing it, the plan for the refuge of faiths wasn't her idea, she told me. When she first came to the Baca in the late 1970s, a local mountain man named Glen Anderson showed up at her front door and proclaimed, "I've been waiting for you to arrive." He then explained a vision that had been communicated to him by archangels, about the world's religions establishing villages at the Baca to demonstrate how mankind can live in harmony. (Anderson also claimed that in a former life he was a compatriot of the Sioux warrior Crazy Horse. Like prophecies and energy fields, reincarnation is an accepted phenomenon among many locals. According to one of the newspaper articles she gave me when I left, a Buddhist lama recognized a grandson of Hanne Strong's as the third incarnation of a saint who lived in Tibet nine hundred years ago.) After outlining his vision, Anderson told Hanne: "You're here to do it. This is your job." She agreed.

Whether it was a revelation or mere shrewdness, Anderson had selected the right person to carry out his vision. Maurice Strong, Hanne's husband, a wealthy Canadian oil and mining tycoon and United Nations environmental diplomat, had become owner of the Baca in 1978 when he took control of the company that had started the retirement community. The 14,000-acre Baca Grande development was eventually sold to local developers. Strong and other investors retained the bulk of the ranch and unveiled the project to tap the aquifer; after the proposal began stirring up heated controversy, Strong sold his interests to his partners. In the meantime, the Strongs donated parcels of land to the religious groups that wanted to put up temples, retreats, sweat lodges, and hermitages, and through a foundation they set aside 2,000 more acres for new additions to the future global village of faiths.

"This is something beyond a human plan. It's predestined," Hanne said. "Unless mankind transforms from the material to a more spiritual, harmonious consciousness, this little planet is through. World religions need to transform, too. They've gone off the Path. Religions have to go back to the source and renew themselves. Then maybe the teachings can go forth. Basically, this is a place for mystics."

THREE TIMES THE SIZE OF RHODE ISLAND, SAGUACHE County offers plenty of room for mystics. The western half, where the Continental Divide angles across the upper corner of the county, is filled with the humped flanks of the San Juan mountains. The Sangre de Cristos, their spiked peaks higher than 14,000 feet, form an awesome rampart along the eastern border, edging toward the Divide at the north. In between is a wedge-shaped alpine desert, elevation 7,000 feet, flat as a tabletop and covered with clumps of sage sprouting from the alkaline soil. From Saguache, the county seat in the north, you can see the Great Sand Dunes 40 miles away: the dunes are that big, the air is that clear, the view is that unobstructed. Hugging the edge of the Sangre de Cristos, San Luis Creek struggles to run the length of the desert and reach the Rio Grande, which plummets out of the San Juans just below the county line before turning south toward New Mexico. But the two streams never meet. San Luis Creek, barely visible in the first place, except during spring runoffs, disappears into a sand sink near the dunes. Hydrologically, it's called a closed basin: a small-scale Nevada or western Utah.

The county's basic economy is ranching, potato farming, and a little tourism. The ranchers graze cattle in the mountains' foothills, often on national forest leases; the potatoes are grown at the valley's southern end, where water can be diverted from the Rio Grande or pumped from underground sources and where the flat land accommodates big tractors; the dunes attract a few people, but the main tourist routes lead somewhere else and skirt the county's boundaries. The result is one of Colorado's poorer counties, with one of its highest unemployment rates. An economic closed basin.

Eyebrows arched a little when the Baca started attracting new people, most of them college-educated, many of them relatively affluent, and some of them believing in reincarnation, vision quests, or the power of healing crystals. "Weird" and "flakes" were words I often heard when other residents talked about their new neighbors, but the term usually was used good-naturedly. They are tolerated as eccentrics.

Crestone-Baca children attend school in Moffat, where officials said the ranch kids accept them gladly. The only visible adjustment is the addition of vegetarian meals to the lunch menus; field trips include visits to cattle brandings and the ashram. Dr. Victor Sierpina, the "Country Doc" who moved to the area from Chicago in 1988 and became Moffat's first doctor since 1900, said that offering acupuncture helps him "bridge the belief systems" between the two communities. "I almost have to apologize for being a doctor to some of the people in Crestone, who call me a pill pusher and a knifer," he said, "but I'm not going to treat pneumonia with herbal tea."

Some people groused about Crestone-Baca residents feeding the deer herd that roams, protected from hunting, in the development. There are so many deer, and they are so tame, you have to drive slowly not to hit them on the streets. I almost bumped into a small group on a walk at twilight; I was more startled than they were. One homeowner, I was told, once called for help when two emboldened deer had her pet dog cornered in its dog house. Another time, a mountain lion visited for a venison buffet.

When the temples started going up, Hanne Strong said, a Christian fundamentalist in the area had threatened to burn them down, but he moved away, and other initial antagonisms eventually evaporated. One local told her, "I'd rather have them move in from Tibet than New York."

Other long-time residents seem simply bewildered by the influx of new people. "A lot of them come, hit one winter, and leave," a woman in Moffat said. "The people in Crestone call it a . . ." she raised her eyebrows and rolled her eyes, "high energy area. I don't know if it's that. I always just thought of it as home."

At the Agape Market, next door to the Free Spirit Christian Church, a nondenominational, "full-Gospel" Pentecostal church in Moffat, Ruth Jones said she has become friends with one of the Buddhists from the Baca. "It turns out we believe in a lot of the same things," she said.

The religious community represents less than a third of the 300 people in Crestone-Baca. Another third are retirees or others associated with the Baca Grande development, who view the emerging global village with a mixture of bemusement ("They'll provide all the rice we can eat," one man joked at a homeowners' meeting I attended, when someone asked about an upcoming volunteer effort to build a bridge) and recognition that the shrines, temples, people, and homes for the Refuge for World Truths contribute to the economic viability of the area. The rest, while not directly associated with any of the religious groups, nevertheless probably wouldn't have settled there without them. They attend the various concerts, lectures, and celebrations, but follow their own path. They include a former director of training at the National Institutes of Health, who now sells real estate; a former Merrill Lynch stock trader, now a reporter on a local paper; a woman who gave up a high-paced job and a bicoastal marriage to open a flower shop and live in the fire station; a former design engineer for IBM, seeking, she said, the "chance to get away from corporate America," who works on a ranch for room and board and bakes bread for the Bistro; and a man who makes his living by making replicas of English long bows.

"The one thing that sets it apart is the spiritual community that's here. It's an eclectic place," one woman said. "It makes for a real interesting community, almost like an international community in your backyard."

Spiritually charged or not, it is a pretty place, even more so in contrast to the desolate desert valley and the supernatural dunes at its feet. Crestone, about four square blocks of small, tidy homes, straddles a clear mountain creek that supports pastures and groves of cotton-woods and aspens as it cascades from the mountain snowpack. The Baca is less centralized, but equally watered by fresh creeks. Its homes and religious shrines, hidden among the piñon pines, are spread along gravel roads in the foothills. The view westward across the valley toward the San Juans holds the gaze. Sunsets redden the backdrop peaks of the Sangre de Cristos and explain why the Spanish explorers gave the mountains their blood-name. Some new residents compare Crestone-Baca to Telluride, Vail, Santa Fe, or Sedona, without the glitz, tourists, or high land prices. The lack of jobs, the remoteness, and the unforgiving climate keep their numbers small.

On the whole, the county's reaction to the Refuge of World Truths seems to have been like the valley floor's to San Luis Creek: quiet absorption. What got everyone's attention, however, was the proposal to pump up to 200,000 acre-feet of the Baca's aquifer to the big cities on the other side of the mountains. (One acre-foot of water is enough to supply ten people for a year.) Even without the benefit of a Bovis scale, it was clear that the water project generates a lot of negative energy.

Depending on your point of view, the Strongs are going to be instrumental in either saving the earth's spirit or despoiling the county's ecology and economy. "Many view Maurice as the man who brought this calamity to the valley," a friend of Strong's told me. When he resigned from the water development company, Strong told the local paper that his partners didn't like his association with the spiritual communities and that he "wanted to develop the water in a socially and environmentally responsible way. They are bottom-line oriented."

Virtually no one in Saguache County supports the water plan. Locals perceive the issue as a battle pitting themselves against rich outsiders with designs on the future of their homes and no concern for their opinion, or well-being. They feel that because they live in a place that doesn't have many people, much money, or a lot of political muscle, they are being picked upon by places with all three. They are angry and frightened. Some even suspect that the religious retreats above the aquifer are merely a New Age smokescreen masking a bald water grab.

The proposal has been working its way slowly through the state's water courts, but several opponents said it might not stop there. "I don't think a pipeline will be built," a woman in Crestone told me. "I think local people would blow it up. There would be people shot. They'd have to hire armed guards."

American Water Development Inc., the company that owns the Baca and the water rights underneath it, contends that the water to be piped to Denver would not be missed, that it merely evaporates each year in the closed basin anyway or exists in billions of unused gallons in the aquifer; that the project would create jobs and quadruple the county's tax base; and that opponents are being short-sighted and unduly paranoid.

"Remember the Owens Valley," is the common reply. At the turn of the century, officials from water-hungry Los Angeles had surreptitiously purchased the water rights in Owens Valley, a remote and sparsely populated closed basin in Inyo County, California. Within years after an aqueduct started moving water several hundred miles to Los Angeles, Owens Lake, where large ore boats once plied, was a dry and windswept alkali bed and nearby farms and ranches went out of business. San Luis Valley residents are aware of that history. Some Owens Valley officials had been brought in by opponents of the plan to recount their tales of woe; and a production company, seeking a location to make a film of Mary Austin's *The Land of Little Rain*, about life in the Owens Valley before the aqueduct, had selected Saguache County because it looked so much like Owens Valley once had.

News that American Water Development had on the one hand reduced its water-export plan (to 60,000 acre-feet), but on the other hand was using the name of other companies to buy up more water rights in the region deepened everyone's distrust. Despite the company's assurances to the contrary, some people in Saguache County said that Los Angeles, not Denver, is the ultimate market for their water. The price of water in southern California is a lot higher, they reasoned; without making the pipeline much longer, it could reach over the Continental Divide and feed into a tributary of the Colorado River, a major source of Los Angeles's supply. In their view, pumping their water for the benefit of city folk in Colorado would be bad enough. But Los Angeles . . . The thought turned anger to white fury.

Buddy Whitlock, a garrulous former Forest Service employee who serves as the water company's lightning rod in the county—"They were lookin' for someone who could take the heat from people without cussin' at them"—said he had received some threatening letters and phone calls, and someone had blown up his mailbox. But he was confident of success. "The water's here and *someone* will develop it," he said. "There's a need for water—where the people and the votes are."

IN SOME WAYS, SAGUACHE COUNTY WAS UNIQUE among the counties I encountered. I certainly didn't find any others where Birkenstock sandals are almost as commonplace as cowboy boots, where the Fourth of July barbecue features carrot juice, or where the list of coming events includes a Sufi whirling dervish. But, oddly, in some ways Saguache County is also more similar to the old frontier than the other areas. Land is being marketed to people who have never seen it, on the basis of dreams rather than hard facts. Wealthy investors, none of them local, are locked in conflict with resident settlers over the disposition of a natural resource. And people are gathering in a spot—partly because they think it is a holy place, partly because it offers them remoteness, and partly because the price seems cheap —where they hope they can practice their religions in peace.

Land, a quick profit, a refuge. Those had been the three main magnets that drew people to the western frontier more than a century ago. Whether driven by greed or lofty ambitions, gullibility or a desire to escape and be left alone, for those who came west every new frontier settlement was once a "dream corridor." In Crestone-Baca, all three magnets are exerting their pull, although with a distinctly modern inflection: a late-twentieth-century reincarnation of the old frontier.

"MY PEOPLE MUST BE TRIED IN ALL THINGS, THAT they may be prepared to receive the glory that I have for them, even the glory of Zion, and he that will not bear chastisement is not worthy of my kingdom." Thus, through the medium of Brigham Young's voice, spoke the Lord to the several thousand Mormons—the Camp of Israel—huddled in the midst of misery, malnutrition, and deadly disease on the banks of the Missouri River in January 1847.

Since its founding by Joseph Smith in 1830, the Mormon church had already suffered its share of trial and chastisement. Expelled by enraged mobs from northern Ohio, then from western Missouri, and finally from Illinois, where their prophet had been martyred in 1844, the Latter-day Saints were on the move once more. Zion was as yet undiscovered, but they believed it lay somewhere to the west, in a place so isolated and unpopulated that they could build their kingdom unmolested by the unbelievers they called Gentiles. By the end of 1847, where the river they named Jordan empties into the dead sea of the Great Salt Lake, Young and an advance scouting party found their Zion. From there the call was issued for the final gathering. By wagon, handcart, and foot, a great hegira set forth. In the years immediately following, while others streamed west for gold in California and for free land in Oregon, the Mormons went for faith and freedom from persecution in the Great Basin.

Much of the contemporary frontier lies in the original Mormon kingdom. When Brigham Young first petitioned Congress in 1849 to create the State of Deseret (so named in honor of the industrious honeybee), it covered virtually all of Utah, Nevada, and Arizona, and parts of Oregon, Idaho, Wyoming, Colorado, and southern California. The principal characteristic, extreme aridity, that had promised the Saints sanctuary from crowds of Gentiles still works today to keep population density low, even in those places no longer closely associated with Mormonism.

Many of the people I met were descendants of early Mormon settlers. Because genealogy is important to their religion, and because the Mormon migration contains so many dramatically epic elements, they all had stories to tell of their pioneer ancestors. Even without subscribing to their beliefs, it was impossible not to be awed by the power of faith to impel a people into such a harsh environment and sustain them through the tribulations of surviving in it.

The family story of Adair Merrell, a farmer in Hidalgo County, New Mexico (population 5,958; 1.7 people per square mile), is a good example.

In 1863, young Harry Payne, Merrell's maternal grandfather, immigrated with his family from the squalor of English coal country, where they had been converted by Mormon missionaries. While Harry's father stayed in Pennsylvania, working in a coal mine to pay back the church's immigration fund, the rest of the family, a mother and four children, joined a large contingent of Saints trekking to Zion from the staging ground near what is now Omaha. The route was more than a thousand miles, and they walked virtually all of it. A young cousin died early on the journey, and then, about halfway, at a place called "Bitter Cottonwood," Harry's two-year-old brother also succumbed. He was buried in a red dress and a sheet, with part of a wagon box laid over his body. Harry, age six at the time, and the rest of the family made it to Utah, where his mother gave birth to another child a few weeks after their arrival. At age twelve, with the family still owing money to the immigration fund, Harry went to work building grades in the mountains for the first transcontinental railroad. By his late twenties, he was a bishop in the church, prosperous, and, in accordance

with the Mormon doctrine recommending plural marriages, husband
to two wives. In the late 1880s, after Congress passed a law forbidding
polygamy in the territories, he was arrested for "unlawful cohabita-
tion," fined $300, and sent to prison for six months. Payne was pound-
ing rocks in a striped suit when church leaders, paving the way for
statehood, issued the manifesto abandoning polygamy. Rather than
split his family, Harry moved in 1891 with his two wives and six children to northern Mexico, where like-minded Mormons were establishing polygamist colonies where the deserts of Chihuahua meet the
Sierra Madre. They arrived in Colonia Dublan with their horses and
wagons, $80 in Mexican currency, and started over. By 1912, Harry,
a carpenter, mason, and farmer, was prospering again. He had seventeen children and brick houses for each of his wives. But his trials
and chastisements weren't yet over.

Mexico was where the two limbs on Adair Merrell's family tree
joined. Charles Merrell, his paternal grandfather, had made the walk
of faith from the Missouri River to Utah in 1852, losing his father on
the fourth day of the migration; was dispatched by the church to help
found a settlement along the Little Colorado River in Arizona, where
he married his second wife and where malaria forced the settlement's
abandonment; and in 1887 moved his multiple family to the polygamous refuge in Mexico, where he died twelve years later after falling
from a tree he was pruning. Eight-year-old Orson Merrell, Adair's father, began shouldering a lot of the work to help support the large
family.

In 1912 the Mexican Revolution was in full swing. Though neutral
in the conflicts, the Mormon colonies were in the thick of it. Lucinda
Payne, Harry's daughter, a teenager at the time, remembered it this
way: "First the government troops would pass through the country;
then the rebel troops; then the ones we were most afraid of, the bandit
groups, who were in it just for thrill and plunder. Each group would
take whatever they wanted—horses, grain, or hay for their animals,
or whatever they saw that they wanted—of course, in most cases without paying for it." That July, Pancho Villa arrived in Dublan with a
thousand men, set up machine guns at the town border, and demanded
that the residents surrender their weapons. He granted permission for
the women and children to leave the country. Yet another Mormon
exodus was prepared.

The night before the evacuees were loaded into boxcars on a train to El Paso, Orson Merrell came courting for Lucinda Payne. He brought a bouquet of roses and took her for a buggy ride confined, because of Villa's troops, to the town center. Just before midnight the next night, as 1,200 people waited for their train, Orson sought her out again for one last ride. "There was a feeling of excitement and of sadness," Lucinda would later write, "and as we passed our homes we would give them a last loving look and wonder if we would ever see them again. We wondered, too, if we would ever meet our friends again and just what the future had in store for us. . . . It was a beautiful moonlit night, and I will never forget it." After the ride in the moonlight, Lucinda and Orson promised to try to stay in touch, and said good-bye.

Needless to say, they eventually got back together, otherwise Adair Merrell, their son, would not be around to tell their story. Reuniting wasn't easy. Orson and the other men of Dublan were chased and shot at by Villa's troops as they escaped with Dublan's munitions once the women and children were safely across the border. Nor were the early years of marriage easy, especially when the couple tried to reestablish themselves in Dublan while the revolution was still in progress. Orson decided to give it up after the Mexican army impressed him and his wagon into service, separating him from his family for a month.

With twenty other former colonists, Orson Merrell bought 800 acres along the Gila River in New Mexico. They broke it into parcels, some good bottomland coupled with uncultivated upland, they platted lots for a town (which they named Virden, after the Gentile who had sold them the land), and they drew numbers from a hat: the lowest numbers got first pick of the farm parcels, but last pick for a town homesite. Like the honeybees they admired, they worked together to dig irrigation ditches, start farms, build a church and school, and found a town, now shaded by the trees they planted.

Old Harry Payne was in his sixties by this time. He had followed his faith from England to Utah to prison to Mexico and now to another fresh start in Virden, burying kin virtually all along the long trail. As one of his first acts in the fledgling village, he took a son with him on a clear night and, using strings and stakes and the North Star to guide him, laid out plots for a town cemetery. To avoid more trouble with the law, he moved both wives to Virden but lived only with one. He died in 1940, at age eighty-three. "When I was a kid," Adair Merrell said of his grandfather, "I didn't think he amounted to much. He didn't own a car, probably couldn't even drive one. He just tended an orchard and his farm. But that was when I was a kid. Now, I think he had a rich heritage, lived a rich life, and survived a lot of hardship."

Adair—tall, erect, taciturn, businesslike, about the same age as his grandfather was when he came to Virden—is no stranger to hardship himself, although he didn't travel as far to find it. "I've stayed right where I was born, in the same county," he said. After he married his wife, Mary, he decided "that little old valley [around Virden] just wasn't big enough" and started a cotton farm near Animas, a dusty little town on flat land that butts into the Peloncillo Mountains about 30 miles south of Lordsburg, the only town of any size in Hidalgo County. There were no paved roads, no electricity, no phone, no water faucets, no sewer when they made their home in the corner of an old metal airplane hangar. "The wind!" Mary remembered. "It would push that door, 'BANG, BANG' all night." She washed their first baby's diapers in an irrigation ditch. This was in the late 1940s.

From that start, the Merrells have thrived. Adair and one of his sons now run the state's biggest hog farm; he and his wife have six children, twenty grandchildren, are active in the church, and between them log 200 miles a day driving to meetings, work, and town. When I visited with them in their modern ranch house, Adair was watching Brigham Young University's basketball team play a tournament game on a special Mormon church channel, courtesy of a satellite dish. In the parlor was an upright piano, the only surviving possession from his mother's last exodus from Mexico, and a drawing of the Merrells' daughter who died at age ten after a freak playground accident. They gave me a copy of the Book of Mormon to keep and we walked outside. The Peloncillo Mountains were turning amethyst in the setting sun. A desert breeze was sweeping up the valley floor from Mexico.

"When I came here," Adair said, surveying the scene, "I thought it would be for a few years. It's turned into thirty-nine."

Mary turned toward him, smiled, and as he put his arms around her, said, "You didn't tell *me* it would be for just a few years."

ON DECEMBER 3, 1975, A CONVOY OF ABOUT TWENTY vehicles turned off U.S. Highway 89 in the red rock desert of Kane

County, Utah, and headed north along a treacherous dirt road toward Cottonwood Canyon. About 14 miles up the road, they came to a quarter section of private land where Alexander Joseph and his family and friends had been living for two years. There was an octagonal wooden house, a small bunkhouse, a corral, a garden plot for melons, squash, and carrots, and a trailer with a 50-gallon barrel on its top, where water was stored for showers. The convoy rumbled past onto land supervised by the Bureau of Land Management. Handmade signs welcomed them to Bac-Bone, Utah, warned of children at play, and, where a bulldozer had cut roads across the rocks and sand earlier that year, announced streets named Liberty Avenue and Constitution Boulevard. Here the convoy stopped and disgorged about a hundred men, all of them armed, including a special SWAT team of federal counterterrorism agents.

Facing them was a small contingent of people who had filed homestead claims on the BLM land and had begun the initial work of improvements by hauling in the trailers, prefabricated cabins, and army tents they called home. Some had lost their earthly possessions, and nearly their lives, in a flash flood that summer, but had started over. All of them believed that federal law still permitted them to homestead, or at least that the Constitution prohibited the government from stopping them, and most of them, including the women and children, had included gun practice among their weekly chores in case their interpretation was challenged. That moment appeared to have arrived on this crisp and windy day.

At the head of the homesteaders was Alex Joseph, who had been quoted in newspapers as saying that if authorities tried to remove them, "we will make Wounded Knee look like a picnic." He was holding a center-fire carbine.

Alex, thirty-nine at the time, was accustomed to controversy. Argumentative, a ravenous reader and quick wit, alternately gruff and mischievous, charismatic in a rough-hewn way, he seemed to attract either avid admirers or bitter enemies, but always attention. He had been a marine in his teens, a policeman in central California, a forest firefighter, car salesman, insurance salesman, debate coach; had converted to mainstream Mormonism in the mid-1960s, but had been excommunicated when he joined a splinter sect of Saints in Pinesdale, Montana, that furtively practiced plural marriages and occasionally warred with rival polygamist groups who claimed to be the true disciples of Joseph Smith; and then he had broken off on his own, convinced that the others had become murderously obsessed with doctrinaire squabbles and used the secrecy surrounding their polygamy principally to enhance their economic power and to excuse their tyranny over their adherents. In the early 1970s, he set off on a search for "a place that nobody else wanted; if it was ugly enough, barren enough, and hostile enough, everyone else would leave us alone." He also wanted a place where the winters weren't as cold as Montana. Utah's Kane County seemed to fit the bill.

In Cottonwood Canyon, an old man showed him ginseng plants growing wild and told him that some people believed in the medicinal powers of its root and were willing to pay good money for it. With some like-minded friends, he bought 160 acres, installed some of his wives on the land, and began making a modest fortune selling his roots to Californians. Trouble soon found him again, and Alex did little to avoid it.

He made no secret of his plural marriages, in fact seemed intent on being as public as possible, hoping to expose what he considered society's hypocrisy about the issue. "If you had six girlfriends, it was all right," he said. "If you had six girls living with you, great. But you'd better not represent that you had two wives. I was in Nevada once. Down the street, people were gambling; prostitution was going on in a nearby brothel. I was having a quiet picnic in the town park with two of my wives and some of my kids, and *I* was committing a felony." Alex was arrested once for polygamy, but his jailer saw a television report about two gay men getting married in San Francisco and released him the next morning.

By 1975 he was living with ten wives, ages sixteen to twenty-nine, and five children. (He had been married thirteen times, but three wives, including his first, had left him.) With Cottonwood Canyon not ready to house them all, some of the family was staying in Glen Canyon City, a former camp for construction workers on the nearby dam on the Colorado River and a coal-fired electricity plant across the border in Page, Arizona. Among the several dozen trailers, they had the only house and operated a small bar/café. After running some local drug dealers out of the area, they had gained the reputation of being friendly but potentially militant. When Kane County officials decided to arrest him on charges of selling illegal fish from Lake Powell, they sent six deputies: they weren't afraid of Alex being violent, they said, but they weren't sure about some of his wives.

The homestead filings in March 1975 got the federal government's immediate attention. Based on the fact that Congress had never explicitly repealed the Homestead Act of 1862 and as late as 1955 had included homestead provisions within veterans' benefit laws, the applications posed a direct threat to prevailing federal policies on the use of public lands. Alex and his twelve homestead disciples were promptly enjoined from further activities on the land, but allowed to remain until the courts sorted out the legal mess. Characteristically, Alex made his first court appearance with two wives at his side and an eagle feather stuck defiantly in his headband: "I was a *walking felony*." The judge, who had prosecuted the last celebrated polygamy case as a Salt Lake County attorney in the 1950s, decided to overlook this challenge and concentrate on the land issue. The media, however, were more interested in Alex and his wives. The family started showing up on nationally televised talk shows, where discussion of homesteading laws took a distant back seat to the presence of a long-haired polygamist with beautiful and articulate wives, three of whom had been college roommates at the University of Montana.

Early in the fall, the court ruled for the government and gave the homesteaders thirty days to vacate Cottonwood Canyon. Alex answered by presenting 113 new applications under a different statute that allowed ranchers to file for 640-acre desert grazing parcels. The media blitz had brought in a wave of letters, plus ten dollars for application fees, from people around the country. The new claims totaled nearly 75,000 acres, including part of the coal-rich Kaiparowitz Plateau, where environmentalists and utility companies were already preparing a struggle over development. The judge threatened a contempt citation, and when the applicants announced they would vacate their homesteads, it looked like the battle was over. A seemingly defeated Alex told a wire service, "The very things that built this country and made it great—town-building, homesteading, mining—have been brought to a screeching halt."

But instead of vacating the canyon, the homesteaders moved their dwellings onto a different parcel and, under yet another provision of the century-old law, filed a townsite plat for Bac-Bone. On Thanksgiving Day, after a community dinner, they elected town officers. One of Alex's wives was named mayor; the patriarch himself became town marshal. A few weeks later, the SWAT team arrived.

Alex Joseph is a complex man with many facets: a flair for flamboyance, to be sure, and a simultaneously playful and serious knack for poking the ribs of established authority; a renegade intelligence that drives him to study things until he masters them, from computers and helicopters to Egyptian hieroglyphics and chess; the kind of person, one of his wives said, who if he met Joseph Smith, the Mormon founder, the evening wouldn't be spent with discussions of doctrine but "would more likely begin with a wrestling match and end with whiskey and card tricks." At the same time, his belief in polygamy is based only partly on the conviction that it reflects Old Testament patriarchal fundamentalism, the kind that Abraham, David, Moses, Solomon and, he contends, Jesus practiced, and "if you're going to understand the Bible, you have to adopt the life-style of those who wrote it." What further appealed to him, he told an interviewer at the time, was the notion of a "responsible masculine figure; polygamy demands that I take on the attributes I've wanted to develop anyway: patience, tolerance, judgment, and industry." Being an avid card player, he also knew when to call a bluff and when not to, when to hold 'em, when to fold 'em. All of those multiple facets crystallized as, rifle in hand, he confronted the federal agents, and his followers, all armed as well, including his wives, looked to him for the first move.

Besides his carbine, Alex had his Bible with him. He opened it to Ecclesiastes 9:4, where it is written, "For to him that is joined to all the living there is hope: for a living dog is better than a dead lion." He handed over his gun. The others followed suit. Then he grimly watched as the families were evicted from their homes, and the agents confiscated trailers, trucks, and generators. Not long afterward, bulldozers arrived to remove any trace of Bac-Bone, Utah, and the other homesteads, where sagebrush has now reasserted its prior claim of ownership.

WHEN I MET ALEX JOSEPH IN THE FALL OF 1990 HE was supervising additions to his family's compound on a dusty hill in what had formerly been Glen Canyon City, where they had resettled after the homestead fight. Two prefabricated homes had just been towed in and set at a right angle to a large wooden building and bunkhouse they had built in the late 1970s to serve as a combination assembly hall and living quarters for most of the family. He had nine wives and twenty of his twenty-three children with him in town, some of them living in other houses down the gravel street. His goal is to consolidate everyone into housing around a courtyard that will eventually be shaded by the tree one of his sons was planting with a backhoe when I arrived.

The minds that had named a prospective town Bac-Bone and given its roads the names of Liberty and Constitution are still much in evidence. The big house is named Long Haul, a pun on its 144-foot length and a reflection of the travails the family had endured to find a final home. It rests at the crest of Concord Bridge Street. And the town itself, which the Josephs led to incorporation in 1984, is now officially Big Water, Utah.

"Big Water sounds Indian, and suitably, in Indian country," said Joanna Joseph, a cheerily intent woman, wholesomely pretty, one of the three roommates who had married Alex while in college, a graphic designer and mother of one, responsible for many of the namings. "It calls to mind the lake in our backyard [Lake Powell], our greatest commercial asset. It bespeaks the element most valuable in a desert place: water, which in abundance spells wealth, contentment, health. Big Water most fundamentally reminds me of mortality, the experiment in living, the Great Abyss into which we are cast to sink or swim."

Big Water (population 328) is now the second-largest of the four towns in Kane County (5,169 people, 1.3 per square mile). It is 56 barren miles east of the county seat, Kanab (population 3,278), where the county's first and only stoplight was recently installed. The impermanence of its construction camp days, when it was merely a cluster of trailers on a treeless patch of rocks, the kind of place you occasionally encounter in the deserts and feel sure will be gone with the next wind, is slowly giving way to a more solid look. A school was under construction, to replace the trailers that comprised classrooms for the students from kindergarten to the senior class of two. There is a motel, a bar, a cabinet shop, a boat storage facility, and a gravel business. None of the streets are paved, and most of the dwellings are still mobile homes, but gentling the otherwise unremittingly harsh plateau landscape are some young saplings, more than a thousand of them the work of Erick Lassen, a compatriot of Alex's whose third wife is Joanna's twin sister.

Alex, his family, and associates are now heavily outnumbered by Big Water's newer residents (none of the others are polygamous), but they are its most influential members. They had, in effect, founded the town, named it, and are associated with most of its enterprises. One Joseph wife runs a real estate office, another is town attorney. The family publishes the Big Water newspaper. Alex, the man who had gone to the desert to be left alone and had fought the government in court and nearly with a carbine when he wasn't, the patriarch who openly flaunted his plural marriages in the face of Utah's laws and the decrees of its principal religion, the rebel spirit prone to saying things like, "I'm not a big fan of democracy, I'm a monarchist; you can't help but be anything else if you're a Christian"—Alex is serving his third term as mayor of Big Water.

He has mellowed in his middle age. His long hair, which he once wore in braids with an Indian headband, has given way to a cut that just covers his ears. His beard and mustache, salted with gray, are well kept. His face is worn and weathered from the years and desert wind, somewhat tired except for the eyes that still burn with a mischievous fire. He looks like country singer Merle Haggard and has the same deep-gravel voice.

He normally stays up most of the night, working in his office in the second floor of Long Haul. The office has a powerful computer on its desk; bookshelves lined with volumes about Joseph Smith, the Old Testament, genealogy, and municipal waste laws; a globe and poster of a time line of world history; pictures of President Bush and of Alex with a town softball team; and a drawing of an Egyptian pictograph that Alex translated into a book. It was about noon when I arrived. Alex had just gotten up and was having a cup of coffee and a cigarette in the courtyard.

"Religious persecution made this frontier," he said. "This used to be 'cohab alley' when people were escaping the law. I moved here [Big Water] on the recommendation of the federal government; they stuck a machine gun in my face. I was going to move out there, raise my family, mind my own business, have some control over my own life. I just wanted them to leave me alone. I guess that was naive."

I asked whether "they" left him alone now.

"There's no 'they' anymore," he answered. "*I'm* 'they.' Polygamists come out here and say they're hiding. 'From what?' I ask them. Senator Hatch [one of Utah's U.S. senators] sent a staff member down here recently just to see if I'm happy. The governor picks me out of receiving lines to talk. I don't know *what's* going on." He seemed bemused by the irony: from outlaw to accepted public official, without altering his beliefs.

His wives echoed the theme: they aren't the ones who have changed, rather it was the attitude of society around them, a growing "live and let live" ethos toward all forms of nontraditional living arrangements.

"You couldn't find a bigger women's libber group than us," one wife told me. "We have careers, independence, and our family—like something out of *Cosmopolitan*."

Reflecting the change, legal authorities no longer file charges against polygamists. In Big Water, there's an extra dimension. "Who would prosecute me?" Alex laughed. "My wife, the town attorney?"

For Alex and his extended family the homestead fight in Cottonwood Canyon had been a crucible, a formative experience in the same way that the Mormon pioneers were affected by their flight from Nauvoo to Salt Lake. Except for Alex, who grew up dividing his time between Okie tenant-farmer grandparents and Greek immigrant parents, most of them come from comfortable middle-class families, and they never considered themselves part of the 1970s counterculture movement. But living in tents and trailers, without electricity or running water, had bound them together, made them feel even more separate from modern society than did their belief in plural marriage.

"I see someone on television complaining about conditions, and it makes my blood boil," said Patricia Graffam, who had homesteaded as Erick Lassen's first wife (she's now remarried, but lives in Big Water, where she teaches at the school). "I want to scream, 'I was in a cold shack in the winter, delivering a baby on a *stool*!' Modern society is draining the grit out of people." Like the others, she was transformed into an ardent anti-government conservative by their eviction from the canyon; they vote Republican but consider themselves libertarians. "I learned that it doesn't work the way you learn in civics books," she said. "If the government wants to do something, it doesn't matter what the law says."

Alex was more philosophical about it. Relocating to Big Water had, in the end, been "providential," he said. With coal deposits and Lake Powell nearby, Big Water is destined to grow (its population increased 52 percent in ten years) and his expanding family would prosper with it in ways it never could have in the remote canyon. "We're adding a million dollars a year to the tax base," he said. "By the year 2050, if my sons do what I've done, there will be thousands of people living here named Joseph."

Speaking to a reunion of the homesteaders, most of whom had dispersed to other areas after the eviction, Alex ended the first day's ceremonies with a short speech to the next generation: "Examine your environment to see what's wrong and decide how much of it is your fault. The more that is your fault, the better. Be thankful for that, because you can fix it. You can't fix the part that isn't your fault—those things that you'll be victimized by. You must get out of their way."

GET OUT OF THE WAY OR YOU'LL BE VICTIMIZED. IT could be considered one of the slogans of the old frontier, joining ranks with the better-known "Pikes Peak or Bust" or "Go west, young man, and grow up with the country." The West's original Indian inhabitants certainly learned that bitter lesson the hard way. Of the various stains on the nation's history, the two darkest have been slavery and the treatment of Native Americans. In one, whites chained people of another race into bondage and brought them against their will to the new land; in the other, a different race already living on the land that the whites coveted were forced from their homes, and America's oldest way of life was essentially extinguished.

Black or red, they faced the cocked gun of racism. Not surprisingly, then, the group called Seminole Negroes, combining both colors, got it from both barrels. Even when they tried to get out of the way, they were still victimized. Their odyssey for freedom makes the Mormon exoduses seem like a church outing by comparison. It ended in Kinney County, Texas (population 3,119), where the rocky hills of the Edwards Plateau give way to a brush-speckled dry plain north of the Rio Grande. But it began in a far different climate: the densely forested, sodden swamps of Florida.

Starting in the early 1700s, slaves escaping from plantations in the

Carolinas and, later, Georgia found refuge in Spanish Florida, beyond the jurisdiction of the British colonies, where they were accorded freedom. The principal tribe in the area was named Seminole, meaning "runaway" or "separate ones," because they had broken off from the larger Creek tribe and moved south. Some of the Seminole chiefs owned black slaves, although people who visited the region reported that "vassals and allies" would have been a better term. The Seminole Negroes had their own villages, raised their own crops and livestock, and since many of them knew more about farming than their titular masters, they frequently became comparatively wealthy. Only an annual tribute of corn to their chief distinguished them from the free blacks among whom they lived.

The blacks adopted the Seminole way of dressing: colorful turbans, draped shawls, leggings, and moccasins. Intermarriage was not prohibited, but also not extensive. Being conversant in both the Seminole language and English (they spoke a version called Gullah), the leading blacks became important to the tribe in its dealings with whites. Having a strong motivation to avoid conquest—if they were captured in battle, they might be sent back to plantation slavery—they were even more invaluable whenever the Seminoles went to war. Which was quite often.

The Seminoles of Spanish Florida presented a double irritation to their white neighbors to the north, hungry for more land and anxious to eliminate any haven for runaway slaves. Sporadic fighting went on for nearly a century, before and after Florida's annexation in 1817, and culminated in the Seminole Wars of the 1830s, the nation's most costly Indian conflict. The fierceness of the resistance can be measured by apocryphal anecdote and by statistics. The anecdote: Seminole women were said on occasion to have killed their young children in order to free themselves to fight alongside their men. The statistics: the U.S. army lost 1,500 soldiers and spent $20 million in the hostilities. Finally defeated, the Seminoles were shipped to Indian Territory in Oklahoma; the Seminole Negroes (at least those that hadn't been killed or sold back into slavery during the wars) went with them.

Indian Territory offered little better sanctuary. Friction arose when, despite promises to the contrary, the Seminoles were assigned land among the Creek Indians and told to abide by Creek laws. The Creeks held a more traditional view of how black slaves should be treated.

When the Seminole Negroes, many of whom had been free for generations, began establishing separate towns according to their custom but in violation of Creek law, tensions mounted. The tensions soon erupted when Creeks started abducting blacks and selling them for a hundred dollars apiece to Arkansas slave traders.

Wild Cat, a Seminole chief who had been one of the last holdouts in Florida and felt particularly betrayed by the government's promises when he arrived in Indian Territory, decided in 1849 to lead his people to freedom. After scouting the Southwest, he made a treaty with the Mexican province of Coahuila: in exchange for protecting Mexicans against raiding Indians, they could have eight square miles of land south of the Rio Grande. A year later, Wild Cat returned to his tribe, announced the deal, and invited anyone who wished to join him in the new home. With the help of the black leader John Horse, 300 Seminoles, of both colors, were recruited.

The journey of the exiles was perilous, especially when word spread among the slave owners in Arkansas and the Creek nation that another freedom trail was being blazed. A Creek party pursued Wild Cat's group, fought a battle, and lost. Marauding Comanches captured a number of blacks in a raid and ransomed them back to the Creeks. A separate group of slaves, trying to catch up with the main body, were attacked by Comanches in Texas. All of them except two girls were killed in the battle. The girls were tortured—the Comanches scraped off some of their skin to see if they were also black underneath—and then sold. Deeper in west Texas, Wild Cat made a peace treaty with the native Indians for safe passage, and his band reached the Rio Grande without further incident. Fording the river near Eagle Pass was an indelible moment, still fresh in the memory of an old Seminole Negro woman who recounted the story in her Gullah English to an anthropologist eighty years later: "Now we was glad dat we done git away fo de American race people, and we felt dat we could be safe if we can git across de ribber."

Over the next years more black runaways, many of them Seminole Negroes who had been enslaved in Arkansas, some of them slaves of other tribes, would join the group in Mexico. As promised, the Seminoles would fight and defeat Indian raiders in northern Mexico and be granted land near Nacimiento, and then they would fight and defeat bands of slave-trading Texans who considered them "black gold" for market on the north side of the Rio Grande. Wild Cat would die from smallpox and be replaced in leadership by John Horse; most of the full-blooded Seminoles would decide that Indian Territory was better than the bleak desert of Coahuila and return to their reservation in Oklahoma. With the Civil War in progress, the Seminole Negroes would decide it was safer to remain *south* of the Confederacy. By 1870, the Civil War was over, American slaves had been emancipated, and the U.S. government was desperate for help along the west Texas frontier, where small bands of Comanches, Apaches, Lipans, Kickapoos, and Kiowas were wreaking havoc among the settlers while the army seemed incapable of stopping them. The Seminole Negroes—with battle experience from Florida to Oklahoma to Mexico—were just what the army needed.

Another deal was struck: the Seminole Negroes would become cavalry scouts, draw regular pay and supplies, their families would be provisioned at forts along the Rio Grande (eventually consolidating at Fort Clark in Bracketville), and at the end of their enlistment they would be granted what they had always wanted, land of their own in a slavery-free United States. At Fort Clark, they were assigned land near the spring-fed headwaters of Las Moras Creek, where they built thatched and adobe huts discreetly separated from the stone barracks and officers' quarters at the other end of the fort's lands.

The scouts were assigned to Lt. John Bullis, whom they admiringly called "the Whirlwind," and under him served with distinction. They could track trails that others thought too "cold" to follow, survive for weeks in the desert on short rations, find water where no one else could, and, as they always had, fight fearlessly. At one of the decisive battles of the southern Plains, in the Palo Duro Canyon of Texas's panhandle, one of the scouts, Adam Payne, was awarded the Congressional Medal of Honor for bravery. A year later, three others earned the medal when they rescued a surrounded Bullis from certain death.

Within ten years, most of the serious Indian depredations in west Texas had been brought to an end. Remarkably, the Seminole Negro scouts suffered no casualties in combat. They credited their good fortune to the prayers of their families and to the good luck they associated with the clear and abundant waters of Las Moras Creek, next to which, for a time at least, their people lived happily and securely.

In gratitude for his services, west Texans dubbed Bullis "The Friend of the Frontier" and presented him with a fancy sword. Engraved on the scabbard were the words: "He protected our homes—our homes are open to him." The scouts he led, however, received something quite different.

The settlers treated the Seminole Negroes with contempt, considering them riffraff, half-breeds of the two races that whites were accustomed to loathing. That the Seminole Negro community was cultivating crops in a corner of fort property coveted by area farmers only exacerbated the strained situation. Relations with the black "buffalo soldiers" bivouacked at the fort often weren't much better. Many of the black soldiers viewed the scouts and their families as savage Indians. The scouts, on the other hand, proud of their frontier skills as well as the fact that for generations their people had stubbornly resisted American bondage, often seemed to condescend to the black soldiers relatively fresh from plantation slavery. (To the whites, this pride cast the group as "uppity niggers," yet another reason for hatred.) As a result, the scouts' immunity from combat fatalities didn't extend to life around the fort. John Horse's nephew was killed in a barroom fight with a border outlaw. A little later the chief himself and another scout were ambushed in the dark on fort grounds; the chief escaped but his partner died. Adam Payne, the Medal of Honor recipient, was murdered when someone stuck a double-barreled shotgun in his back and fired.

In the meantime, the scouts' appeals for the land they had been promised were denied. The army backed their claims—even Phil Sheridan, credited with coining the phrase, "the only good Indian is a dead one," argued on their behalf. But the Bureau of Indian Affairs, apparently with the encouragement of Seminole leaders in Oklahoma, stalled and dodged. The bureau's position was that the tribal rolls had been formally established in 1866. Anyone who wasn't in Oklahoma at the time therefore wasn't a Seminole and entitled to land in the Indian Territory: they shouldn't have left in the first place, but since they did, they weren't welcome back. Case closed.

For the aging John Horse, this was the last straw. He had been part of some of the greatest Indian victories against the United States in the Seminole Wars, only to discover concessions won in the mangrove swamps of Florida reneged upon by the government in the hills of Oklahoma. With his friend, Wild Cat, he had led his people from the turmoil of Indian Territory to the arid desolation of Coahuila. And then, at the invitation of the American government, he had brought them back to Texas. His life had been one fight after another for freedom and land of his own. Now he was being betrayed again. Bitterly, he and some others again forded the Rio Grande into Mexico, where the land wasn't as good but at least promises were kept. They were put back to work fighting Indians, and John Horse never returned to the United States.

Most of the scouts and their families, however, remained at Fort Clark and waited patiently for their cause to prevail. It never did. In 1914, the contingent of scouts was officially disbanded and the Seminole Negroes were unceremoniously evicted from their homes on the fort grounds. After nearly 200 years of fighting and fleeing for their freedom, they found themselves once again dispossessed.

FORT CLARK CLOSED AFTER WORLD WAR TWO (ITS last service had been as a camp for German prisoners of war). All of its twentieth-century wooden buildings were dismantled and sold for salvage; the sturdy nineteenth-century structures, made of stones from the fort's quarry, were left vacant. Bracketville, the Kinney County seat on low land adjacent to the fort, shriveled when the soldiers left. Twenty of the town's twenty-one bars quickly went out of business. Ranchers started grazing cows where Gen. John Wainwright, the hero of Bataan and Corregidor, and George S. Patton, who brought the cavalry into the armored tank era, once staged mounted maneuvers.

Then in 1971 the core of the fort was purchased and turned into Fort Clark Springs, a private retirement community. Elderly couples now live in the stately former officers' houses or in condo apartments carved out of the century-old barracks. They play par-three golf on the former parade grounds lined by pecan and live oak trees, they swim in the spring-fed pool, and they dine in a restaurant that formerly was the officers' club. Built to provide military protection so that the surrounding countryside could be opened to settlement, the fort itself is now the area's principal residential development. Fort Clark Springs is already more populous than Bracketville, and its growth is the reason Kinney County moved from just below to just above two persons per square mile between 1980 and 1990, one of only three counties to make that transition.

"It's very pleasant," one resident told me. "There's everything you need to keep busy. If you're an avid duplicate bridge player, they'll wear you out. The only thing we don't have is a shopping mall. Some of the ladies get in a bit of a twit over that." Then he pointed to the security gate at the entrance. "And it's safe. As safe as you can get this close to the border."

Several dozen descendants of the Seminole Negro scouts remain in the area, though none of them at Fort Clark Springs. One of them is Miss Charles Wilson, age seventy-eight, a large, kindly woman who lives in a small wooden house on a gravel street in Bracketville. Her mother's father, Sampson July, had been born in Florida and accompanied Wild Cat and John Horse to Mexico; her father's father, Billy Wilson, had escaped slavery in Arkansas to join the group on its way to the border. During the years at Fort Clark the July and Wilson families had contributed twenty-four Seminole Negro scouts to the service. (Every generation of Wilsons has had a Charles, hence her name; people call her "Miss Charlie.") She was born at Fort Clark, baptized in the waters of Las Moras Creek, and was still a toddler when the scouts were evicted.

"The government just went down there and told them they had to go," she remembered. "They *did* give them their horses and some rations, but there was no place to go. They just went everywhere, wherever they could stay. We're about depleted now."

Like many of the scouts, her father found work as a cowboy on a ranch while the family stayed in Bracketville. Her mother, and the girls when they got older, served as maids and cooks for the officers at the fort. Miss Charlie later became a teacher at Bracketville's black school prior to integration. (Originally, the district provided a school only through the eighth grade; after troops of black soldiers were assigned to the fort in the 1940s, a separate black high school was added.) In retirement she has devoted her time to preserving what's left of her people's culture.

Together, we drove through the old fort. It was February, but warm enough for golf. A light rain the night before had greened the grass and settled the dust. Along officers' row, she pointed out houses where she had earned twenty-five dollars a month cooking, cleaning, and babysitting. With its two-story, historic buildings, its mature trees along the road and sidewalk, and its parade ground in the center, this part of the development looks something like a New England village with an oversized town common. At one corner of the parade ground stands Patton's former house, now divided into two retirement homes. Miss Charlie had served food at parties for the general there. Beyond the stone buildings lies a mesquite-covered plain, with roads winding through a mobile-home park and RV camp, both hidden from view.

We came at last to the headwaters of Las Moras Creek, where the Seminole Negroes had lived. Huge cottonwoods and oaks shaded the stream, and the grass was luxuriantly emerald near the cool waters. Miss Charlie smiled at the sight. "Oh how we used to 'shout by the river' here," she said. The scouts' families were Baptists, but at wakes, dressed in the bright-colored attire of tribal tradition, they would chant in Seminole, not Gullah, she said. "I asked my mother what they were saying," Miss Charlie recalled. " 'Hush,' she answered, 'I don't know either.' We have all types of cultures in us." Along one bend of the creek, near where her family had lived in a dirt-floor hut, is a new three-story condominium building and the clubhouse for an eighteen-hole golf course.

Most descendants I met were bitter about the fort-turned-development. "I think *we* should put up a gate to check *them* when they come over here," one man in Bracketville told me. Like other descendants of the scouts, he believes a treaty exists somewhere, either long lost or perhaps deliberately hidden, that would prove the Seminole Negroes' rightful claim to some land, maybe even the parcel of the old fort along the creek where foursomes were driving golf carts down the fairways. (Historians don't argue that there was an agreement with the Seminole Negro scouts that wasn't fulfilled, but doubt that there ever was a formal treaty.) He resents the fact that he can't fish or visit without paying a fee. "Do you have a *membership*?" he sarcastically imitated the question asked at the security post. "It's economics, is all it is. Our people wanted work and wanted land and they got cheated out of it. The most we get from the government is a flag for our cemetery."

Miss Charlie is more forgiving. She likes the development. It is one of the area's major employers, along with the Border Patrol, and has at least kept the fort from decaying. "I hated to see it vacant and locked up," she said as we left. "It seemed like such a sacred place to me."

Several miles away, we came to a small clearing surrounded by mesquite and cedars: the scouts' cemetery. "They were buried out there so they wouldn't be next to the white soldiers," a local historian had told me. When the fort was closed, the remains in the white soldiers' cemetery had been reinterred in another military graveyard; the scouts were left where they were, and the land had been part of a parcel sold to a nearby rancher. Miss Charlie had formed a cemetery association that eventually reclaimed it and now maintains it. No one is sure how many Seminole Negro scouts are buried there, or, for that matter, exactly where. "We might be walking on some right now," she said, concerned, as we stepped across the rocky soil. There are some wooden crosses, a few old gravestones, and, near the center, four white marble headstones that the association recently got from the army to commemorate the Medal of Honor recipients.

This, then, was the end of their odyssey, the only American land they had been granted in return for their services on the frontier: about an acre of hardscrabble where their warrior heroes are buried. Even this had not come easily, but at the end of a legal and political battle.

Miss Charlie adjusted some flowers at one of the headstones. I asked her why she thought the Seminole Negro scouts and their people hadn't been treated better.

"I don't know," she said quietly. "Maybe because we're just a forgotten people in a forgotten part of the world. What do you think?"

REFUGEES OF ANY SORT ARE UNCOMMON IN THE CONtemporary frontier. By overwhelming proportions, the people I met do not live miles from nowhere because they want to escape some more populated place or some previous life. They were neither drawn nor driven to the least-inhabited fringes of America seeking a permanent haven. Most often they had been born there: it is what they prefer because it is what they are accustomed to.

In the more stunningly scenic spots, there might be vacation homes owned by urbanites who enjoy the solitude and majestic landscape, speak dreamily of how they wish they could stay year-round, and then vote with their feet when they return to the city and their jobs after a month's stay. A few might make a stab at transplanting themselves. Within a year or two they usually confront the wide distinction between a change of pace and a change of life, and then they are gone. Living 70 miles from a movie theater or a different restaurant or even some variety in the groceries requires a greater motivation than novelty.

I encountered scattered pockets of young adults associated with tourist businesses—river rafters, outfitters, hiking guides—who try to scrape by between seasons and say they enjoy it most when they have the wild places to themselves. For them, adventure is the attraction. They are fleeing boredom. At this point in their existences, life, like their livelihoods, is a wilderness vacation. My lingering impression was that if I came back several years later I would find a new wave of adventurers in their place, enjoying the same prerogatives of youth.

On the other side of the age divide, retirees comprise a significant portion of the non-native frontier residents in some counties. In the southwestern deserts, many of them are "snowbirds" who spend the winters in their RVs and trailers where the sun is warm and the land inexpensive; summers they are on the road, visiting their children, or back at homes in northern climes. Important as they might be to the local economy, they aren't considered integral parts of the community, merely a variation of tourists.

Some retirees, however, move in permanently. Low housing costs were the principal reason most of them gave to me, followed distantly by lack of crime, a more leisurely pace, the scenery, and a lifelong itch to live somewhere other than where their careers had kept them.

Lucille Muchmore, a gregarious white-haired woman I met near Big Bend National Park on the Rio Grande, had relocated from her native Waco, Texas, to one of several retirement developments carved out of the rocks and cactus in the area. "My kids thought I was crazy," she said. "I sold my Plymouth Fury and bought a pickup truck. I got a camper. And then I bought some property. Then they *knew* I had gone crazy. It was joyous. I hated Waco."

Likewise, deep in the mountains of Idaho, in the little settlement of Yellow Pine—a place that relies on a two-way radio for communication with the rest of the world because it has no telephone service, where the mail in winter has to be flown in three times a week, and where until recently once the snows began in earnest the only way out to the nearest real town, Cascade, about 60 miles away, was by snowmobile—I found a small group of retired school teachers. They wish they could have lived in Yellow Pine in younger years, but it would have been unrealistic, they said, because of the lack of jobs. "Summer people use Yellow Pine as an escape," one said. "It's the same reason we're here. You don't need anything here beyond your home and your food and your clothes—you're talking basics." Their main concern is the distance to medical services, particularly during emergencies in winter.

Among the age group in between young adventurers and retired urban escapees—for those people trying to earn a living and raise a family, but not wanting to do it in a city or suburb—I found few transplants, with the exception of teachers or employees of various federal agencies whose jobs require their presence and guarantee them a salary. In two different parts of Utah, I met men who are computer experts with employers in California cities; they report to work by turning on their computers and hooking up their modems to the telephone line. In Lake City, Colorado, a hamlet on the Continental Divide, a document preservation specialist had migrated from Texas and carries on his business through the graces of regular UPS service. Dennis Parks, a renowned potter, and his wife, Julie, moved their family eighteen years ago from California to the mining ghost town of Tuscarora, Nevada (population eight), seventy sagebrush-covered miles from the nearest town, to open a pottery studio and summer school. "At the college where I was teaching, people used to sit around and talk about what could be done to make the Los Angeles basin more livable," Dennis told me. "It finally came to me, the old proposition that if you're not part of the solution you're part of the problem. The best thing to do is to move out to the country."

But all these newcomers to the frontier, "modern pioneers" I guess you could call them, are exceptions to the rule. The sparsely settled lands as a whole no longer function as magnetic poles for the restless, the landless, and the ambitiously mobile, or the persecuted pilgrim. Not even for the recluse. "Some people come here not only to get away from cities, but from people," a retiree in Yellow Pine told me. "Yeah," said his friend, "they don't last long."

The western frontier once represented wide-open economic opportunity. People moved there and endured its hardships because they thought it offered them the chance to make money. To a great extent, the people moving there now do so only after having already made their money somewhere else. And as a potential sanctuary for escape, the western frontier now serves mainly as a place for vacationers, for occasionally used second homes for the wealthy, or for retirees who either are particularly hardy or can't afford anyplace else.

Most of the residents are the firmly planted descendants of the much-traveled. They seek the opposite of escape. For them, the challenge is in the staying. That usually is challenge enough.

CHAPTER 4

BOOM AND BUST

IN 1864 FIVE PROSPECTORS SCOUTING THE DIAMOND
Mountains of central Nevada discovered a ledge rich in silver ore and
quickly formed a mining district to protect their claim. They named
it Eureka. Promising as the strike seemed, it initially didn't amount to
much. Firmly locked in lead ore, the silver couldn't be freed by the
traditional crushing and chemical treatments of the day. For five years,
the site languished. Eureka in 1869 consisted of two log cabins along
a small creek in a mountain canyon. Within the 4,175 square miles of
what now is Eureka County lived fewer than a hundred people. By
1870, however, new smelting and refining techniques, using intense
heat from blast furnaces, had been perfected. Suddenly Eureka's deposits were commercially valuable.

Before the year ended, a real town had been born. Three stages were serving it and plans were under way for a rail line. Several local newspapers were circulating. During the summer of 1870 one of them reported that forty-three houses had gone up in a single week, most of them carted in from towns nearly a hundred miles away, since lumber was selling locally for two dollars a foot. In October 1870, Eureka's population was 2,000; a year later, 4,000; and by 1878, when it peaked, nearly 9,000, making it the state's second-most important mining city after Virginia City, home of the fabulous Comstock Lode.

Two large corporations, one financed by San Francisco investors and the other British-owned, bought most of the Eureka claims in 1871 and built smelters and refineries whose furnaces required so much charcoal that for 50 miles in every direction the mountains were denuded of their piñon pine, dwarf cedar, and mountain mahogany. Smoke from the furnaces, heavily laden with arsenic and lead, hung over the crowded city, coating the new buildings with soot and killing off the vegetation and birds and, sometimes, a few of the residents. "Beauty, Eureka has none," wrote a town booster in a promotional booklet. "Her scenery is rugged and wild, but the drear hills that environ her contain the germs of untold treasure." Others called it the "Pittsburgh of the West."

During its twenty-year heyday, Eureka survived several conflagrations among its tightly packed buildings and a flash flood that swept through the center of town, killing fifteen people, including a reporter for one of its papers who died as his office was carried off by the tide. A smallpox outbreak caused the board of health to warn residents to "abstain from mingling promiscuously with outside people." Lack of fresh food, the harsh climate, and the lethal smog gave the town high infant mortality rates. But Eureka still thrived. People amused themselves at an ice-skating rink, opera house, two race tracks, and the saloons, dance halls, and brothels common to all mining boom towns.

By 1890 Eureka's boom was over. The mines were either played out or too expensive to operate. The smelters closed and people moved on. Some intermittent mining continued, but Eureka survived principally because there is no other town within 70 miles. Area ranchers needed a trading center, the county needed a seat of government, and travelers on U.S. Highway 50 needed gas, food, and lodging.

According to the latest census, 1,547 people (0.4 per square mile) now live in Eureka County, about half of them in town. Minimal as that population is, it represents a 28 percent *increase* from the previous decade, and nearly double the county's population of 1970. Compared to its recent experience, if not its inception, Eureka is booming again. Part of it is due to another technological advance in hardrock mining that has set off the biggest gold rush in the West's history in terms of amount of rock mined and money made, if not in numbers of people employed. Using a method called heap-leaching, mining companies can now profitably extract microscopic flecks of gold that old-time miners ignored. Entire mountains are excavated and turned into holes. Waste rock, called overburden, is dumped and leveled on the side— the growing piles look like pyramids under construction—while the low-grade ore is heaped on a rubber pad and soaked with cyanide, which leaches out the gold (and silver) as it seeps through. The solution is then further refined to produce gold ingots. Through this reduction, one ounce of gold is gleaned from 200 tons of waste rock and 40 tons of ore. The picks and shovels of the old mining boom have been supplanted by huge cranes and dump trucks; honeycomb mine shafts have been superseded by open pits that can reach a thousand feet deep and a mile across; airborne pollutants have been replaced by cyanide-saturated leach ponds that environmentalists say are killing migratory birds and threatening underground water supplies. Since former high-grade mine areas are the first locations where companies look for low-grade ore, places like Eureka, with several mines nearby, are to an extent reliving their past.

But mining isn't the only reason Eureka has revived. In 1986, *Life* magazine dubbed the 260-mile stretch of U.S. Highway 50 through central Nevada the "Loneliest Road in America." The American Automobile Association advised travelers: "It's totally empty. There are no points of interest. We don't recommend it. We warn all motorists not to drive there unless they're confident of their survival skills." Residents and merchants along the highway were initially offended. Then they noticed that traffic was picking up. Travelers started rerouting their itineraries to check it out. Motorcyclists seemed particularly attracted to the lure of a Lonely Road, as were European tourists. The state tourism department began offering a "Highway 50 Survival Kit" with a flashy brochure and a "passport" to be stamped at local businesses for an official "I Survived the Loneliest Road in America" certificate. "What we've done," said one merchant, "is turn lemons into lemonade."

Figuring that if a little loneliness is good for business, more loneliness might be even better, Eureka staked a claim as the "Loneliest Town on the Loneliest Road in America." The boast makes a certain amount of sense. Eureka sits nearly dead center in the biggest chunk of sparsely settled real estate in the Lower 48. Virtually all of Nevada (with the exception of the counties including Las Vegas and the Reno–Carson City region) has fewer than two people per square mile, modern mining boom or not. Contiguous to this tract are contemporary frontier counties in California, Oregon, Idaho, and Utah. Combined with the Nevada core they cover 144,124 square miles, two and a half times the size of New England, larger than any state save Alaska, Texas, California, and Montana. Yet the current total population of this region is only 170,962 people. From Eureka it's a good day's drive in any direction to reach a metropolitan area.

This is basin and range country: one string of mountains after another, most of them peaking out at 9,000 or 10,000 feet and stubbled with small pines and cedars, interspersed with flat, sage-covered valleys that eons ago were at the bottom of a vast sea. Look at a topographical relief map of Nevada, someone told me, and it appears that a swarm of caterpillars is wriggling from north to south. Highway 50 runs east-west, up and over an endless series of caterpillar backs and across an equal number of valleys. The transition from map to actual locale quickly disabuses the caterpillar image: in the midst of the vastness the mind turns from worms to imagining a higher being. The region seems like God's construction site—mounds of rock, occasional piles of sand, and smoothly scraped plains on a titanic scale, a place where He might have practiced before making the moon. Distances and proportions become hard to gauge because there are so few man-made things for comparison. Up ahead, you see columns of dust kicked up by a pickup on a gravel road; you reach the intersection 20 miles later. At night, you dim your high beams for an oncoming car; it takes several minutes before your vehicles finally whizz past each other. At first glance even the mining sites with their craters, waste-rock pyramids, and busy machinery look like small boys' puny, pathetic imitations of their father's grander work. Then you get close to one and see that the

holes could swallow a good-sized town, the rock piles are small mountains in their own right, and the tires on the dump trucks are taller
than a basketball player.

Eureka momentarily ends this confusion of scale. There's no mis-
taking that this is a small town. Having crossed yet another parched
basin and started the ascent of yet another mountain range, the Loneliest Road rounds a bend and becomes the Loneliest Town's main street
for about ten blocks. Century-old brick and stone buildings, many of
them recently restored, some of them in sorry shape, line the street;
the residential district extends three or four blocks on either side. It's
too small and quiet for a standard boom town, too busy for a ghost
town, a step or two short of quaint but seemingly aiming in that general
direction. Bars outnumber restaurants six-to-five; the obligatory video
rental outlet is in a gun shop. Small as it is, Eureka has six motels and
hotels with a total of about a hundred rooms, a fact I discovered when
I tried to get a bed for the night. The search took an hour and I got
the last available one in town. Tourists, surveyors, geologists, and tran-
sients looking for mining jobs had taken the rest.

Being both lonely and near some recently activated mines had filled
Eureka up. People looking to move in permanently face the same problem I did in seeking lodging for one night: vacancies are hard to find.
Most of the new housing is far outside of town, in developments and
trailer parks in the Diamond Valley, where a dispute over whether
ranchers' irrigation pumps constitute a noise nuisance for the newcomers was headed for settlement in court. When the current mining
boom ends—most people think it has ten more years of life—Eureka
is counting on its self-promotion as a tourist mecca to cushion the
economic blow. Voters were about to be asked for $2 million to turn
the old opera house into a mini–convention center. (Perhaps the Lonely
Hearts Club would book it for annual meetings.) Magazine advertisements challenging people to "come find us" were eliciting thousands
of responses. Being the Loneliest Town on the Loneliest Road in America, local boosters hope, is better for the town's long-term health—
economic and otherwise—than being the Pittsburgh of the West.

Finding a truly lonely story in Eureka turned out to be difficult.
The best I came by was told by a woman who moved to the town from
the French Basque region, where the mountains are lush and green
and the towns are close to one another—the exact opposite of central

Nevada, except for similar high elevations. On the long, dry drive from Reno to Eureka across Highway 50, she said, her mother cried the whole way. But that was forty years ago. "I guess maybe it's lonely here," she said, "but there is something about it that's, how do you say it, it's peaceful. I feel like it's more serene. It's a good town to raise kids; you know where they are." When she recently visited her birthplace in the south of France, she was homesick for Eureka. For one thing, the humidity made her feel like she needed to take a shower three times a day.

At the Nevada Club, a bar and casino and dance hall that calls itself "The Loneliest Bar on the Loneliest Road," a few dozen people were spending Sunday afternoon playing pool, video poker, and the slot machines and having some hair of the dog that had bitten them at the dance the night before. Two women who obviously had partied straight through the night were sharing drinks, flirting with a few of the miners, and apparently discussing Nevada's second-oldest profession. "You're going to make a *killing* in this town, I can tell," the older one said to her younger friend.

There are roads lonelier than Highway 50 and towns lonelier than Eureka. I found a lot of both during my travels across the contemporary frontier. But I'm not going to say where they are. It might set off a boomlet nobody could control.

LIKE COWBOY BALLADS AS SEEMINGLY LONG AS THE trail drives they describe, the Song of the West has an endless number of verses and many local variations. But the repetitive refrain is the same: boom and bust, boom and bust. Exploitation and collapse, sudden growth and precipitous decline, ballooning hopes and burst bubbles are the cycles of the region's convulsive history. Whether they were based on beaver furs or buffalo hides, farming or livestock, oil or gas, precious metals or other ores; whether they occurred in the last century or last year; whether they lasted for several decades or several months, each boom was eventually paired with a bust. Not one place seems to have been immune.

By the eleventh century the Anasazi ("the ancient ones") of the Four Corners region were living in elaborate villages, sometimes including multistory apartment complexes with hundreds of rooms, in the rock cliffs and canyons. Three hundred years later the villages were empty. No one knows exactly what happened. Perhaps a prolonged drought, invasions by nomadic enemies, or depletion of the wood supply or soils made living in such concentrations untenable. Their adobe ruins hold clues but no final answers, just mute and eerie reminders that the land enforces its own limits, that mankind's dreams of permanent ascendance are laughable compared to the enduring realities of wind, sand, rock, and sun. Indians had named Hovenweep the "deserted valley" long before the first white men came upon the scene. Despite a brief uranium-mining boom in the 1970s, what is now San Juan County, Utah, may have experienced its peak population about the time William the Conqueror invaded England.

In western Wyoming in the 1830s, in what is now Sublette County, mountain men would gather every summer to exchange a year's worth of fur pelts for another year's worth of supplies. Most of the time they lived in isolation, trapping beaver to supply the current trend in men's hats in England. But in late summer, when the beaver were shedding their fur and therefore not worth trapping, the men would converge on one corner of the vast amphitheater-like valley near the headwaters of the Green River and turn it into a teeming tent city. Besides the "free" trappers and salaried employees of fur companies at the rendezvous were various Indian tribes, suppliers with pack trains from St. Louis, and occasional painters, journalists, European adventurers, priests, and preachers. Accounts of the annual gatherings make them seem like frontier versions of raucous Shriners' conventions held in the Central Park of the West, where the grandeur of the Wind River and Bear mountains substituted for Manhattan's skyline.

There were "contests of skill at running, jumping, wrestling, shooting with the rifle, and running horses," recorded Benjamin L. E. de Bonneville. "And then their rough hunters' feastings and carousals. They drank together, they sang, they laughed, they whooped; they tried to out-brag and out-lie each other in stories of their adventures and achievements. . . . The presence of the Shoshonie [sic] tribe contributed occasionally to cause temporary jealousies and feuds. The Shoshonie beauties became objects of rivalries among some of the amorous mountaineers." The arrival of supplies from the East made things even wilder. "Every freak of prodigality was indulged to its fullest extent, and in a little while most of the trappers, having squandered away all their wages, and perhaps run knee-deep in debt, were ready for another hard campaign in the wilderness."

Marcus Whitman, a doctor and missionary attending the rendezvous of 1835, removed an arrow point that the Blackfeet Indians had shot into the legendary mountain man Jim Bridger three years earlier. At the same gathering, a French trapper, after beating up several men, bragged that he could whip anyone in the camp, a challenge accepted by Kit Carson. The two mounted their horses and charged at one another. "We both fired at the same time, and all present said that but one report was heard," Carson wrote later. "I shot him through the arm and his ball passed my head, cutting my hair and the powder burning my eye, the muzzle of his gun being near my head when he fired. During the remainder of our stay in camp we had no more bother with this French bully."

The rendezvous of 1836 witnessed the arrival of the first white American women to cross the Continental Divide, Whitman's wife, Narcissa, and Eliza Spalding, wife of another missionary, bound for Oregon to convert Indians. Sir William Drummond Stewart, a Scots nobleman and one of the West's first "dudes," who after fathering an illegitimate child had left his homeland to hunt in the American wilderness, paid solicitous court on the pretty Narcissa. The more bashful trappers trooped by her tent and doffed their caps. The women recorded that they could have disposed of enough Bibles to burden several pack animals.

Father Pierre de Smet is said to have performed a mass for 2,000 people at the rendezvous of 1840, which would have made the impromptu parish twice the size of the biggest town in today's Sublette County. The Reverend Samuel Parker, a Presbyterian missionary, had less luck at the rendezvous of 1835. "I did not feel any disposition to upbraid them for their sins but endeavored affectionately to show them that they are unfit for heaven and that they could not be happy in the employments of that happy place unless they should first experience a great moral change of heart by the grace of God," he wrote of his sermon. Midway through his discourse a buffalo herd appeared in the distance and his flock took off in pursuit.

By the early 1840s silk had replaced beaver felt as the hat of choice among London's style setters. Half a world away on the cold streams of the Rockies, men who had become the symbol of rugged independence and self-sufficiency were thrown out of work by a whim of fashion. Fifteen years after its start, the era of the fur trappers' rendezvous closed.

More than a century later, a different type of rendezvous hit Sublette County. Oil and gas deposits had been discovered and a billion-dollar dehydration plant was under construction. (An earlier proposal to detonate atomic bombs underground to increase the gas flow had been defeated; Sublette County wanted a boom, but not that kind.) In 1985, a temporary "mancamp" housed a thousand workers, about half of the work force employed in building the plant and pipeline. Some families were squatting in tents and trailers along the Green River; others slept in their cars. Sales tax receipts doubled in a year. Prostitutes masquerading as magazine salespeople worked the long lines outside of Big Piney's bank on paydays; lines at the liquor store were a hundred people deep. Enrollments outstripped the schools' capacities and Big Piney and Pinedale, the two principal towns, built new ones. A new jail was constructed to handle the jump in crime. Then the first phase of construction was completed and the anticipated second phase was cancelled. The place emptied as quickly as it had when the trappers used to head back to the mountains to get more beaver pelts and nurse their hangovers in solitude.

Today's Sublette County (4,843 people, one person per square mile) is still suffering its own hangover. "Please Lord, give us one more boom," read a bumper sticker I saw on a pickup. "We promise we won't piss this one away." Pinedale (population 1,181), the only county seat in Wyoming without a stoplight, has a surplus of houses for sale. When I first pulled into town I had to stop a block from the business district while two stray horses lazily crossed the main street. Big Piney (population 454), in the southern part of the county and closer to the gas plant construction site, has a number of boarded-up businesses, including two rather new but defunct minimarts. The mancamp that once housed a thousand workers in metal dormitories is now just rows of concrete pads and light poles and electric junction boxes rising from gravel, all enclosed by a chain-link fence. It looks a little like a multiple-missile launch site gone to seed. But the main legacy of the boom is Big Piney's school, a $60-million complex that includes a fine arts center with an auditorium big enough for an audience of 575, a professional-quality recording studio, facilities for a radio station, a gymnasium that can seat 2,000 people, and an Olympic-size swimming pool with separate diving tank, wading pool, six-person Jacuzzi, and seating for 600. The high school had been built to hold 450 students; it had 192 when I stopped. Pinedale's new schools are almost as elaborate and were equally half-filled. With Exxon footing most of the bill, and with the anticipation of continued growth, the towns had decided to "do it right," according to one of the principals.

"The oil boom came and gave us this brief, giddy sense of what things could be like," said John Perry Barlow of Pinedale, a fourth-generation resident, former cattle rancher, an expert on computer "hacking," and a lyricist for the Grateful Dead. "I don't care how smart you are, if your income triples you're going to change the way you live. Now it's returned to business as usual but it seems like a depression. This economy is basically us passing money between ourselves. We're running at carrying capacity. It's a struggle. That's what these places are about. It's hard ground. That's their blessing and their curse." Like a number of other ranchers in the area, Barlow had given up the cattle business out of debt and exhaustion and sold his place to a wealthy easterner who uses it for a vacation home. Pointing to the state's license plate, where a cowboy is depicted holding onto the arched back of a bronc suspended in mid-leap, he said of his ranching days, "It was a uniquely Wyoming experience: that son of a bitch never stopped bucking." The same could be said of almost any other enterprise in every other part of the West. What goes up, comes down—and the landing is rarely gentle.

Other places have a lot less to show for their booms than Sublette County and its impressive school buildings. Mogollon, New Mexico, accessible only by a tortuous mountain road that dwindles to a single lane in the final switchback descent to the town, once had 5,000 residents. Its gold and silver mines closed in 1942. The school burned to the ground ten years later and wasn't replaced. Of the fourteen year-round residents now, one is of school age and is taught at home.

Ingomar, Montana, on the long sweep of prairie in the eastern half of the state, had the world's largest sheep-shearing plant and 600 residents in the early 1900s. The ranges emptied once a year as sheep-herders drove their huge flocks to the town's pens. A sheep rendezvous. In 1911, some 170,000 of them were relieved of their wool. Ingomar in 1923 had twenty-three businesses, including five hotels. Four trains a day stopped at its station. All that's left is a few wooden buildings leaning toward collapse, some trailers, a grid of dirt streets, and a population of 19. Even the iron rails and wood ties on the railroad grade have been removed.

But Ingomar still has the Jersey Lilly, the town's only business, a bar and grill in an old bank building that specializes in pinto beans served in a tin pan with "sheepherders' hors d'oeuvres" (an orange peel, onion, and crackers). The rest rooms are outdoor privies in the back lot; in front is a wooden sidewalk with a horse rail waiting for someone to ride in and tie up, as a few locals still do on occasion. The spittoons on the sawdust-covered floor aren't there for decoration. The Jersey Lilly survives not on the strength of its local clientele (they're loyal but there aren't enough people to support the business) but because of a word-of-mouth cult following spread across the state and beyond. Good as the beans are, they're not enough by themselves to draw the bar's aficionados from hundreds of miles away. It's more out of a quirky affection for the place and its owner, Bill Seward, whose father founded the Jersey Lilly in a pique that Ingomar's other bar closed each night at nine o'clock. "I'd rather spit in church than have a bar closed at nine; I'll open my own," he had said. Seward, now in his seventies, has something of his father's spirit: keeping the Jersey Lilly open keeps Ingomar on the map. He wears a U.S. Navy cap on his head, over a piece of string he configured to keep his glasses from slipping off his nose; eats cold beans for breakfast every morning and then starts a fresh five-gallon batch on the stove; and, in a friendly, soft-spoken way, says things like, "I spent time in Chicago, Bozeman, the South Pacific, but it ain't Ingomar" without traces of either irony or braggadocio. When he eventually passes on, Ingomar will probably go with him.

On the plains of northeastern New Mexico, farmers from the Midwest swarmed in during World War I's wheat bonanza and plowed up the virgin grasslands. Union and Harding counties had 15,457 people in 1930 before drought turned the exposed, sandy soil into the center of the Dust Bowl. Survivors I met recalled sitting in their homes during wind storms with wet cloths over their mouths so they could breathe, having their doors drifted shut by piling sand, hauling dirt that had sifted in through window cracks out of their living rooms and bedrooms in three-gallon buckets, finding tractors buried to their seats in sand. On Palm Sunday of 1935 a late-afternoon dust storm rolled into

Clayton, New Mexico, a "boiling caldron of black and sand-colored clouds" that created a "darkness blacker than night and terrifyingly quiet," according to the local paper. Visibility collapsed to two feet. Drifts closed the highways and stranded cars. The Santa Fe railroad had to reroute trains because the tracks were impassable. Two months later a hail storm broke windows, killed calves, and ruined what few crops were left. Insulated by the dust on the ground, the hail didn't melt for a week. Union County had the state's highest caseload for government food assistance, and a headline in the Clayton paper in July warned, "Looting of Stores Talked as Relief Budgets Dwindle." Farms were abandoned by the hundreds. The federal government bought 166,000 acres (260 square miles) in the two counties, put people to work replanting grass seed, and created the Kiowa National Grasslands.

The two counties now have 5,111 people (0.8 per square mile), half of them within the city limits of Clayton. The dry winds of the Dirty Thirties had blown away two-thirds of the population along with the topsoil.

Ronald McKay, a rancher in the area, drove me around his grazing leases on the national grassland. I had trouble conceiving of the terrain in either of its two former modes in this century: a flat tableland of grass so thick and high that in 1900 the short wife of a neighbor of McKay's grandfather couldn't see over it and laid her washing out on its tops to dry; and then a flat expanse of furrowed farmland. Instead, McKay's pickup rose and plunged over rough hummocks like a small cutter bobbing and disappearing on a choppy sea. He helped me interpret the broken land. Wherever the soil had been exposed—planted fields, barnyards, cow paths—the Dust Bowl winds had scoured it off and left a depression. At sites where the wind eddied—fence lines, hedge rows, or sometimes just a well-rooted Russian thistle—the sand and dirt had deposited to form ridges and piles. Former pastures were the flattish stretches between gouges and ridges. From one rise we could see twelve former homesteads, each one with an old windmill rattling in the breeze, all of them now part of a grazing parcel.

A few miles farther in the distance, in the Texas Panhandle across the county and state line, farmland predominates. Equally blasted and contoured by the dust storms of the Dirty Thirties, it too had initially been put back to pasture in the aftermath. But it sat over the southern

John Streiff and the Sand Hills, McPherson County, Nebraska.

Margaret Stafford, homesteader, Garfield County, Montana.

Missouri River Breaks near Hell Creek, Garfield County, Montana.

OPPOSITE: Lisa Peterson and the student body of the one-room, log-and-chink Ross School, Garfield County, Montana.

The Reverend Harvey Senecal, pastor for both Presbyterians and Lutherans, Jordan, Montana.

Main Street, Jordan, Montana.

Reinhart Rath gives a haircut in his combination barbershop and liquor store, Jordan, Montana.

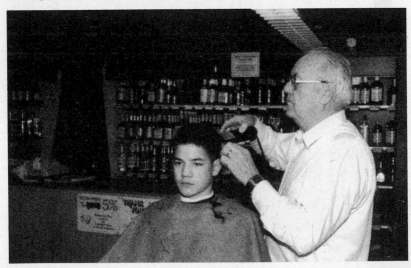

Sheriff Jim Bilberry, De Baca County, New Mexico: In the tradition of Pat Garrett, he lost his job for doing it too avidly.

Miss Charles Wilson at the cemetery for the Seminole Negro scouts,
Fort Clark, Texas.

Father Dave Denny at the Carmelite monastery, Crestone-Baca, Colorado.

Ram Loti (Deborah Wood) at the Crestone-Baca ashram,
Saguache County, Colorado.

Adair and Mary Merrell, Animas, New Mexico: A Mormon family's odyssey finally leads to a permanent home.

Polygamist Alex Joseph and his wives, Big Water, Utah: From social and legal rebel to mayor of his town.

Downtown of Yellow Pine, Idaho: The town has no telephone service; winter access until recently was by snowmobile.

Glen and Alan Akins, prospectors, Inyo County, California.

Bill Seward, proprietor of the Jersey Lilly, the only business left in Ingomar, Montana.

Ruins of Metropolis, Nevada, one of Municipal Darwinism's victims.

OPPOSITE: Merriman, Nebraska,
on the edge of the Sand Hills.

Lloyd Goodrich of Loving County, Texas, the nation's most sparsely populated county.

BELOW: Larry and Lolly DeRieux, the prime boosters of Fields, Oregon, population nine.

ABOVE: Rancher and rodeo
rider Margaret Hawkins, in
front of the rig she drives,
Arthur County, Nebraska.

Jonay Ward and his
"mail order" bride, Audrey,
in front of their bar in
Quemado, New Mexico.

ABOVE: Jerry McComb's UPS truck slows down for cattle in the road, Presidio County, Texas.

LEFT: Mark Maryboy, leader of the all-Navajo political slate, San Juan County, Utah.

OPPOSITE: Father Melvin LaFollette at the chapel in Paso Lajitas, on the Mexican side of the Rio Grande: four services, 200 miles, 11 hours, 25 people in one Sunday.

Robert Chambers and John Littlejohn, on the trail of mountain lions,
Presidio County, Texas.

Janet Gordon and a picture of a bomb blast at the Nevada Test Site;
her brother, one of the "virtual uninhabitants" caught in downwind fallout,
died of cancer.

extension of the Ogallala aquifer, the trapped runoff from the last few Ice Ages that forms an underground freshwater lake stretching from northern Nebraska to west Texas. When a diesel-powered centrifugal pump was invented in the 1960s that could bring water from below ground, a second swarm of farmers descended on the area. The land was leveled and plowed once more. Shelterbelt lines of trees planted in the wake of the Dust Bowl catastrophe were cut down to make more room for corn, sorghum, and cotton—all crops previously unheard of here because of the heavy moisture they require. No one worried about another big blowout. With cheap fuel and an aquifer relatively close to the surface, who cared if the skies were cloudless? By the mid-1970s, grassland that had brought a hundred dollars an acre a decade earlier was selling for a thousand dollars or more. The money being made seemed so relatively easy and endless, the center-pivot irrigation sprinklers were called "Wheels of Fortune."

Then oil prices tripled and the constant water-mining started to lower the aquifer, making it more expensive to create an Iowa-on-the-Plains. The second big farmers' boom headed downward. The bottom has not yet been hit, but it was easy enough to imagine from McKay's land. "Say that water quits coming up," he said. "You get your drought. You get your wind. It'll blow again. A lot of these problems we created for ourselves. We get greedy when times are good."

In Edwards County, Texas, the good and greedy times occurred more than a century ago. After the Civil War, cattlemen overstocked the grassy hills, and when settlers started showing up in the 1880s the cattlemen's answer was to crowd even more animals onto the land. At a stockmen's meeting where someone was trying to promote better grazing techniques, they interrupted his speech and passed a resolution: "Resolved that none of us know, or care to know, anything about grasses, native or otherwise, outside of the fact that for the present there are lots of them, the best on record, and we are after getting the most of them while they last." Mesquite, once confined near streams, started spreading onto the overgrazed uplands, along with cedar, prickly pear, and other brush. Pastures that had fed 300 head of cattle per section were so depleted they could support only 50. Now Edwards County (population 2,266; 1.1 people per square mile) raises more angora goats than any county in the nation, goats being good at eating what cattle won't. Many landowners supplement their earnings by sell-

ing deer-hunting permits to people from the cities; some have introduced exotic game animals from Africa as a special lure. Half the stores
on the central square of Rocksprings, the county seat, are vacant. "The
story here," one rancher told me, "is that there's damn few of us who
survived and we damn well don't want any more people coming in."

Ticaboo, Utah, went bust before it got the chance to really boom.
A modern uranium-processing plant was completed in the 1980s, just
in time for the bottom to fall out of the American market. The plant
sits vacant and never used in a gully of the Henry Mountains. On a
flat spot of desert nearby are paved streets, sidewalks, fire hydrants,
junction boxes for underground utilities—still waiting for the houses
and people that never showed up. A ghost town without even the lingering presence of ghosts. Thousands of years from now archaeologists
will find Ticaboo even more inscrutable than the cliff-dwelling Anasazi,
who at least left houses when they moved on.

BY ITS VERY NATURE, MINING IS A BOOM-AND-BUST
enterprise. You take out the ore until either there's none left or what
remains is no longer profitable. You close down and move on. If the
metal offers the prospect of quick and fabulous riches, the boom frenzy
is that much more intense. If the strike is located in a place where
there is little else to sustain a concentration of people, the bust is that
much more complete. Gold and silver are those kinds of metals. Nevada
and Death Valley are those kinds of places.

Nevada is America's mining boom child. Prior to 1859 it was known
as a desolate, deadly obstacle on the way to California, the thick sands
of its Forty Mile Desert between the Humboldt and Carson rivers littered with the rotting carcasses of dead oxen and the discarded be-
longings of those who had crossed in the rush for Sutter's Mill. The
discovery of the Comstock Lode, the world's richest deposit of silver,
interlaced with vast amounts of gold, turned Nevada from obstacle to
destination overnight. Nothing quite compares with the two words
"gold" and "silver"—which more commonly appeared as "GOLD!" and
"SILVER!"—for luring people to places they would otherwise consider
preposterously uninhabitable.

By 1861, Nevada had been carved from the Utah Territory to form
its own territory. A brief three years later, even though it had fewer

than 10,000 residents, it was a state; Abraham Lincoln needed the gold and silver (as well as two more Republican senators) for the Union cause. In 1866 the state was still so unpopulated and unformed that when Henry Blasdell, Nevada's first elected governor, decided to travel in a direct line from Carson City to a new mining district in the southeastern corner, his group was the first ever to attempt such a crossing. (Among other things, Blasdell wanted to check whether the mines were actually in Nevada; no one was sure.) They temporarily lost their way, ran short of food and water, and nearly perished. One man died. The others survived by eating lizards.

The naturalist John Muir visited the state in the late 1870s and found five deserted towns for every thriving one. "Nevada is one of the very youngest and wildest of the States," he reported. "Nevertheless it is already strewn with ruins that seem as gray and silent and timeworn as if the civilization to which they belonged had perished centuries ago." Thinking the boom was over for good, he wrote, "The fever period is fortunately passing away."

Muir's diagnosis turned out to be only partly correct. As the first mining strikes played out and boom towns like Eureka and Virginia City slid toward dormancy at the turn of the century, Nevada's population shrank by half. Then the fever hit again, this time in and around America's most forbidding location: Death Valley.

Hyperbole comes naturally to Death Valley. A wagon train of forty-niners, on what they thought was a shortcut to the California gold fields, blundered down the rocky alluvial fans and onto the arid valley floor and were stranded for nearly a month before being rescued. Although only one member of the group died, as the parched survivors were heading for safety one of them looked back, took off his hat, and intoned, "Good-bye Death Valley." The name stuck and gave the area its compelling mystique. Not that it needed much help.

Death Valley is the hottest, driest, and lowest spot in the Western Hemisphere. It lies just across the state line in Inyo County, California, where the Amargosa River, said to be the world's longest underground river, curls in from Nevada and sinks into Badwater Basin, 282 feet below sea level. The *average* high temperature in July is 116.2 degrees; temperatures above 100 degrees have been reached in eight of the twelve months; the record high is 134 degrees. The average annual rainfall is 1.66 inches; the most on record for one year was 4.6 inches, and in two years there was no measurable precipitation at all. The humidity, which averages 20 percent, can go down to 3 percent on summer days, an aridity that will split wood.

Skeleton Valley might have been a more descriptive name: it and the mountains surrounding it look like New Hampshire's White Mountain region with the flesh of vegetation scorched off by a flame thrower. Dante's View, an overlook on a peak of the Amargosa Range, perches 5,755 feet above Badwater Basin, where the temperature is 25 degrees hotter. Directly across the valley is Telescope Peak, elevation 11,049 feet, which in the clear air looks close enough to touch. This drop and rise is one of the sharpest topographical reliefs in America. "The limits of population are quickly reached in this desert," says a sign at the overlook. "It's too hot and dry. The resources for abundant life just aren't here."

But the barren mountains contained mineral treasures, and so Death Valley experienced some spectacular booms, many of which were based more on mining the pockets of gullible investors than on mining gold, silver, or copper. Being remote and having the name Death Valley had its advantages, not the least of which was to prevent investors in San Francisco and the East from actually venturing out to inspect what, if anything, their money was buying.

In one fraud, stock speculators claimed to have established a productive mine and town named Kasson. To bolster their marketing they convinced the government to designate Kasson as a post office; Rand McNally's *Indexed Atlas of the World* included Kasson on its maps. But on further investigation, postal authorities discovered "not a soul living within twenty-five miles." During what became known as "the monumental mining-stock swindle of the century," more than a hundred copper mining companies sprang up in the valley in the early 1900s, staked claims covering 150 square miles, offered a quarter of a billion dollars' worth of stock, found buyers for tens of millions of shares with advertisements promoting "an inexhaustible deposit of copper in the rapacious maws of this man-devouring monster," and then disappeared like a mirage. In the end, only one mine had shipped any ore —worth $2,625.09.

Among Death Valley's inexhaustible supply of con artists, the most brazen was probably Walter Edward Scott, a bronc rider for Buffalo Bill Cody's Wild West Show whose knack for flamboyant promotions equaled those of the old scout. With a few chunks of high-grade gold ore from a mine in Colorado, Scott convinced a banker he met in a New York City bar in 1902 that Death Valley was the next El Dorado. The banker grubstaked him for $1,500 to return to the valley, where Scott said he had discovered the gold, and develop a claim. When his money ran out he would wire back news to his financial angel: "I am about burnt up fearful," or "Hot, great God! Got in the lower end of the Valley—liked to die," or that his burros had died, that he had walked 145 miles for water, that he was on his way back East with a satchel of rich ore but it got stolen, that the mine was progressing and showing good promise, and *always* that he needed a little more money to keep going. Over three years, he milked the banker for $10,000. When the New Yorker finally pulled the money plug, Scott found a new sucker in Chicago.

Scott had a camp in Death Valley, which he visited often enough to seem knowledgeable about the area, but he spent most of his time in Los Angeles bars where the heat wasn't as withering, the liquid refreshments more plentiful and not as alkaline, and there were more people to listen to him spin tales of his exploits. In 1905, with the help of a reporter for the *Los Angeles Examiner* he had met at a bar rail, he emerged as "Death Valley Scotty" and hit the big time.

Bankrolled by a stock speculator who wanted people to believe the valley was loaded with untapped riches, Scotty was portrayed as a "Death Valley Croesus," a mining magnate who lit cigars with ten-dollar bills and left hundred-dollar tips. His biggest publicity stunt was hiring a train, dubbed the "Death Valley Coyote," to try to break the speed record between Los Angeles and Chicago, a coup that inspired reams of news copy, songs, a paperback novel, and a play, all of which kept the equation of Death Valley and easy money firmly before the eyes of potential investors. (Secondary to this main purpose, the train broke the existing record by four hours.) Scotty became such a celebrity that an appearance at the New York Stock Exchange brought trading to a halt as brokers cheered this hero of brash capitalism. People from all over the world sent him letters asking for money, usually just addressed to Death Valley Scotty, Death Valley.

In yet another flimflam, Scotty led representatives of skeptical investors into Death Valley, where they were to investigate a supposed mine, but staged an ambush to scare them off. Even after admitting in court in 1912 that he had no mines and no money of his own, his fame continued unabated. A rich industrialist from Chicago—who had been fleeced repeatedly by Scotty—began building an elaborate estate in the north end of Death Valley and allowed Scotty to live there. It soon became known as "Scotty's Castle" and people were paying him a dollar to tour the home he didn't own. Right up to the end, he was the darling of reporters more eager for a juicy yarn than the dry facts. "Every Scotty story is an exclusive one," a grateful reporter said. "He never tells the same one twice."

Death Valley had its legitimate mining strikes—minuscule in comparison to the watered stock that flooded the country for a quarter-century, but enough to lend credence to the scams and foster some real booms. Bullfrog was the biggest. When the news reached Tonopah and Goldfield, two Nevada mining towns in the midst of their own booms, that high-grade ore had been discovered on the northern edge of Death Valley, a human stampede began. "It looked like the whole population of Goldfield was trying to move at once," one miner recalled. "Miners who were working for the big companies dropped their tools and got ready to leave town in a hurry. Timekeepers and clerks, waiters and cooks—they all got the fever and milled around, wildeyed, trying to find a way to get out to the new 'strike.' In a little while there wasn't a horse or a wagon in town, outside of a few owned by the big companies, and the price of burros took a big jump. I saw one man who was about ready to cry because he couldn't buy a jackass for $500.00. A lot of fellows loaded their stuff on two-wheeled carts—grub, tools, and cooking utensils, and away they went across the desert, two or three pulling a cart and the pots and pans rattling. When all the carts were gone, men who didn't have anything else started out on that seventy-five-mile hike with wheelbarrows; and a lot of 'em made it all right—but they had a hell of a time!"

Half a dozen instant towns sprang up along the Amargosa in 1904, but when it quickly appeared that one mine, near Rhyolite, was going to be the real producer of the Bullfrog district, most of the others folded overnight. One booster of Bonanza died of heart failure as he watched its residents pack up everything and move en masse to Rhyolite, which at age six months had 50 saloons, 16 restaurants, 19 hotels, 6 barbers, and one public bath for its 2,500 residents. Ice sold for $400 a ton, a price higher than the gold ore was fetching. By 1907, Rhyolite had telephone, telegraph, and electric service, water mains and concrete sidewalks, three-story buildings, its own stock exchange, a school, hospital, and ornate opera house, and a population of 4,000. Since Nye County officials wouldn't let the town incorporate, Rhyolite's municipal services were financed by bake sales, donations, dances, and license fees on dogs (three dollars a year) and on prostitutes (five dollars a month). A thoroughly unionized town, Rhyolite experienced one labor dispute, when a group called the Concert Girls posted notices asking union men not to patronize the Unique and Adobe concert halls because Tessie Alfred, Kitty La Belle, Mazie, Skidoo Babe, and Fay and Little Fay were "unfair girl workers." The town's two churches were the Amargosa area's first.

The Bullfrog district yielded $3 million worth of gold, a respectable amount, but far short of the extravagant promises of the two hundred companies that had foisted more than 200 million shares of mining stock on the public. Six years after its founding, two years after its peak as a desert metropolis, Rhyolite was already well on its way to the kind of ruin John Muir would have recognized. The census counted 611 residents in 1910; ten years later the official population was 14. In 1924, a *Los Angeles Times* motor tour pulled into Rhyolite and found no one there, just some concrete shells of buildings slowly crumbling in the shimmering heat.

Other mining towns shared Rhyolite's fate, although few of them quite so spectacularly. Unalloyed by the mirage of instant wealth, arid heat engenders a different kind of fever: the hots to emigrate somewhere more hospitable to human life. On the eve of World War II, Nevada had just five towns with populations above 2,500. Four of them, including the two largest—Reno (21,137 people) and Las Vegas (8,422)—had never been mining camps. Instead of ore, they had water.

NEVADA IS BACK IN THE BOOM BUSINESS. THE BIGgest and longest, generated by gambling, tourism, retirees, and government installations (mostly military), is concentrated in two small corners of the state around Las Vegas and Reno–Carson City, where 92 percent of Nevada's population of 1.2 million people lives on about 10 percent of its land, making the state not only the nation's fastest-growing but also its most disproportionately urban. The Las Vegas area is increasing at a clip of about 6,000 new residents a month. Two months of growth in Las Vegas brings in more people than live in eight of the state's rural counties.

The other boom is more in keeping with Nevada's history. The new cyanide-based technology quadrupled gold production in five years. Nevada, at the center of the modern West's gold rush, is producing 5 million ounces of gold a year, more than half the nation's total and greater than the output at the peak of the California bonanza a century earlier.

In the vast, empty middle of the state, the new gold rush had increased the population of the ten counties with fewer than two people per square mile by 53 percent in ten years—a big jump to be sure, and the only dynamic growth in all of the contemporary frontier. But percentages can be deceiving. The counties cover 87,582 square miles (twice the size of Pennsylvania), yet even with the recent spurt of new residents their population totals 97,162, barely more than a person per square mile. Traversing this part of the state, "boom" is not the first word that comes to mind. The primary evidence of activity in the countryside is white plastic pipes stuck in the corners of mining claims—ubiquitous enough to be dubbed the "Nevada state tree"— and occasional huge pits and waste piles and leaching ponds. In other words, not so much people as what they leave behind.

The people are in the towns: This is the first commuters' gold rush. In the old frontier, towns were thrown up at the mine site; now, the workers usually congregate in preexisting settlements and are bused to and from the mines. As a result, about half of the people in Nevada's ten most sparsely populated counties live in just seven towns, none of which at first glance seems connected to gold fever and the scars being gouged in the distant mountainsides.

Elko, population 14,736, is the biggest such town—and, at twice the size of any other town in the contemporary frontier, a veritable New York City compared to the others. But Elko is no Rhyolite revisited. Unless you ask, you wouldn't know that a gold boom is the reason that housing developments are going up, and that rather than one closed movie theater the town now has three open, with more under construction. The mines are 50 to 70 miles away, some of them in other counties. Elko is more like a suburban island in an ocean of sage. Although its recent growth is due to gold mining (Elko's population nearly doubled in the last ten years), its very existence is due to its being halfway between Salt Lake City and Reno on Interstate 80, on being a hub for the myriad governmental natural-resource agencies, and on being the only retail center within a radius of 125 miles. When the mines play out, said George Boucher, the county manager, "maybe we'll have a lot of rooms for rent and homes for sale, but it wouldn't annihilate the community."

The only new town created by the recent gold rush is Hadley, near the Round Mountain mine in the south central part of the state. The mine is too far from any established town to accommodate commuting workers, so the company purchased a nearby ranch, moved in more than two hundred modular homes, built a school, swimming pool, golf course, tennis courts, library, and grocery store, installed a medical clinic and a twenty-four-hour day-care center, and created Hadley. But it, too, seems more like a quiet suburban housing development than boom town. Hadley doesn't even have a bar. Round Mountain, already 300 feet lower than its original height, is being disassembled at a rate of 130,000 tons of rock a day. It is producing gold—more in a year than Rhyolite in its lifetime; more, in fact, than the Bullfrog scam artists *promised* their sucker/investors—but not, I think, many legends.

Rhyolite itself, the town built by rainbow chasers and flimflammers, is the best example of the differences between the old mining frontier and the new. Bond International Gold, a Canadian-owned company, purchased the former Bullfrog district and started a modern heap-leach operation. Beatty, Nevada, six miles away, once a poor cousin to Rhyolite, which had escaped total ghost status earlier in the century by virtue of a federal highway going through it, is now the beneficiary of the renewed mining activity. It has grown from 500 people to 1,500 in two years, a quantum leap in percentages, but almost leisurely and orderly compared to the heady days of 1904 when men streamed in on burros and behind wheelbarrows, and Rhyolite went from a barren spot on the desert to a town of 1,200 in its first two weeks. During that first rush, a con man named William Phillips announced plans to make Beatty the "Chicago of Nevada." He posted signs where, he said, a grand hotel, hospital, city hall, and other civic structures would be located. He sold hundreds of house lots. Then he vanished with the cash, finally ending up in jail for selling lots through the mail for the nonexistent Amargosa town of Velma. Like Eureka, the former "Pittsburgh of the West," Beatty no longer has pretensions of mimicking a big city back east; it isn't complaining about the recent gold boom, but seeing tourism as a steadier bet for its future, it now calls itself the "Gateway to Death Valley."

Death Valley, as hot, dry, and far below sea level as ever, still trades on the mystique of its intimidating landscape and ghoulish name, but in a different way. When the first mining bubble burst, the valley switched from relying on gullible investors *not* daring a visit to counting on tourists flocking to see "Nature's Inferno" and "the Mystery Spot of America." By the late 1920s, with the rise of automobile travel, a toll road had been built and a luxury resort was under construction. One advertisement that helped set off this new stampede said: "View the dire and dreadful Death Valley—with all danger removed and all thrills retained." Described by the *New York World* in 1894 as "the dominion of death . . . forever destined to stay in its state of primitive desolation and barrenness . . . it will ever be avoided alike by man and beast," it is now a national monument (and proposed as a national park) visited by 700,000 tourists a year, many of them including Scotty's Castle on their itinerary. Mining, meanwhile, is being phased out within Death Valley's federal boundaries; the tourists prefer seeing the vestigial ruins of former mining bonanzas to modern ones in action.

The ghost towns of Rhyolite and Bullfrog, along with their cemeteries and trash dumps, designated as historically significant, have been spared from the wholesale excavation going on around them. Even this is a change from past procedures. The discovery of a high-grade deposit at the Pioneer mine had caused a brief burst of migration within the Bullfrog district in 1909. Many structures from neighboring towns were hoisted and moved intact to the new site, including Beatty's best hotel and at least two Rhyolite houses that were stolen from their owners. One legend holds that when Pioneer's first casualty was being laid to rest, his friends at the graveside spotted a trace of gold in the hole, called off the funeral while they sank a shaft, and ended up burying the man somewhere else.

Compared to that kind of gold fever, the modern boom in Bullfrog and other places is a mild temperature. It has less outward frenzy to it. It is less quirkily human and more inexorably mechanistic—and ultimately more profitable. Only a few independent prospectors still wander the barren mountains and valleys of the Amargosa region in search of new strikes. Alan Akins, forty-eight, and his father, Glen, seventy-six, who call themselves "the last of the burro prospectors," live in an electricity-less trailer west of Death Valley and occasionally pack into the Inyo Mountains looking for signs of gold and silver. "Most prospectors live on dreams without too much behind it," Alan said. "A lot aren't even rational, like compulsive gamblers." During twenty-seven years in the region, Alan said, "I've never met anyone who made his entire living by prospecting." He and his father and some partners had developed some modest claims, but most of the time they rely on Glen's government pension and Alan's part-time jobs to support themselves. During one prolonged stretch in the field, they lived on a budget of forty dollars a month for four people. "Beans is what that mainly was," Glen remembered. "Then beans went up."

"The prospector days are over," the manager of a modern mine told me. "You can't do it yourself because of the upfront money that's necessary." Most of the work, like the industry itself, is a thoroughly corporate undertaking, as colorless as it is efficient in rearranging the landscape.

In all likelihood, this will be Nevada's final gold rush. Once entire mountains have been dismantled and chemically stripped of microscopic gold, there's not much left to go after. Standing in front of the concrete husk of Rhyolite's former stock exchange building, you can see and feel the future. In the near distance stands a small mountain, whose far side is being whittled away by giant cranes and bulldozers. The earth trembles when dynamite charges shake loose a little more to be hauled off. At the moment, the stock exchange and mountain are two facades facing each other, one man-made and one not, one protected as a landmark and one not, both symbols of the same desire for gold but of different times and technologies. When these new mines close, the people will leave again. Time and technology can't change that sequence. The desert will reassert itself. Towns like Elko, Beatty, Eureka, and their counterparts will contract again to their pre-boom sizes, but survive as trading centers; Hadley's modular homes will be carted away and the town, such as it is, will disappear without a trace. The bulk of Nevada will return to its former self: a home for the very few, an obstacle to cross for the many.

A hundred years from now, Rhyolite's ghosts and the shells of buildings they inhabit will still be here, along with a historical marker commemorating the wild tales of its first gold boom. There probably won't be a historical marker for the final gold rush. Just a breeze up out of the depths of Death Valley, brisker and hotter because the mountain currently in front of Rhyolite will be gone.

TWO TYPES OF REAL ESTATE BOOMS HAVE MARKED United States history. One was the initial white settlement of the land. As the country's boundaries expanded from one coast to the other, national policy called for the transfer of public domain lands (purchased, ceded, or simply appropriated from the Indians) to private ownership as quickly and completely as possible. Thomas Jefferson and other founders of the American republic believed in the ideal of the yeoman farmer: democracy would flourish when property and wealth were distributed among small landholders rather than concentrated in cities or an elite class as they were in Europe; America's greatest blessing was its vast supply of tillable soil waiting to be parceled out. A majority of the laws that Congress passed in the nineteenth century dealt in one way or another with this disposal. Often, much of what the government did was merely an attempt to keep up with the land rush going on with or without its official approval. From December 1831 to June 1832, President Andrew Jackson signed ten thousand land patents but was still ten thousand behind and losing ground on the waves of paper. In 1833, Congress created the position of official patent signer to relieve the logjam and impending presidential writer's cramp.

Proclaiming 1890 as the close of the frontier, Frederick Jackson Turner had this land boom in mind. The country had not been completely settled—four times as many homestead claims would be filed in the West after 1890 as before that year—but in Turner's view the movement of people onto the public domain would no longer be the defining story of the nation. Even with the supposed end of the frontier, the nation still preferred to see itself, and was viewed by others, as a frontier country. "In the United States there is more space where nobody is than where anybody is," wrote Gertrude Stein. "That is what makes America what it is."

The westward expansion, however, only masked the other real estate boom. This one ran counter to the Jeffersonian model and inspired fewer myths, but it nonetheless proceeded virtually uninterrupted from the nation's beginnings and only accelerates in the present: the urbanization of America. Even from 1790 to 1890, when the theoretical population center of the United States migrated from the east bank of Chesapeake Bay to Indiana, the urban population grew 139-fold while the national population grew 16-fold. For every laborer who left the cities and went into agriculture, one study of the Homestead Act and the frontier-as-safety-valve theory revealed, twenty farmers moved to an urban area; for every farmer's son who became the owner of a new farm, ten became city dwellers. By 1920, for the first time in history more Americans lived in an urban area (a town with at least 2,500 people or unincorporated suburb with at least 1,000 people per square mile) than in a rural area. Seventy years later, the urban majority has swelled to encompass more than 75 percent of the population, nearly half of them in suburbs, where the real boom is under way. (Contrary to their locales, people still apparently believe in the Jeffersonian ideal even if they don't live it. Asked in a 1989 poll if they would prefer living in a city, suburb, small town, or farm, 56 percent of the people chose a small town or farm, although 80 percent of the poll's respondents lived in a metropolitan area.)

Against that backdrop, the counties of the contemporary frontier present a double anachronism. Having only marginally shared in the peopling of the countryside—few of them, even at their height of settlement, had ever surpassed two people per square mile—they also have witnessed more towns decline and disappear than grow. In an urban/suburban nation becoming increasingly more so, they aren't just rural, they are ultra-rural and usually headed farther away from the national norm. Consider the size of their ten biggest towns:

Elko, Nevada	14,736 people
Pahrump, Nevada	7,424
Winnemucca, Nevada	6,134
Alpine, Texas	5,637
Ely, Nevada	4,756
Hawthorne, Nevada	4,162
Dillon, Montana	3,991
Moab, Utah	3,971

| Tonopah, Nevada | 3,616 |
| Glasgow, Montana | 3,572 |

Half of these towns owe a significant portion of their current population to the recent gold boom, which means that sometime in the early part of the next century they can expect a severe contraction. After the top ten, there are about a dozen additional towns with populations above the Census Bureau's minimal "urban" standard of 2,500 people. During my travels, I became accustomed to regarding a town of 500 people as a major settlement. I also became acquainted with what I call "Municipal Darwinism."

Founding a town on the western frontier was both an act of faith and an exercise in false advertising. Some promoters had every intention of building a settlement that would last forever and be their lifelong home. Many others planned only to get things started while land prices were cheap, sell out at higher boom prices, and then move on to begin the process all over again. Either way, the same techniques of hyperbole, boosterism, and bald lies were all essential tools in creating a town out of bare land and getting people to move in. After touring the West in 1859, Horace Greeley, editor of the *New York Tribune*, reported that the gap between most fledgling towns' claims and what he encountered was "enough to give a cheerful man the horrors . . . Land speculation here is about the only business in which a man can embark with no more capital than an easy conscience."

From the moment of their birth the frontier towns struggled to survive—against their rival neighbors for the rights of being county seat or for a railroad's business, against the boom-bust economic climate that could wipe out settlements as easily as it created them, and finally against entropy, the dwindling numbers of farmers and ranchers upon whose trade they relied. Anyone with some stakes and twine could lay out a townsite, water it with heavy doses of inventive puffery, and get a settlement planted. Getting it to take root was another matter. The winnowing process of natural selection started immediately. The odds of success were long.

Being a county seat meant a lot to a young town. As the place where land titles would be registered, where political decisions would be made on taxes and the location and upkeep of roads and schools, where the sheriff would have his office and where trials would be held, a county seat might also expect to emerge as the merchandising hub of the immediate area.

Town promoters also realized that designation as a county seat was the only inoculation against extinction. If everything else failed, a county would always need a town for its official business. Roberts County, Texas (population 1,025; 1.1 people per square mile), shows how spirited—and critical—the fight could be. The towns of Miami and Bennett contested for the honor in 1889. Miami was larger but was located in the extreme southeast corner of the Panhandle county; Bennett was hardly more than the idea of a town, but it was closer to the center of the county and therefore easier for the rural population to reach. Miami won the election in balloting that the courts invalidated as fraudulent, but the disqualified county officers opened a courthouse in a vacant store in Miami anyway. The legally elected county authorities responded by hiring a gunman, who captured the county records and brought them to Bennett, where the local boosters placed the documents in a safe and hurriedly erected a building around it. The new county seat hung on for a while, long enough to change its name to Oran and then Parnell and grow to about twelve residences, a few businesses, a hotel, and a post office. Miami, however, had railroad service and in 1898 enough voters to force a new vote and win it fair and square. With fewer than 1,000 people living there, Miami is now the only town left in the county. All that remains of Bennett-Oran-Parnell is a historical marker and a pasture where cattle graze.

Railroads played an equally important role in determining which towns lived and which ones died. In the eastern plains of Colorado, the surviving towns of Kiowa County (1,688 people, one per square mile) lie in an east-west line along the tracks. Even their names came from the railroad company, whose president indulged his daughter by letting her label them in alphabetical order: Arden, Brandon, Chivington, Diston, Eads, Fergus. Sheridan Lake was one of the few exceptions. Its promoters, who had purchased a marshland and former buffalo wallow, hired a public relations man to sing its praises, calling the dredged marsh a lake which Gen. Phil Sheridan considered his favorite camping spot. It attracted enough buyers of town lots that the railroad was forced to stop at its station (although the townspeople had built the station themselves) and accept its out-of-sequence name.

As crucial as it was in the early shakeout of survival-of-the-fittest among municipalities, hanging a town's future on the railroad often turned out in the long run to be a lot like counting on a mine's ore to be inexhaustible. In 1888, one year after its founding, Chivington, Colorado, one of Kiowa County's "ABC towns," was a division headquarters, with a roundhouse, switching and repair yards, the grandest hotel between central Kansas and the cities of the Front Range, and a population of 1,500. When changing technology allowed the railroads to space out their division points across greater distances, Chivington lost its lifeblood. It now consists of four houses, a church, and an abandoned and crumbling two-story brick school building that would look at home next to Rhyolite's stock exchange ruin.

Immediately north of Kiowa County, in Cheyenne County (2,397 people, 1.3 per square mile), the town of Cheyenne Wells had better luck—and, from its inception, demonstrated both ingenuity and pluck in the Darwinian fight to prevail or disappear. Once a stage station on the Smoky Hill Trail to Colorado's mining camps, the town had literally picked itself up and moved five miles when the railroad initially bypassed it. In 1887, the local Town and Investment Company sponsored excursions for potential settlers, featuring fireworks, a barbecue, a baseball game, and a dance in the brand-new Monte Cristo Hotel, where the prospective buyers were put up for free. The musicians were imported from Denver. A special stage line was established to take people directly to the government land office 70 miles away. Free lots were offered to the first church willing to build a structure worth more than $1,500 and to the first child born in town. Water from an artesian well dug by the government was piped in and offered at no cost to homeowners.

As with all new towns, the local newspaper became the chief booster of Cheyenne Wells' prospects and its vocal defender against other settlements vying for preeminence in the region. The rival in this case was the town of Kit Carson, 25 miles to the west, which by the 1880s had already gone through one boom and bust. For a brief period in the 1870s, as the westernmost railhead on the Kansas and Pacific, Kit Carson had grown to nearly a thousand residents and earned a reputation as a center of gambling, prostitution, and thievery. When the territorial government created Greenwood County in 1870, Kit Carson was named the county seat. Four years later, with the railroad completed across the Plains, the population was so diminished that Greenwood County was abolished; by 1880, only 28 people lived in Kit Carson. When homesteaders entered the region in the late 1880s, the town grew again, and began regarding the younger Cheyenne Wells as a pretentious upstart. The *Kit Carson Bee* and the *Cheyenne Wells Gazette* locked horns.

"More money was paid on September 13th [1887] for Cheyenne Wells town lots than has been contracted for Kit Carson sand since its miscarriage into this world," the *Gazette* gloated after the first successful townsite auction.

The *Bee* buzzed when Cheyenne Wells' water pump broke and "pure sparkling water" from Kit Carson had to be hauled in. The *Gazette* responded that the water made Cheyenne Wells people sick.

"This year will show to the world that Kit Carson does not lay claim to being the best and most progressive town between Wallace [Kansas] and Denver without just grounds for the assertion," the *Bee* boasted in 1888. The *Gazette* retorted with a news item: "Dr. Corporan visited Kit Carson for the express purpose of getting out of the bustle and excitement of Cheyenne Wells for one day, and recover his equilibrium. He says Kit Carson operated on him like an ancient graveyard and had the soothing effect desired."

Cheyenne Wells got the last word again in 1889, when Cheyenne County was formed and the upstart town was named county seat, then division headquarters for the railroad.

"Push, enterprise and perseverance are essentials of success in making a city," the *Gazette* editorialized. "Towns are easily started, but it is the next step that requires the guidance of able and energetic citizens."

A hundred years later, Cheyenne Wells is still taking those next steps. It has survived the pullout of the railroad headquarters, suffered through the great drought of the 1930s, when dust storms lifted the plowed soil and carried it all the way to the Atlantic Ocean, and then reeled again from another severe dry spell in the 1950s, losing people with each setback. A spurt of oil discoveries in the last ten years has breathed some new life into the economy and pushed the town's population back above 1,000. Booming it isn't, but compared to the other towns in the region, most of whom look as if they are waiting for their last handful of elderly residents to turn off the lights and pass on, Cheyenne Wells at least seems active instead of moribund. The only larger town within 75 miles is Burlington, which is on an interstate, the modern equivalent of the railroad for a town's lifeline.

"We're the kind who go out and fight to keep our town alive," said Shirley Pelton, a member of the Chamber of Commerce who had recently opened a florist shop on Main Street. The town has built a new swimming pool and golf course and fire station; it has a one-doctor clinic and is offering a reward of $10,000 to anyone who can bring in a second doctor; and it is trying to entice new businesses and people by touting its low taxes, plentiful water, and available land and work force.

Were he still alive, the first editor of the *Gazette* would probably object to the town's latest publicity campaign, identifying it as part of "Colorado's Outback," hardly the progressive image he once strove so hard to project. But he would appreciate the fact that in Kit Carson, a town barely clinging to life by comparison, the water supply was recently condemned and the old rival is asking Cheyenne Wells for some of its supply.

TOWNS IN FARMING AREAS WERE USUALLY SPACED at intervals according to the "team-haul" principle, which provided for a settlement close enough for the area's farmers to reach it and return home in one day. The two crucial variables for sustaining a town that depended on rural customers, therefore, were the density of homesteaders and their means of transportation. In the initial frontier land rush, a homestead of 160 acres was considered enough to provide for a large family, and people traveled by horse and wagon. If each family had five members on its quarter section, the rural density was 20 people per square mile; a town in the center of a circle with a 10-mile radius had more than 4,000 patrons living within a half-day's haul. Change the average size of the farm to a full section of 640 acres, and the number of people drops by three-quarters. Two people per square mile would be even less: a family of five on 1,600 acres, about 400 potential customers within a 10-mile radius.

It doesn't take a degree in mathematics or city planning to see what happened to a lot of towns in the semiarid West that sprang up on the mistaken assumption that the homesteaders filing on quarter sections (and later half sections and full sections) would be around for a long time. As farming methods that had been developed in the moister regions to the east proved futile west of the 98th meridian, the countryside population quickly thinned out. Without a critical mass of customers, many towns lost their reason for existence. John C. Hudson, a cultural geographer, found that within a space of ten years "nearly all Plains towns were marked for either growth or stagnation, whether by circumstances of geography or by the entrepreneurial skills of their business people."

The advance of technology also worked against the odds of a rural frontier town's survival. With new machinery, one farmer could do the work of several; the size of one family's land unit expanded, meaning even fewer people on the land. Horse and wagon gave way to automobiles and trucks, altering the other variable in the "team-haul" equation. The fewer remaining farmers could travel greater distances to do their shopping and sell their products. The miles between viable trading centers lengthened again.

"The two big changes in my lifetime around here have been fewer people and greater conveniences," said Ladd Pendleton, whose parents brought him to their ranch on the Mexican border in Hidalgo County, New Mexico, in a covered wagon in 1917. At the time, there were enough people in the area to support the town of Cloverdale, about five miles from Pendleton's home. Now the closest town is Animas, a tiny crossroads settlement 45 miles north; Lordsburg, where the Pendletons get their groceries and gas and do their other shopping, is an additional 30 miles farther up the road. Cars, phones, television, electricity, refrigeration—all the things that on the one hand make living miles from nowhere easier are part of a larger technological process that, on the other hand, has made existence more physically isolated.

"Ladd's ranch isn't the end of the world, but you can see it from there," a person in Animas had told me. When I arrived, Ladd was getting off his horse after a day in the saddle checking on the cattle that graze on his 16,000 acres. His wife, a school teacher, and two young children were in Animas, where they live during the week. Besides ranching, he also runs a real estate business from his remote home. That night we turned on the television set, adjusted to receive a particular satellite's beam, and watched an advertisement for a ranch he was selling. "It's the best way to reach buyers," he said. "There aren't enough people in the local market."

The same problem and solution has occurred to others. On a ranch in southeastern Oregon, where the nearest town of any size is 80 miles away, most of it on rough gravel roads, the Miller family prides itself on its old-fashioned ways. They make their own ropes, breed and break their own horses, use teams and wagons to carry feed to their cattle in the winter. "This is about as close to the old West as you'll get," their hired cowboy said. But instead of hauling or trailing their cattle to an auction barn for sale—which would be time-consuming and expensive, cause their steers to lose weight from the stress, and, at a small auction barn, not guarantee a price they are willing to take— they hire a firm that videotapes their herd and shows it over a "satellite auction" in which cattle buyers around the country participate. They don't have a town nearby, but then again they no longer need one.

Farms getting larger and small towns dwindling is not unique to the contemporary frontier. It's been happening—and continues— throughout rural America. The process had simply been quicker and more dramatic in the places I visited. Because their terrain and climate are so hostile, they were the last places to witness a land boom. For the same reasons, they were the first to see it go bust. Their populations hadn't so much grown and declined as they had exploded with the opening of lands to white settlement, and then collapsed.

What other rural but more densely populated parts of the nation are experiencing so agonizingly and steadily, these counties went through a generation ago. Their towns are already fewer, smaller, and farther apart, and the people have already adjusted to that fact. Life at or near the irreducible minimum is something they accept stoically. They are used to it. Accordingly, even though 93 of the 132 contemporary frontier counties lost population between 1980 and 1990, and even though 12 new counties slipped below two people per square mile, there is less of a sense of despair in their communities than in other parts of the Farm Belt that are facing the irreducible minimum for the first time.

In many of the contemporary frontier counties, both the hope of growth and the panic of sharp decline are distant memories, replaced by a determination to make do, hold on, and hold out. When I asked people to predict what their counties would be like in thirty years, the overwhelming response was "fewer people," but in saying that they were talking about someone else. Others might leave, but, by God, they didn't intend to.

As for their towns, there aren't many left to lose. People still need gasoline, mail, schools, groceries, churches, and other basic services (including, of course, movie videos and hairdressers), and there are limits of how far they will drive to get them. Barring some next step that makes modern automobile travel as outdated as the horse and buggy, those limits have pretty much been reached. In thirteen of the counties, the only remaining settlement is their county seat. In the contemporary frontier, Municipal Darwinism seems to have just about run its course.

The ladder of devolution ends in a town like Amidon, North Dakota. Amidon, population 24, is the county seat of Slope County (907 people, 0.7 per square mile), in the southwestern border of the state, where the Little Missouri River wriggles through coulees of lignite and bentonite bluffs which sometimes smolder when struck by lightning. In 1915, around the time of its formation, Slope County had 4,945 residents. In 1990, having lost 250 people in the last ten years, it became North Dakota's first county since 1900 to fall below a population of 1,000. Modern Amidon consists of a small, woodframe courthouse, a school (30 students from kindergarten through eighth grade; high school students attend classes outside the county), an office for the federal Soil Conservation Service and local grazing association, a post office, a few houses, a Lutheran church, and a country store, the town's only business.

Jerry Erickson, who owns the store and manages it with his wife, Carolyn, is the Lutheran minister. (He also serves two Congregational parishes in the area each Sunday.) The store sells gasoline, snacks, perishables like milk and bacon, and serves coffee and lunch. I had lasagna the day I was there, baked in Carolyn's home kitchen and brought on order to the small table in the store. A couple of elderly ranchers came in, picked up some lunches to go, signed for them on their account sheets, and left. Erickson said the store doesn't make money for his family, but that wasn't why they opened it in the first place. "It creates and maintains a sense of community," he said. "Without the store, you wonder what would hold the community together. I do some ministry just by being here."

WITH FEW EXCEPTIONS—PLACES WHERE THE GOLD boom is under way and in a few tourist or retirement spots—the land fever of the frontier passed a long time ago. Like so many of the people, it has migrated to the cities and suburbs. In the contemporary frontier, the era of town-building has given way to town-saving. Finding modern equivalents of the old-style boosters, who talked hyperbolically about opportunity and glowing futures for their locales, is a rarity. Three of them are worth noting.

Cody, Nebraska, sits between the Niobrara River and the South Dakota border in Cherry County (6,307 people, 1.1 per square mile). More than three-quarters of the county is covered by the northern edge of the Sand Hills; its few towns all lie beyond the dunes on an arc of the railroad and U.S. Highway 20, as if they had been swept out of the interior by a sand storm. At first glance, Cody, in the middle of the arc, appears to be like innumerable other Plains towns living on borrowed time, except that its clustered old houses are freshly painted and a billboard on the edge of town proclaims it as "The Town Too Tough to Die."

"This is an active community involved in the survival process," said John Johnson, Cody's mayor and owner of Western Vet Supplies, a store that sells cow medicine, horse tack, farm sundries, and locally made arts and crafts. Four years earlier, he said, leading townspeople had decided that without strenuous effort Cody would expire. "What it was in jeopardy of was its own attitude," he said. "Attitude is the biggest obstacle. It takes foresight and enthusiasm to get rid of that damned 'can't do' attitude. There are leaders in a community—don't call them leaders, call them dreamers—and they need to be nurtured."

The town formed committees, started a redevelopment commission, searched for federal and state grants, attended workshops on preserving communities, and went to work. The old dance hall in the two-block business district was renovated for community events. Showers and RV hookups were installed in the town park. They built a new softball field—"One of the finest in the state," according to the mayor, "a real boost to the community because everyone was involved. You could find a dime in the outfield with those new lights." They started refurbishing the closed theater for plays and movies, and they held community clean-up contests with prizes for those who did the best job sprucing up their houses. Against the recommendations of the state, they refused to close their high school. "Without the schools, people would shop where their kids go to classes and the town would collapse," a local businessman told me.

Mayor Johnson, a small man in his early forties, was a bundle of energy as we took a brief tour of Cody. He proudly pointed out two of the town's newer businesses—a furniture refinisher working in a metal barn and the Mane Tamer, a recently opened hair salon—and when he spoke it was often in aphorisms that seemed to have been culled from a small-town Chamber of Commerce primer a hundred years out of date. "I think the future is in rural America," he said. "*This* is the new frontier. Anything's possible here."

One of the things he was proudest of was that, between the 1980 and 1990 censuses, Cody had not lost any population. It is still home to 177 people, exactly what it had been a decade earlier. In a different time on the frontier, holding even would hardly have been a sign of victory. But in the contemporary frontier, a town too tough to die is something to boast about.

Sweet Grass County, Montana (3,154 people, 1.7 per square mile), is undergoing the second land rush of its history. The first came at the end of the last century, when the former Crow Indian reservation was opened to white settlement and the Northern Pacific platted the town of Big Timber and made it into a major wool-shipping point. A Big Timber real estate firm had run the following advertisement to spur development:

HEALTH, WEALTH, HAPPINESS
Made by
Sunshine, Pure Air, Pure Water,
Industry, Good Soil, Fine Markets,
Excellent Climate and General Prosperity.
MONTANA, In the Infancy of Development,
Invites You to Come
Come and Help Build a State
Come While Lands Are Cheap and Opportunities Abundant
Come Now, Before the Wave of Immigration
Has Equalized Values

Better Be a Big Frog in a Little Pond
Than a Little Toad in a Big Puddle

The modern land rush arrived in two waves. The initial one included artists, artisans, and urban refugees—people like Suzanne Wilson, who sold a restaurant in a Colorado ski resort and bought a ranch of a section and a half in Sweet Grass County for the price of a house lot in Vail and then opened a bed-and-breakfast in the old Grand Hotel in downtown Big Timber; a couple from the East who operate a hydroponic greenhouse; a surrealist artist from Virginia who works on the side as a sheep shearer; some sculptors who started a small foundry for their work; and two businessmen who make reproductions of famous Old West rifles. "Around here," one of them said, "you have to come up with something you can do independently and make a living."

They were attracted by the scenic beauty of Sweet Grass County, one of the prettier counties in a state with a lot of them. In the northwestern part of the county, rolling plains collide with the Crazy Mountains. In the south, the ramparts of the Absaroka and Bear Tooth ranges lift into the clouds, near the northeastern boundary of Yellowstone National Park. The Boulder River, a premier trout fishing stream, cascades down from the Absarokas to meet the Yellowstone River at Big Timber.

The other part of the first wave was, to borrow from the terminology of the nineteenth-century advertisement, big frogs from big ponds. Among them were actors Michael Keaton and Brooke Shields, author Tom McGuane, musician Dave Grusin, network newsman Tom Brokaw, and Robert Haas, chairman of Levi Strauss & Company and owner of the Oakland Athletics baseball team. They liked the scenery too, but didn't have to figure out how to make a living within the county; with the exception of McGuane, who lives on his ranch year-round, they purchased their ranches as vacation homes.

The first wave was generated by happenstance and word of mouth. The second, bigger wave hit once word of the local celebrities spread through the national media. A story about the "Great Montana Ranch Rush" in *The New York Times* used the Big Timber area as its prime example of the statewide phenomenon of movie stars, professional athletes, industry CEOs, and other wealthy out-of-staters buying up ranches in the state and contributing to what one person decried as the potential "Aspenization of Montana."

Within days of the story's publication, the phone in the office of Sonny Todd, a Big Timber real estate agent quoted in the article, started ringing off the hook. In three months' time, he received nearly a thousand inquiries about land in the area. "One woman from New York was real frantic," he said afterward. "She asked, 'Will there be any left if we don't get there right off?' I assured her there was plenty." Two national television news shows, along with other print and radio reporters, turned up to do features about Big Timber.

"All of sudden our little county is pretty popular," Todd said. He had sold a couple of million dollars' worth of real estate almost immediately. Compared to four years earlier, land prices had doubled from the sudden demand of people trying to "come now, before the tide of immigration has equalized values."

There is some evidence of the overlay of part-time Westerners to be found in the town. The newspaper boxes in downtown Big Timber include ones for *USA Today* and *The Wall Street Journal* alongside those for local papers, something I didn't see in other county seats. At the Grand Hotel, an absentee ranch owner from the East was treating her young hired hands to a fancy dinner. They were freshly scrubbed and, without their cowboy hats, their foreheads were pearl white from never having been exposed to the sun. She was talking about the case against raising cattle—"So much energy is wasted transferring grain into beef . . ."—and they were probably wondering if they were about to face the choice of looking for cowboy work somewhere else or becoming workers on a sprout ranch. Big Timber's tiny airport is undoubtedly the only one in the contemporary frontier where private Lear jets land with regularity. And a woman at the Chamber of Commerce complained about people stopping to ask for directions to tour past the celebrities' ranches.

But if Big Timber is on its way to becoming Aspen, it still has a long way to go, which is just fine with people in the area. They have other, more common issues to deal with. A fund-raising drive had just been held to keep the local hospital afloat. A woman involved in search committees for a doctor and a minister for her church said the major questions for prospects were "Can they stand the wind? Can they stand the winters? More important, can their wives stand it?" At one of the several local bars, a man told me the Grand Hotel is "still the only place where the bartender has to know how to do more than pour beer and shots." And like so many other contemporary frontier counties, Sweet Grass County still lost population since the previous census.

Todd, as a real estate dealer one of the clearest beneficiaries of the land boom, believed the best part of the new activity is that "this is not a leveraged market. These folks aren't speculators. They aren't dividing things up in twenty-acre lots. We'll be a ranching community for a long time. It's just an independent, surviving type of town." Some people don't like the influx of movie stars and others buying ranches, but it is providing work for carpenters and cowboys and keeping the land as it was. "One thing that's hard to do in Montana is make money," Todd said. "It's a great place to live but hard to make a living. A few old-timers complain about [the new absentee owners] but not when it comes time to sell their place. I'm a bad guy until it comes time for sellin'."

The smallest town with the biggest dreams is Fields, Oregon, founded in 1881 as a way station for freight wagons because it was at the midpoint in the 240-mile stretch of sage desert and mountains between Winnemucca, Nevada, and Burns, Oregon. More than a century later, Burns and Winnemucca are still the nearest towns of any size, and the final portion of the road, a 60-mile gap with Fields at its center, has only recently been paved. "Congestion," a new highway sign outside of town warns approaching motorists, giving new definition to the term: Fields has a population of nine. Larry DeRieux, the owner of the Fields General Store, is preparing for his town's long-awaited boom.

DeRieux is a newcomer to Fields but its greatest booster. During the 1970s and 1980s, he and his wife Lolly spent their weekends and vacations traveling the Pacific Northwest in a trailer, looking for a business to buy and run themselves. He wanted something that had a potential others didn't see, something that could be bought for the right price. "The secret to business is buying right," he said. "It doesn't matter if it's real estate or horses or a restaurant, buying for the right price is the secret." (Like the mayor of Cody, Nebraska, who could have been his soul mate in enthusiastic optimism, DeRieux tends to talk in maxims and aphorisms.)

Their journeys eventually brought them to Harney County, Oregon's vastest and most sparsely populated county. Covering more than 10,000 square miles—larger by itself than nine separate states—Harney County is home to 7,060 people, 0.7 per square mile, more than half of whom live in the twin towns of Burns and Hines in the county's northern corner. The Fields region, in the south, is so lightly populated that when a group of artists secretly etched an intricate pattern, one-quarter-mile square, in the sandy floor of Alvord Desert in the summer of 1990, no one noticed for several months, until some pilots from the Idaho Air National Guard saw it from the air and briefly touched off rumors that the mysterious design was a launching pad for UFOs.

"If there's anyplace more remote than Fields, Oregon, I don't know where it is," DeRieux said. "It is *the* Outback in Oregon, *the* last frontier." In other words, just what he had been looking for. With his purchase in 1989, he got the Fields General Store, which under one roof houses a small grocery store, a liquor store, a café, a gas station, and a post office (thirty patrons who receive their mail three times a week); an RV park and small hotel; a tire shop (its business, once a major percentage of the trade, dropped off with the completion of the highway paving in 1990); and 144 of Fields' 160 acres—all of the town, in fact, except for a few houses and the small school, where eleven students attend grades one through eight. (High school students attend a public boarding school in Crane, more than a hundred miles away.)

DeRieux has big plans for his town. We didn't have to tour it for him to explain them to me; we could see everything from the yard in front of the store. "This is going to be a destination spot," he predicted. "The world wants to see America like it used to be: the little town in the country. Charming. Our total package will be the Great Escape. That will be our theme." He envisioned a "groomed town" with the appearance of the early 1900s, a campground, tour buses and pack trips to the desert and nearby Steens Mountain, a dramatic escarpment from whose peaks the corners of four states can be seen on a clear day, and a series of "Fields Days" with barbecues and big-name bands. "My goal is to make Fields a place for people to come and stay while they enjoy the rest of the area," he said. "I think we can draw thousands of people here."

He has a sixteen-year plan mapped out for the growth he antici-pates. At the moment, in year one, he was concentrating on sprucing up the hotel and stocking the store ("Nobody wants to buy from a loser," he explained) and building a reputation on extra-thick milk-shakes and burgers made from chuck steak. The rest would come with time and hard work, proving, he said, that "you can still build things in America."

As he talked of his vision of the future, DeRieux grew breathless with excitement. A car pulled up to the café entrance and before he hurried back inside to serve them he had one last maxim to impart. "The two strongest elements of success," he said, "are courage and imagination." Spoken like a true frontier town-builder, for whom *location* appeared lower on the list of necessary ingredients. In DeRieux's Fields of dreams, if he built it, they would come.

CHAPTER 5

BELOW THE
IRREDUCIBLE MINIMUM

FLAT AND TREELESS, ARID AND ROCKSTREWN, ITS unremittingly bleak terrain lightly speckled with low-lying greasewood bushes and sagebrush, Loving County, Texas, on the state's western spur between the Pecos River and New Mexico border, is doubly unique. It is the nation's least-populated county (107 people) and its most sparsely populated (0.16 people per square mile).

"Out here there are plenty of rattlesnakes, jackrabbits, and coyotes—and not much else," said Julian Sanchez, a veteran ranch hand on the Slash Ranch, a spread covering 115,200 acres of land so devoid of good forage that on average it takes 120 acres to support one cow. According to a local saying, the cow has to graze at 15 miles an hour to survive.

People in Loving County are outnumbered by everything: by cattle forty-to-one, by square miles six-to-one, and by oil and gas leases four-to-one. No one knows how many rattlesnakes, jackrabbits, and coyotes there are, but by all accounts there are more than enough. Outside the café in Mentone, the county seat, a small pack of coyotes tends to skulk around in the evening. Residents keep their small dogs indoors so the coyotes won't get them. Out in the country, Sanchez said he never shoots jackrabbits because he wants the coyotes to have something to eat other than his chickens.

Rattlesnakes are a bigger problem, not just a nuisance but a real threat, particularly to children. "You teach your kids from the git-go to watch out for 'em," said Edna Clayton Dewees. "You learn to watch where you step." In the spring, when the rattlers are still lethargic from their winter torpor, people hold rattlesnake roundups to get rid of as many as possible because by summer, when the oppressive heat gets under everyone's skin, the snakes get particularly ornery, mean enough to go out of their way to bite someone. Barbara Creager's line of defense is a house full of cats. Rattlesnakes feed on mice, she reasons, so if the cats get the mice first, the rattlers will stay away from the house. She has fourteen cats—she needs that many to keep her supply replenished, because coyotes consider cats a delicacy equal to puppies —but nonetheless her freezer is full of dead rattlesnakes, whose skins she uses to make hatbands and belts.

Most of the stories I heard during my stay in Loving County broke down into three categories: bad rattlesnakes, bad water, and bad feelings.

Sheriff Elgin "Punk" Jones had one of the most memorable rattlesnake anecdotes: An oil worker a few years back saw a rattler on a gravel road and, following the custom of the region, stopped to kill it. (Passing up the chance to do away with a rattlesnake is the west Texas equivalent of seeing an undetonated blasting cap on a city sidewalk and not getting someone to defuse it: an irresponsible oversight that might cause someone else bodily harm.) The roustabout climbed out of his pickup, took out a shovel, and rammed the edge down on the snake's neck, severing its head from the rest of its long body.

Back in the pickup, he was about to start down the road when he realized that the fangs in the snake's decapitated head might puncture one of his truck tires like a nail, so he got out again and picked up the head to toss it aside. "That head just latched onto him," Jones said. "It flipped and latched onto him and started pumpin' on his wrist." Believing a dead snake couldn't be poisonous, the man went on with his work. Pretty soon, his fingers started hurting. Then his wrist and arms began swelling. He drove to the nearest doctor, 30 miles away in another county, who sent him to a hospital in Odessa, another 50 miles east, from which he was rushed to a bigger hospital in Lubbock, yet another 150 miles up the road, where they were barely able to save his life. That was one vengeful rattler.

The second type of story is about the local water. To begin with, there isn't much. On average, Loving County receives about ten inches of rain a year. "You ought to be here the day we get it," several people joked. (The other oft-repeated local rainfall adage is that a six-inch rainstorm in west Texas means the raindrops fall six inches apart.) Worse than the sparse amount of precipitation is the quality of the water supply. Most well water in the area is loaded with sodium chloride, gypsum, magnesium sulfate, some epsom salts and occasional traces of arsenic. "It'll burn your mouth," said Lloyd Goodrich, a member of one of the county's oldest families. "You couldn't drink enough to kill you, because you couldn't hold it in your stomach. You'd throw up." In some places the water is so "hard" (full of minerals) that it isn't even suitable for toilets; the mineral deposits will eventually plug the system. Not all of the local water is that destructive, but none of it is without some problem. "Salt water would be an improvement," one resident said of some of the best. "It would be like getting a glass of salt water and mixing milk of magnesia in it."

Until 1988, people hauled their water from the town of Pecos, 23 miles away in Reeves County. Now water is piped from a passable well 7 miles north of Mentone to a big tank near the courthouse, where residents can get it for fifteen cents per forty-two-gallon barrel, transport it home, and transfer it to reservoirs elevated on stilts above their houses. Mary Belle Jones, the county appraiser and sheriff's wife, a vivacious woman and the county's unofficial local historian, believes that the bad water is the main reason Loving County has so few residents. "You can't sell a house in Mentone," she said. "Women won't live in a place where you can't have a dishwasher. Even during the last boom [in the 1970s] when they were living in chicken coops and shacks in Kermit [30 miles away], you couldn't get them to move to Mentone." When state tax officials questioned some of her low valuations of local properties, Mary Belle drew on her own experience and wrote back indignantly: "Water from yard wells . . . eats up fixtures and ruins appliances, if one tries to use them, besides leaving clothes stained brown and dishes milky and streaked." The state decided she knew what she was talking about and accepted her appraisals. Her own prize possession is a recent replacement for the 20-barrel tank that had provided only enough volume for drinking water. Huge and black, nearly as big as her house, her new tank holds 500 barrels. To keep it supplied with water from a ranch well in the county, her husband bought a semitruck with a 200-barrel tank. "See that," she said, pointing to the bulky steel reservoir. "I love it. When I die, I want it buried with me."

More than water and rattlesnakes, however, what people talk about is their neighbors. Without exception, Loving County residents were generous and friendly toward me. As with most rural Westerners I've met, genuine hospitality toward strangers was part of their life's code. But also without exception, they all had something disparaging to say about someone else in the county, ranging from an offhand, catty remark to a long string of epithets and pointed accusations. "If you sneeze around here, everyone knows it," one woman told me as we toured part of the county. "Right now, they know I'm driving around with a man in my car." A few days later, a neighbor said of this woman: "She's one of the sweetest people. She can be real nice and then lie right in your face."

None of the animosities are harbored in secrecy. The factions, feuds, and grudges are all fought in public, and they infect every aspect of life in the county except, perhaps, personal tragedies. "You know who likes you and who doesn't, but in a crisis, everybody would be there," said Monique Keen, the postmaster. "It doesn't matter if they didn't talk to you all year or not. They'd *be there*." When a resident's trailer had burned down a year earlier, everyone had gotten together and donated money and household items to help him start over. On the other hand, when a Texas magazine had solicited each resident to gather for a cover photograph including the county's entire population, many of the return letters said things like, "I'll be damned if I'll have my picture taken with ———" and the project was dropped.

With more space per person than any county in the nation (3,840 acres), and despite its name (the courthouse does a brisk business in supplying marriage licenses to outsiders who want Loving on their document), Loving County was nonetheless the most socially claustrophobic and fractious place I encountered. It is inhabited by friendly folks who just happen not to like each other very much and who would prefer that, if they could make the selection, about half the population would live somewhere else.

LOVING COUNTY WAS NAMED FOR A MAN, NOT AN emotion. Oliver Loving, one of the legends in the state's long line of cattle barons, is credited with driving one of the first herds of Texas cattle to a northern market, in 1858. Following the Civil War, he and his partner, Charles Goodnight, blazed the Goodnight-Loving Trail with cattle drives up the Pecos River valley to supply beef for army forts and Indian reservations in New Mexico and to Union Pacific tracklaying crews in Wyoming. On the trail in 1867 he was mortally wounded by Comanches, crawled five miles for help, chewing his gloves for nourishment for several days, was hauled to Fort Sumner for treatment, but died there from gangrene. Goodnight packed his corpse in charcoal and carted it back to Texas for burial. When the state legislature created Loving County in 1893, it gave the new jurisdiction his name because his trail crossed the Pecos in the area.

Mentone was named by a surveyor homesick for Menton, France, on the Riviera. The original townsite, on the east bank of the Pecos, was platted by a canal and irrigation company and had 200 residents in 1896, before the farming effort failed. A year later, with no county officials living within its borders and the money from taxes and sales of school lands missing as well, Loving County became the only county ever disorganized by the Texas legislature. The 1900 census listed 33 residents, most of them employees of a ranch covering 1,200 square miles in three counties.

Five years later, E. L. Stratton, a quick-talking Chicago lawyer, started another land and irrigation company. Comparing the Pecos to the Riviera in his promotions, he sold parcels of the valley to Midwestern farmers. "The truth wasn't in him," said Goodrich, whose grandfather bought some land from Stratton and moved from Michigan. "He could show you a white sandy beach like the Riviera's. 'Course there wasn't any water." In another place, Stratton reportedly tied ripe bananas to the branches of mesquite trees and ran an excursion train past them without letting the prospective buyers out for a closer inspection. "My grandmother felt cheated; my grandfather didn't," Goodrich recalled. "My grandmother hated his guts." Within a few years, most of the Goodriches' neighbors from the Midwest gave up and moved back north.

Oil was discovered in the mid-1920s, and by 1931 enough of a drilling boom was under way for the county to be officially reinstated. A new town was platted. It had five cafés, five filling stations, two hotels, two drugstores, two recreation halls, two barber shops, a dance hall, a machine shop, a cleaning establishment, and a lumber yard. Water sold for a dollar a barrel, ten times what oil was bringing. The town was first called Ramsey, then Porterville (the name of the Stratton town that emptied and moved its buildings to be nearer the oil strikes), and finally Mentone, in order to appropriate the post office designation of the abandoned first settlement. At the height of the drilling activity, an estimated 600 people lived in the new Mentone; in 1940, with the frenzy cooled, the official count for the entire county was back down to 285.

Having literally brought Loving County back to life and sustained it for the last half-century as the population dwindled, oil is still the lifeblood of the county. It defines the landscape. Driving toward Mentone at night, with lights twinkling at regular intervals across the flatness, it seems that perhaps Stratton had been right: this could be rich farmland, perhaps central Michigan, with homesteads on every half section. Daylight reveals something different. The lights denote oil pumps, not homes. Aside from the salt cedars choking the banks of the green and sluggish Pecos River, there are more pump jacks than trees on the barren vista that sweeps uninterrupted to the Guadalupe and Davis mountains, 80 miles to the west and south. A faint sulfurous smell, from one of the gas wells that touched off a brief second boom in the 1970s, wafts across the outskirts of town in the early-morning air.

Mentone itself, the county's only town, has 17 residents. That it once was bigger, with more than one of nearly everything, has to be left to the imagination. Though it's written down in historical accounts, physical evidence that there once were better times has been dismantled and carted away, as if the community doesn't want such reminders in its midst. Except for the school, closed in 1978 (the county's 19 students now attend classes in Wink, 35 miles away in Winkler County) and the old community center/church/school from Porterville, a small clapboard structure built in 1910 and preserved in Mentone as the county's oldest landmark, the town doesn't have vacant buildings, it has vacant lots. All that remains are a gas station, a café, a one-room post office, a few houses and mobile homes, the brick courthouse built in 1935, and a lot of empty spaces. Loving County was the only one I found that has neither a hairdresser nor a place to rent movie videos.

An oil pump bobs slowly up and down a block from the courthouse. More can be seen in the near distance. They mark the county's heartbeat, an artificial life-support system for a county that slipped below the irreducible minimum more than a generation ago. Without the oil and gas wells, and the tax revenue they generate, said Don Creager, the county judge, "we'd be dead. We don't have businesses, we don't have development, we don't have residential growth. We'd have to dissolve." Real estate taxes brought in $8,547 in 1989. Mineral taxes, however, amounted to $666,305. About 25 people—roughly one in four of the residents, even counting children—draw some salary from the county, a government that exists less out of absolute necessity than out of the fact that there is money enough to justify it. Loving County's budget for salaries, wages, and benefits in 1989 was $653,000; most of the elected administrators earned more than $33,000 and had full-time deputies; the four commissioners were each paid more than $20,000 a year. (By comparison, Slope County, North Dakota, with nine times as many residents and twice the area, spent $247,000 in salaries, wages, and benefits; no one, including the sheriff, had a full-time deputy; and each of the three commissioners was paid $7,500 a year.)

The oil and the courthouse are also at the center of the rivalries that split Loving County's tiny population. Beginning around 1960 ranchers organized to collect money from the oil companies for damages to their grazing land from roads, pipelines, and other activities associated with drilling wells and keeping them maintained. The oil men complained that many of the damage claims were excessive—one of the early ones was for $5,000 on land that was selling for $5 an acre and being leased for grazing at ten cents an acre. But the commissioners, who determined whether the roads the oil men needed could be extended, were dominated by ranch interests. No damage payments, no roads. Beyond deciding who got the salaried county jobs, elections took on a heightened importance in the tug of war between ranch and oil interests.

The saying that "every vote counts" is more than a civic slogan in Loving County. Many elections are decided by a margin of two or three. The issue of who is a legally registered voter and who isn't became hotly disputed, occasionally settled by the courts and Texas Rangers posted at the four precinct voting locations. A state election law provides that under certain conditions a person can vote in a jurisdiction even if he or she actually lives somewhere else, and both factions take advantage of it. The result is that for years Loving County has had more registered voters than residents. In 1990, for instance, although there were 107 men, women, and children in the county, there were 110 legally authorized voters. "It gets wicked here around November," one county official said. "Families fight with one another for control of the county government. They just fight and fight."

Write-in campaigns, easy to mount because of the small number of people, became a favorite ploy. A slate would be fielded in secrecy and on election night incumbents who thought they were unopposed would find themselves out of a job. Even after the law was changed to force write-in candidates to announce in advance, the strategy continued. In the election previous to my visit, three write-in candidates beat out three incumbents by votes of 52–46 (a countywide vote for county clerk) and 19–13 and 20–12 (two precinct commissioners).

"You never get one vote accidentally here. *Never,*" said Royce Creager, one of the victors and brother of the judge. "You win nineteen to thirteen and you know every one of those votes. I mean, you *know.*"

Complicated by personality clashes and family feuds (several people referred to the Hatfields and McCoys in their descriptions) and occasional shifts of alliances, with little room for neutrality since everyone knows everyone else and which side each person is on in any issue, the friction spills into other activities. The school once was "the community center, with raffles, dances, games," one resident told me. "It was a delightful place to be. Then politics got involved and the school became a kicking ball" with teachers, being voters, dragged into the other disputes. Some people voted to join the Wink school simply to get education out of the field of fire. When the commissioners voted to donate the historic Porterville building to Texas Tech University's ranching museum in Lubbock, opponents started holding church services in the building and then claimed that Loving County's only place of worship was being torn away from its congregation. After the proposal was killed, the regular services stopped. The local 4-H and home-makers' clubs, both of them riven with dissension, I was told, often hold their fund-raising drives around election time because no one wants to unintentionally slight someone else so close to the balloting: everyone gives.

The newest point of contention is a proposal to locate a toxic waste dump about three miles from Mentone. Not surprisingly, the county's residents are split over it. Some like the prospect of permanent jobs, in case the oil wells stop producing. Others are writing letters and organizing against it. But the main battle lines seem to be drawn along sides of the longer-standing conflicts rather than over the merits of the issue itself. "A lot of people just don't want more residents in Loving County," said one commissioner, who approved of the proposal. "They want it to stay the same—just the opposite of what a Chamber of Commerce ought to be." And yet, another woman used the same argument for opposing the dump, which she said would discourage population growth. "The current political setup doesn't want new people moving in," she said. "It would dilute their power, and they want to stay in charge."

Although most residents said the feuding is now less poisonous than it had been the last three decades, there is still little love lost within Loving County. Several people advised me—strangers being noncombatants and therefore accorded every kindness—not to mention that I had already interviewed them when they learned who was next on my list of visits; with others, their first question was, "Who suggested that you talk to me?" A prominent leader of one faction said he never ate at the local café because his presence might hurt its business with the other faction; he ordered by phone and ate at home.

People offered different reasons for staying. "It's kind of like mother's cooking," explained McKinley Hopper, a descendant of one of the county's earliest homesteaders. "Regardless of how it tastes, it's what you grew up with. It's home."

Judy Crow, the deputy clerk and wife of the deputy sheriff, had lived there for four years. "When I first came out here I couldn't figure out what I'd done so wrong that God was punishing me," she said. "But it grows on you. You learn to live with the inconveniences."

"After we first came here, we were too poor to leave," said Edna Clayton Dewees, a former sheriff and county clerk. "Now we have too much invested to walk off."

Newt Keen had come to the area as a cowboy for one of the big ranches, then ran the café for twenty years before turning it over to his children. In the late 1970s, an armed robber after the café's daily receipts had jumped him in his home. Newt, in his sixties at the time, put up a fight. During the struggle, the bandit fired at close range, hitting Newt in the front teeth. But the old man fought on. "I had a little old pistol in my back pocket," he recalled. "I got a few shots off" before the robber escaped with the money. More than a decade later, Newt still hadn't replaced the four teeth he lost in the scuffle; bits of the shattered bullet were still lodged in his lip, gums, and throat. Now in his seventies, he herds 400 Spanish goats on scrub pasture along the Pecos, spending twelve-hour days in the saddle. "I jumped off a train, blew off a sole on my shoe, and hobbled into Mentone to get it fixed," he said of his introduction to the county. "If I ever get it fixed, I'll leave."

Lloyd Goodrich splits his time between his mother's house in Pecos and the old family home in what once was Porterville, where he raises alfalfa and oats on 18 irrigated acres and tinkers with the rusted equipment scattered over the property. A diminutive man with a burr haircut and straggly beard, teeth blackened from constant pipe smoking (he has been making his own "ever since pipes went over two dollars each"), Goodrich is considered the local eccentric. "Did you know he's a genius? He is, you know," one local told me. He has advanced degrees in electrical engineering and could find a job anywhere in the nation, but said "I like it nice and warm and dry and where there aren't too many people around. Where else can you stand and look eighty miles in one direction and sixty in another? I just like the climate. You'll never hear anybody in this country bitch about it rainin'." Goodrich is also the only one I met not considered a part of any faction, partly because he is such a contrarian. "That Lloyd," one woman said, "he'd argue with a *door*."

He considers himself in the minority as a "real" Loving County person. "Seventy-five percent of the people are just using it on the way to somewhere else. They want to move to east Texas where they can fish in a deep lake, or they're just here to make some money and move on.

"Loving County's no different than any other place, except it's so small that everything's out in the open," he said. "Nothing happens here that doesn't happen in Houston, except that in Houston it gets lost in the crowd."

Is it like a family, I asked. He rolled his eyes and laughed. "Yeah," he said, "if you consider a family that fights."

In the small gas station in town, eighty-four-year-old Mattie Thorp, who runs it for her nephews, said business was slow. "Most of the people in the county get their gas somewhere else," she said, meaningfully. (Like the café across the street, the station does not accept credit cards, adding yet another distinction to Loving County, the only county in America I know of beyond the ubiquitous reach of plastic.) On one wall of the station is a big poster from Menton, France, a lush scene of a tidy, crowded community next to sparkling, azure waters. It had been sent by the mayor of Menton to the citizens of Loving County, which he called *District de l'Amour*. Obviously, he had never visited.

THERE ARE CURRENTLY TWENTY-SIX OTHER COUN-ties in the United States with populations below 1,000. All but one also have population densities under two people per square mile. (Kalawao County, Hawaii, a tiny peninsula segregated from the island of Molokai for a leper colony, is the exception. It has only 130 residents, but since it covers a mere 14 square miles, its density is 9.3 people per square mile.) Among the others, each one has its own idiosyncrasies, its own struggles against dropping below the irreducible minimum of a functioning community.

King County, Texas, population 354, the nation's third-least-populated county, is the home of the 6666 Ranch, whose 208,000 acres cover more than a third of the county. In Guthrie, the county seat, most of the houses are owned by the ranch or the school district. The main ranch house, on a hill dominating the town, is larger than the courthouse, which in 1982 received national attention for finally getting indoor plumbing. Local people are intensely proud of their school, a modern facility that houses 100 students from kindergarten to twelfth, taught by 24 teachers. A good education is important, a Guthrie mother told me, "because we raised our kids with the idea: you get your high school diploma and get out."

Kenedy County, Texas, population 460, is essentially the feudal domain of five huge ranches, most of them with oil leases. In 1989 it was cited in a book on rural America as having the greatest maldistribution of wealth in the nation. A quarter of the households received investment income, mostly oil royalties, averaging $83,000 a year, ranking it thirtieth in the nation in per capita income. But it also ranked near the top in poverty; 35 percent of its residents lived below the poverty line. Other than U.S. Highway 77 and seven miles of county roads, all the roads in its 1,389 square miles (bigger than Rhode Island, smaller than Delaware) are privately owned and maintained.

Nebraska's Sand Hills include nine counties with populations in three digits. Arthur County, population 462, publishes its residents' telephone numbers on a sheet of typing paper. Since there is no doctor or nurse or physician's assistant in the county, the names of the sixteen people who are EMTs are marked with a star, so that in a medical emergency a resident can call the closest one; the names of volunteer firemen are marked with black dots. The county's sole café had recently closed when I was there, but some area ranchers hoped to reopen it, not expecting any profit but unwilling to see the area lose its gathering place. Arthur, the unincorporated county seat and only town in the county, population about 100, is the site of the world's only church constructed of straw. The straw, more readily available than wood in the treeless region, was baled and then stacked and plastered with stucco for the walls of the small church. Built in the late 1920s, the church is still standing, as is a baled-straw house a few blocks away.

In nearby McPherson County, population 546, the state's extension service had to adapt a program for helping small-town businesses, called "Managing Main Street." Tryon, the county seat, no longer has enough Main Street businesses to manage, so the program focuses instead on operating home-based enterprises. Some people said Tryon was named for a historical figure, others said it meant "we're still 'tryin' to make this into a town." The sheriff (he had no deputy) supplements his salary by cleaning septic tanks, running a two-unit motel, operating a leather shop, and marketing his own "Singing Sheriff" cassettes for two dollars apiece. Up until 1973, the area's phones, all party lines, funneled to a switchboard operator sitting in her living room.

Blaine County (population 675) and Thomas County (851 residents) share the Nebraska National Forest, the largest man-made forest in the Western Hemisphere. It was started in 1902 on the hopes that trees would spur development in the Sand Hills by providing wood for homes, fences, and fuel. By the time the trees were mature, most of the homesteaders had long since moved on. Thanks to the forest, however, the porcupine population increased dramatically.

Hinsdale, Mineral, and San Juan counties in southern Colorado, populations 467, 558, and 745, respectively, are clustered together on both sides of a sharp turn in the Continental Divide. Unlike the Texas and Nebraska counties, virtually all of whose lands are privately owned, in these three the federal government owns an average of 92 percent of each county. They are popular summer vacation spots—Creede, the seat of Mineral County, has a renowned summer theater—but their high elevations and remoteness empty them back to their hardy year-round residents in winter. Hinsdale County is the site of one of the most extreme examples of bad neighborliness in the country's history: Alferd Packer's cannibalism of five fellow prospectors a century ago. But its economy is now based on hospitality. Lake City, the county seat, with its neatly restored Victorian homes, is probably the prettiest town in the contemporary frontier, and its café (I had soup and salad, to be safe from mystery meat) served one of the best pecan pies I ever tasted.

REGARDLESS OF THEIR TOTAL POPULATIONS, MANY of the contemporary frontier counties are marked by both a strong sense of community and an uneasy tension between its individual parts. Folks alternate seamlessly between tales of trusting everyone—not locking their doors and relying on handshakes to seal deals—and lifelong feuds that color everything going on in the county, from bitter elections to petty gossip on the telephones' party lines.

Not that this is anything new. In 1931, when the geographer Isaiah Bowman asserted that a large part of the nation still lived a "frontier" existence, he added this sociological comment: "I was surprised to discover in so many communities . . . that hospitality is reserved for the stranger rather than the neighbor. It seemed, in some communities, as if there were very few men who had not a hard word for some neighboring landowner. We are accustomed to extolling the good qualities of the pioneer. Here is one of the weeds in his garden." Bowman also noted land disputes, friction between old-timers and newcomers, bank loans to small landowners being refused at the instigation of large depositors, and "hotly contested local elections with much ill feeling growing out of rivalry for insignificant posts. . . . 'We threw out the old gang,' said a member of the victorious group in a local village election in 1930—a hard saying in a town of fifty families."

But Loving County is different by several degrees. In virtually every other sparsely populated place, even those that redefine how little a community needs to remain intact, it is hard to imagine the county and its one town disappearing—either because of the deep-rooted spirit of the people or simply because the long distances involved still enforce a modern "team haul" rationale for continued existence. Loving County not only has the fewest residents of any county in the nation; among the contemporary frontier counties, it is one of the smallest geographically. Mentone is no longer a "team-haul" town. The only essential service it provides is its water tank, and even that is a two-year-old convenience. As far as I could determine, Loving County is the only one in the United States without any schools at all or any regularly attended church, the two principal binding forces of most communities. The county itself—organized, disorganized, reorganized—stays in business because oil revenues permit it to function. Already well below the irreducible minimum, Loving County is easy to imagine as an entity disappearing once again.

Loving County's fractiousness was the most virulent of any I found. Individually, the people themselves are no different from their counterparts in other places. There are just *so* few of them, living in such a forbidding landscape whose only abundant fluid is petroleum, that their unnatural circumstances seem to foster an extra degree of the in-fighting common to any community. It is as if the intrigues of "Dallas" were being played out in real life by a population the size of a high school drama class: a large, extended family squabbling over an inheritance that simultaneously binds them together against their will, prevents them from departing, and turns them against one another.

For me, the symbol of Loving County's disunity is its lack of a cemetery. I had been in many counties in which the list of what they don't have is longer than what they do have: no doctor, no hospital, no bank, no lawyer, no grocery store, and so on. But no cemetery—that, too, is unique about this county and seems particularly telling. In most frontier towns, one of the first acts of settling had been to lay out a plot of ground for burials. It was a statement of community, that the new land was to be home, for the living as well as for the remains of the departed. The cemetery connected them, to the land and to themselves.

Loving County has two (some said five) isolated graves on ranches. The most recent grave was for Shady Davis, a cowboy dragged to death by his horse in 1912. But no cemetery. Agreeing on a communal spot where everyone might rest together in perpetuity apparently had never even been contemplated. No one I talked to considered it at all remarkable; I thought it spoke volumes about their sense of place. They would endure poisonous water, harsh weather, and myriad inconveniences because to leave would be to surrender to the other side. Like a rattler that bites even after decapitation, they would fight to the day they died, then be buried far away.

CHAPTER 6

RAINBOW OF THE WEST

BARBARA JONES GREW UP NEAR WACO, TEXAS, AND was living in Dallas when a friend arranged a blind date for her with someone described as "a real hick." He was Skeet Jones, the son of Mary Belle and "Punk" Jones of Loving County, and by this time in his young life he had already been a roughneck in Alaska's oil fields, a rodeo cowboy, an itinerant ranch hand, and an oil worker in other parts of Texas. As they started courting, Skeet brought her several times to Loving County, where he wanted to settle because everywhere else seemed so crowded. Once, while they were driving across a bumpy back road during a visit to the county one summer night, the dust rolling in through the pickup windows opened because of the heat, a new dress she had brought along fell from the rack and dropped onto the dirty floor. "Don't you *ever* ask me to marry you and move out here!" Barbara shouted to her boyfriend.

They married a few years later, and at first lived in Wink, a town of about 1,000 people in a neighboring county. It had ten times more people than all of Loving County, but Barbara considered Wink the end of the earth. "I couldn't believe you had to drive eight miles [to the town of Kermit] to shop," she remembered. Skeet was holding two jobs—as an oil pumper and a ranch hand—and was gone most of the time. Barbara cried every day. Skeet took her to visit friends on a ranch in Loving County, a spot so isolated, she said, "I didn't think places like that existed." On the way back to Wink, she said of the ranch wife: "That poor woman. How could anyone live like that?"

Not long afterward, in 1984, Skeet moved the family to a ranch a few miles from the one they had visited. It was nine washboard miles from Mentone, which meant that the nearest store was now more than 30 miles away. The ranch house sat in a concave depression of treeless and fenceless desert plain and had no telephone. The first time Barbara's parents came to visit, her father was so angry about the conditions in which his daughter was living, he wouldn't speak to Skeet. Over time, Barbara acquired a taste for beef (they slaughtered their own), learned to put up fences and check oil pumps to help Skeet with his job, and became pregnant with their second child.

The week the baby was due, she was outside with her two-year-old son, Matthew, when she heard him scream, saw him freeze in his tracks and start shaking with fear. A huge rattlesnake, up on its tail, its neck puffed out as it made a growling sound, was staring Matthew in the eye. The snake was between Barbara and her son, and the standoff continued until their dog came by, barked, and distracted the rattler long enough for her to grab the boy and take him to the house. Then she dutifully took a shovel and headed back out to the yard to rid the world of that snake. She got the shovel edge down on it, but too far back from the head to kill it. Another standoff. She had the rattler pinned down—it was wriggling angrily, trying to climb the handle. But it also had her pinned down—if she raised the shovel, the snake would get her. So she stood there, bearing down on the shovel handle for half an hour. Her forearms went numb. Fortunately, a hired hand finally came by in time to kill the rattler before Barbara's grip gave out.

This was in the fall—roundup time—and Barbara's job was to cook meals and bring them out to the two dozen cowboys helping Skeet with the work. She went into labor at home, at least nine miles from the closest other adult. Unable to call anyone, she headed down the rough gravel road, driving between contractions to Mentone, her arms still sore from the battle with the snake as they now clenched the steering wheel. In town she located her mother-in-law, who drove her the remaining 75 miles to the Odessa hospital in time to deliver the baby.

A year later, when they kindly invited me to the ranch for supper, Barbara, thirty-four, was pregnant again. She didn't have any major complaints about living where they did, except for the rough and dusty roads—she still hated those roads—but said she'd prefer settling in a town. She missed the people, the conveniences, and the trees of her girlhood home, and she said she considered where she now lived the frontier. Skeet, thirty-nine, didn't consider it frontier, and he said the people, conveniences, and trees of a town made him feel uncomfortably confined. He'd just as soon get even farther away. He had broached the idea with Barbara of moving to a more remote ranch, one that didn't have electricity. "Absolutely not," she answered. "That's unacceptable. No electricity—*that's* where I draw the line."

LILLIAN SCHLISSEL, A HISTORIAN WHO STUDIED THE diaries of women pioneers in the West, concluded that the frontier experience for white settlers was actually two different experiences: one male, one female. The decision to head west in the first place typically was made by the man of the family. (And often, it was only the male who went: California's first census, in 1850, found only 10 percent of the population female.) "Women were part of the journey because their fathers, husbands, and brothers had determined to go," Schlissel wrote in *Women's Diaries of the Westward Journey.* "They went West because there was no way for them *not* to go once the decision was made."

For the men, going to the frontier fulfilled a mythic impulse; it was a grand adventure, at least in conception, a chance for proving oneself and moving up the economic ladder. For the women, more often it was a sad leave-taking, an uncertain enterprise filled with foreboding for the dangers, hardships, and sufferings that awaited their families on the trail.

"The heart has a thousand misgivings & the mind is tortured with anxiety & often as I passed the fresh made graves, I have glanced at the side boards of the waggon, not knowing how soon it might serve as a coffin for some one of us," wrote Lodisa Frizzell as her wagon train cleared South Pass on its way to California during the gold rush.

Hardships didn't end with a journey's completion. Already separated from their homes, many women now found themselves also separated from the acquaintances they had made on the trail. Narcissa Whitman and Eliza Spalding, the first white women to cross the continent, were at missions 120 miles apart. By previous agreement, they communed with each other every morning at nine o'clock by silently thinking of each other and praying for the welfare of their households. Narcissa's prayers weren't answered. Her two-year-old daughter, the first white child born in the Northwest, fell into the Walla Walla River and drowned in 1839. The distraught mother kept the child's body in the house for four days before allowing it to be buried. "She did not begin to change in her appearance much for the first three days," Narcissa wrote her parents in the East. "This proved to be a great comfort to me, for so long as she looked natural and was so sweet and I could caress her, I could not bear to have her out of my sight." As the Whitman mission became a way station for Oregon-bound wagon trains, Narcissa became the mother of occasional trail orphans. In 1844, she and her husband adopted seven children from one family who had lost both parents during the journey west—the father had been killed in a buffalo stampede; the mother, weakened from giving birth en route, had died of fever. The overlanders stopping at the mission also brought disease with them, which wreaked havoc on the Cayuse Indians the Whitmans were trying to convert to Presbyterianism. During a measles outbreak in 1847, when the Cayuse saw the whites surviving while their own people perished, they rebelled against the missionaries, and killed fourteen people, including Narcissa, Marcus, and two of their orphan-adoptees. She and the others were buried in the mission cemetery. Narcissa had to be reburied after wolves dug up her body and gnawed off the flesh on one leg.

Pregnancies and child-rearing were not considered impediments to emigrating—an estimated 20 percent of the women on the overland

trails were in some stage of pregnancy—and once arrived in the frontier, mothers gave birth in the midst of their other duties, often without
the assistance of doctors or female help. "The week Rhoda was born
I cooked for fifteen men who had come to help stack hay," reminisced
Annie Greenwood, a farmer's wife in Idaho. "And in the intervals of
serving them I would creep into my bedroom to sink across my bed.
I was so tired. Through the bedroom window I could see the mare and
the cow, turned out to pasture for weeks because they were going to
have their young."

Life on the vast frontier often required homesteading men to be
gone for long periods—for supplies, for a wage-paying job, for prospecting in the gold fields—while the women were expected to stay with
the isolated land claim. When one Kansas pioneer told his wife he was
going on a trip for firewood, she asked to go with him. She hadn't seen
a tree for two years. He relented, and when they arrived at the distant
river bottom, "she put her arms around a tree and hugged it until she
was hysterical."

Another Kansas frontier incident, recalled by S. N. Hoisington in
Joanna Stratton's *Pioneer Women*, gives a darker view of the solitude.
(Along with the tale of Narcissa Whitman's corpse, it also helps explain
some of the modern opposition from pioneers' descendants to reintroducing wolves in the West.) A neighboring homesteader left his wife
in their sod house while he went to work in the nearest city.

He was gone two or three months, and wrote home once or
twice, but his wife grew very homesick for her folks in the east,
and would come over to our house to visit mother.

Mother tried to cheer her up, but she continued to worry until
she got bed fast with the fever. At night she was frightened
because the wolves would scratch on the door, on the sod and
on the windows, so my mother and I started to sit up nights
with her. I would bring my revolver and ammunition and axe,
and some good-sized clubs. The odor from the sick woman
seemed to attract the wolves, and they grew bolder and bolder.
I would step out, fire off the revolver and they would settle back
for a while when they would start a new attack. I shot one
through the window and I found him lying dead in the morning.
Finally the woman died and mother laid her out. . . . After

that the wolves were more determined than ever to get in. One got his head in between the door casing and was trying to wriggle through, mother stuck him in the head with an axe and killed him. I shot one coming through the window. After that they quieted down for about half an hour, when they came back again. I stepped out and fired at two of them but I only wounded one. Their howling was awful. We fought those wolves five nights in succession, during which time we killed and wounded four gray wolves and two coyotes.

When Mr. Johnson arrived home and found his wife dead and his house badly torn down by wolves, he fainted away. . . . After the funeral he sold out and moved away.

With the balance of the genders tipped so heavily toward the male side in the early western frontier, marriageable women were in short supply. Aside from wanting a companionable mate, some of the men were anxious to marry because various federal land acts allowed wives to file additional homestead claims. A few promoters, particularly in the Pacific Northwest, tried to organize special expeditions of eligible women to satisfy the demands of the market. More often, men used the mails to court family acquaintances back East. In *Old Jules*, her marvelous biography of her father, one of the early homesteaders in Nebraska's Sand Hills, Mari Sandoz recounts how women who had been wooed by letters about vast estates in the West would be met at the train station by their bachelor pen pals. The craftier men would hustle their women to the preacher for a short ceremony in town and then immediately set out by buckboard for their remote soddy, before the bride had any chance to compare what she had read in his flowery letters to the less grand reality and change her mind.

None of this is meant to imply that women were all dragged to the western frontier and kept there against their will. Especially in the latter years of homesteading, a healthy percentage of the claimants were single women or widows, as eager as anyone for the chance to exchange their sweat for their own piece of land. From prospectors to cowhands, speculators to outlaws, none of the frontier occupations was exclusively male. That the West was the first region in the nation to accord women political rights—first in the women's right to vote, first woman justice of the peace, first woman jurors, first woman mayor, first all-female municipal government, first women elected to statewide office, first woman sent to Congress—seems to me no accident of history.

Whatever reason brought them to the frontier, women were partners in the enterprise of settlement. Many of them paid their equity in different coinage than the men—in long periods of isolation left to keep a family and homestead intact during a husband's absence, and in the physical risks of child-bearing far from medical attention. Many of them may have had more misgivings about the cost-benefit ratio of the whole business, viewing it from a different perspective than their male counterparts. But partners they were, and quite often full partners at that.

In popular entertainment, the stereotype of the western frontier woman has been confined to a narrow range. From Miss Kitty at the Longbranch Saloon to the weekly parade of cameo women in "Bonanza," destined to die within the hour once one of the Cartwright men fell in love with them, women have been portrayed as minor—and weaker—characters in a male saga. Often, their role and presence have simply been overlooked and forgotten.

Traveling through the contemporary frontier, I came across the fuller picture, both of the past and the present. Margaret Stafford, flinty and resilient and still homesteading by herself in Garfield County, Montana; Miss Charlie Wilson, fighting to save at least one plot of ground for her people, the Seminole Negro Scouts; the feisty Joseph women of Big Water, Utah; the myriad school teachers bringing education to students in remote one-room cabins and living in tiny trailers next door; and Barbara Jones, as resourceful at living miles from nowhere as she had been reluctant to move there: they all had experiences that paralleled or at least echoed those of earlier frontier women. And through their stories, they all demonstrated that in the sparsely populated places hardship and isolation are still equal-opportunity employers presenting special challenges to overcome. A few more such stories are worth recounting.

IN 1910, WHEN HADIE SEALE WAS SIX YEARS OLD, A Mexican stranger rode up to the family ranch in the stony hills of the Edwards Plateau in southwest Texas and asked for her father, a cattleman and former Texas Ranger who had given the town of Rock-springs its name in 1878 after establishing a herd on Contrary Creek. The father wasn't home, which Hadie's mother told the stranger, using her young daughter as an interpreter. As they were headed back toward the porch, the man raised his rifle and shot the mother through the back. Then he walked over and put another bullet through her head. Little Hadie was standing just a few feet away.

The killer was captured by a posse the next day and brought back to the Rocksprings jail, where he confessed to the murder, saying he shot the woman because she spoke harshly to him. That night, a mob of a hundred men stormed the jail, dragged the man south of town, chained him to a tree, and burned him alive. His burial stone in the Rocksprings cemetery says: Antonio Rodrigues, Died Nov. 3, 1910, "Burned at Stake." One local legend of the incident holds that Hadie lit the fire. "I wasn't even there," she told me, appalled at the thought. "A girl of six . . . my *goodness*."

The frontier had some more bitter cards to deal to Hadie's hand. In the spring of 1927, a tornado struck Rocksprings. Large buildings collapsed, entire houses were tossed in the air, pieces of linoleum were scattered with such force they were found spiked on mesquite branches, fires broke out. One father saved his family by tying a rope around everyone and anchoring it to a dirt floor; the house blew away, but they survived. The twister killed 72 of the town's 1,000 residents. If it had arrived a half hour later, when the senior class play was scheduled, most of the population would have perished when the school auditorium's roof fell in. Hadie and her husband were at their ranch south of town, where the wind hardly blew during the storm. When they arrived at the disaster, they found her brother, his wife, and two of his three children among the casualties.

The 1930s were even harder. A 12-inch rain in 1935 raised the West Nueces River 54 feet. Hadie and her family reached higher ground just before the floodwaters lifted their house off its foundation and carried it away. Two years later, a two-year-old daughter died of a heart ailment. Then the bank foreclosed on their ranch—Hadie's husband and five-year-old son herded their livestock 80 miles by horseback to turn them over—and from that time on the family worked other people's land.

I met Hadie the week that the First Baptist Church in Rocksprings had proclaimed "Hadie Day" to acknowledge her volunteer efforts, particularly the free lunches she organized twice a month for elderly people in the area. She didn't consider her life unusually marked by hardship. She had known other people with equal shares. A neighbor of hers, for instance, had been abducted by Indians as an infant—they murdered his mother and threw her body into the bushes in front of him—and then he had been sold to a Mexican woman in exchange for two horses. "He didn't talk about it much," she said, "but he would if you asked him." Hadie, eighty-six, was the same way about the story of her life. You had to ask before she would tell you. The eyes in her gaunt but strong face misted a little when she reached the parts about each death in the family.

"This is my hometown," she said. "I was born here and I'm going to die here. A lot of people think it's a . . ." she paused to consider an adjective, ". . . *little* town, but it's my hometown, Rocksprings."

A SIGN ON THE WALL OF THE SALMON RIVER EMER-gency Clinic in Stanley, Idaho, says: "A woman has to do twice as much as a man to be considered half as good—fortunately it isn't difficult." It was placed there by Marie Osborn, a nurse practitioner and the sole medical provider in a mountainous area covering 6,600 square miles. Stanley sits at the base of the aptly named Sawtooth Range, near the headwaters of both the main Salmon River (sometimes called the River of No Return) and its middle fork, and in the midst of a collection of federal wilderness and recreational areas. Like virtually all towns in the contemporary frontier, Stanley's elevation (6,260) exceeds its population (about 200). But from Memorial Day to the end of the fall hunting season, a million and a half people come to the region to raft and fish the rivers, hike the mountains, hunt the elk, and gawk at the breath-taking scenery. A certain portion of them end up at Marie's clinic.

She was born in Indiana, eventually settled in Boise when her husband's company transferred him there, and started vacationing in the Stanley area. When four teenagers were hurt in an accident in the early 1970s and it took two and a half hours for an ambulance to arrive, she began lobbying for better medical care, went back to school for her nursing degree, and opened the clinic in 1972. Originally, it was to be open only in the summers, but after the first year the community asked her to stay year-round, an invitation she accepted and which led to the breakup of her marriage.

Her practice ranges from primary care for the residents to emergencies for the tourist hordes. "We go through a lot of sutures," she said, "a lot of fish hooks in arms and legs. In the early seventies, when Stanley had three bars, I used to stay open for an hour after the bars closed to sew up hippies who got clipped by cowboys. After awhile they all had the same length of hair." The ambulance and volunteer EMTs get dispatched about thirty times a year, for heart attacks and injuries from climbing, skiing, logging, snowmobiling, and car accidents; the nearest doctors and hospitals are in Sun Valley and Salmon, respectively 61 and 117 miles in either direction along mountain roads. Sunday nights in the summer, when tourists arrive and prepare for week-long raft trips and wilderness pack trips, she usually gets called in because hers is the only pharmacy in the region. "The floaters realize they forgot their birth control pills, insulin, or medication," she said. "They realize they're in the boonies and it becomes an emergency, especially the birth control pills."

Having been initially attracted to Stanley for its scenery and solitude, Marie found herself burning out from working seventy-five hours a week. When we met in late 1990, a second nurse practitioner's position had been approved to share the load. After eighteen years as the frontline dispenser of medicine in an area not much smaller than New Jersey, she was looking forward to the help. "I'd like to hike into some lakes I haven't hiked into, before I'm too old to do it," she said.

The number of tourists is increasing each year, requiring more medical help. And winter business has been on the rise as well, because of more mobility, she said: "People go to Boise to shop, and bring back the flu." But Marie doesn't foresee Stanley's resident population enlarging much in the future.

"It's a harsh place to live, especially in the winter," she said. "It really feels like a frontier in the wintertime. The women who stay here are unique."

UNLIKE ITS PREDECESSOR A CENTURY AGO, THE CONtemporary frontier is no longer lopsidedly male. Montana in 1890 had twice as many men as women, and most of the other frontier areas in the West had what the Census Bureau called "excess" males of more than 20 percent. Even Utah, which was to outlaw polygamy that year, was 53.13 percent male in 1890. The nation as a whole was split 51.21 percent male, 48.79 percent female—the "excess" female in the Northeast and Southeast counterbalanced the West's disproportion of men. Today, the West is 49.9 percent male, compared to a national percentage of 48.7.

Nonetheless, one of the many practical repercussions of living where people are sprinkled over the landscape as lightly as desert rain is that finding a suitable mate can still be logistically difficult. The main difference is that it now affects both sexes.

In Valentine, Texas, population about 300, where the tiny post office does a land-office business every February from people all over the world who want their Valentine's cards postmarked with the local stamp, the high school serving the area had four seniors and four juniors in 1990. The seniors were all girls; the juniors were all boys. It made dating difficult. The school had even dropped its annual Valentine's dance and naming of a queen. In another west Texas county I met a twenty-four-year-old woman, tall, pretty, a former Miss Texas Rodeo, who said she hadn't had a date from within her county in years. She knew virtually all of the local men in her age group and they were married; the county was the size of Rhode Island. A rancher's wife in western Nebraska told me about a friend of hers, a young divorcee running her own ranch. "I don't know how she's going to meet someone," the friend said, worriedly, "unless it's at a bull sale."

Men face the same predicament. Jonay Ward of Quemado, New Mexico, a tiny crossroads town near the Arizona border in Catron County (2,563 people, 0.4 per square mile) solved his the old-fashioned way: he got her through the mail.

Jonay is an urban refugee from California who in the early 1970s "got tired of the rat race, the smog, and the people. I also wanted to get away from the dope scene. This was kind of a new life, a new start for me. I wanted to prove myself, that I could do it, be self-sufficient." He bought 30 acres for $500, felled trees to build a small cabin, raised his own chickens, pigs, cows, and vegetables for food, cut his long hair, took off his earrings, and generally struggled to survive. "It's a neat kind of country," he said of his surroundings, "if a person wants to live that kind of life, go through those kind of hardships, and work their way up." After a few years of this, his first wife left and returned to California.

In 1976, Jonay took out a personal ad in *Mother Earth News*, saying he lived in a cabin in the mountains of New Mexico and was looking for a permanent partner to share it with him. He hoped to get a few responses. He got 120, all from city women. After responding to them all ("I appreciated their letters"), he narrowed the list of possibilities down to about ten, then four. Three of the "finalists" came out for a visit, which narrowed things a little more. The fourth, a divorcee with a small son from Decatur, Illinois, a city of about 100,000 people, was Audrey, who said Jonay's was the only ad she answered, on a dare from one of her friends.

Audrey had never been west of the Mississippi River, and her job at the time didn't allow her to make an on-site inspection. They courted by letter and telephone for three months, until Jonay flew east to meet her in person. They got married during his visit. When school was out that spring, Jonay flew back to Illinois, loaded up his new wife and son and their possessions in a U-Haul truck, and brought them home. They arrived at two o'clock in the morning. The three-room cabin wasn't big enough for her furniture ("He built me some sheds in a real hurry," Audrey said; later he added eight rooms) and the next morning, with her first look at her new environment by daylight, Audrey's first question was "Where's all the people?"

"It was a big culture shock," she remembered. "I missed my family and friends. I didn't like the isolation, the vastness. I was afraid of the chickens, I was afraid of the dark, I was afraid of everything. I missed the shopping, just for the shopping. I would drive to Springerville [population 1,500 and 50 miles away in Arizona] every day just to get a Coke. It took me a good four years to get used to it. My son adapted better than I did."

Time and the frontier have changed both Jonay and Audrey. Jonay has transformed from a countercultural back-to-the-lander to Quemado's main entrepreneur. He runs a trash service and septic service, sells firewood, has a trailer park and three rental houses in town, and operates the only bar within a 50-mile radius. "I'm trying to earn myself an income for when I retire," he said. "I like to work. That's one of the things I like to do—that's *all* I do. I'm happy. I've never had it so good."

Audrey helps him in his various business enterprises. She said she was happy, too. "I don't know if you'd call it fate, or what," she said of the unusual circumstances that brought her to Quemado. "I just knew immediately Jonay was the right one for me—someone I wanted to spend the rest of my life with."

I asked whether she would have married Jonay and made the move if she had visited the area first.

"No," she said immediately. Then she smiled and laughed as she shook her head. "No. No." Jonay, listening while he tended bar, smiled and laughed along with her.

IN A RETIREMENT VILLAGE NEAR BIG BEND NATIONAL Park in southwest Texas, the brides who had gone West were not so sanguine. As in several other parts of the contemporary frontier, much of the in-migration to this part of Texas has been spurred by people seeking low land prices, a change of scenery, and mild winters while they spend their latter years living on a fixed income. Call them silver-haired pioneers—a far cry from their nineteenth-century counterparts, who more often were young people for whom the frontier represented a place of economic opportunity in which to *start* their lives. What they shared in common was a desire for cheap land and, at least within the group I spent a morning with, a decided split between the sexes on whether moving to a remote area had been a good idea.

It was a Sunday morning when I met the retirees in a café outside the boundaries of the park—four couples who had vacationed in Big Bend a number of times before deciding to move in permanently once the men no longer had jobs tying them to their homes in the East. The development where they now live is not so much a retirement village; it is a former ranch split into parcels of two to five acres of rock and cactus, with winding gravel roads bulldozed seemingly haphazardly across the landscape. There are some gas stations, a few cafés and convenience stores—and at least two hairdressers—in the immediate area. Big Bend National Park, one of the nation's least-known yet most spectacularly scenic parks, where the Rio Grande curls as it slices through majestic canyons, is just a few miles away. Alpine, Texas, the closest town, is 80 miles north. The men and women were sitting at separate tables. I sat with the women first.

"*They* wanted to get away from the noise of their jobs," said one woman from New York, motioning with her head toward the men's table. "*They* like the outdoors, the quiet. *They* like all the space and the lack of people. But there has to be more than getting up each morning and looking at that mountain." She and her husband go to Alpine about once a month to shop, she said, "and it seems like we're always buying *tires*."

A woman from New Jersey said that when she and her husband moved to the area about sixteen years ago, they were living in a trailer with a house under construction when her husband had a heart attack. Their phone, one of the few in the area at the time, saved his life. She called the local EMTs, who met her with an ambulance at the highway, about four miles away, and revived him on the way to the closest doctor and hospital, in Alpine.

"You're lucky," she said to the woman next to her, who lives in a mobile home. "You didn't build a house. Any time you want you can . . ."

"Inflate the tires and leave," the other answered, as if the notion is an everyday part of her life.

"I wish we had *never* built that house," the New Jersey woman said. "Now we can never sell it and get our money out of it. And what is *he* doin'? He keeps addin' on, addin' on. First a porch, then a three-car garage. Now he wants a tool shed. It's costing money we'll never get back."

The fourth woman, originally from Maryland, described what sounded like a quasi–nervous breakdown from the isolation. Her husband had finally bought a house for her in Alpine, where they now spend part of the year. "God has some challenges for me, and I haven't found them here," she said. "This has been a learning experience, don't get me wrong, but I need something more. It's a lonely country, a harsh country."

When I moved over to the men's table, they all said their only regret was that they had to wait until they retired to move west.

MARGARET HAWKINS DOESN'T CONSIDER HERSELF A feminist, but "bein' a woman never kept me from doin' what I wanted to do." Here's what she does because it's what she wants to do:

She runs a cattle ranch in Arthur County, Nebraska (population 462; 0.7 people per square mile), that covers 16,000 acres of the Sand Hills. The ranch has some machinery—when we met, Margaret was getting ready to relieve her daughter, disking a field with a seventeen-year-old tractor; her son was working a different part of the ranch—but much of the labor is still done with horses. Not just riding horses to check on the cattle herd, but using a team and wagon to spread feed during the winter. "I spend two to ten hours a day on or behind a horse," she said. "If you're ridin' a'horseback, you're in good shape. It's good for ya'." One advantage of horses over tractors for getting a wagon of feed to a herd of cattle in a bitter Sand Hills winter, she said, is that "a horse will always start when it's thirty below."

Besides her cattle operation and Belgian workhorses, she has sixty quarter horses, which she breeds and trains. Her grandfather and father had both raised horses. "I grew up handling horses," she said. "I even handled stallions, which at the time shocked a lot of women in the area."

Petite but with strong and rough hands that are disproportionately large, Margaret constantly shifts her shoulders while she sits and talks, like an athlete trying to stay limber. She speaks with the blunt directness (and occasional profanities) of a cow boss used to giving commands and having his opinions given full consideration. Her husband, Virgil, had been thirty-five years older than Margaret; when they married, she said, it was "the scandal of the county." She has been in charge since his death in 1977. "It never bothered me to know that I'd have to raise children and run the ranch by myself," she said. She is proud of having kept the ranch going during one of the toughest decades for agriculture since the Depression and credits her success to sticking with the old-time practices Virgil and some of his neighbors had inculcated in her. "Those *progressive* farmers are always the first to do this and that," she scoffed. "I don't hear much about those boys anymore."

Her love of the land is as mystical as it is fierce. "I don't think I ever ride a day that I don't see and enjoy the beauty of the Sand Hills," she said. "Riding in the hills there's no doubt about there being a higher power. It's there before your eyes. It gives you a peace, a tranquility. They're God's gift."

She is considering some improvements to her home, which sits in a broad valley, eight miles from the highway, and is a hybrid of old homestead dwellings that Virgil had hauled from other locations and joined together. In the Sand Hills, where there is no such thing as an accidental tree, the cottonwoods and elms that shelter the yard had been brought and transplanted from the Platte River, 40 miles away. The home and setting are cozy and comfortable, but Margaret thinks they could stand a little sprucing up. "The yard doesn't contribute to payin' for the ranch, so it's always a low priority," she said.

She has a small plaque with a favorite quotation on it, resting on the kitchen counter. (She eats beef for every meal, she said. "It keeps ya' goin'.") The plaque says: "Whether you think you can or you think you can't—you're right." Another dimension of her personality is encapsulated in something she told me: "Stick-to-it-ness and bullheadedness are the very same quality—it just depends on whether you're doin' what people think you're supposed to do."

She and her daughter, Virgilene, travel and compete in the Women's Professional Rodeo Association in barrel racing. Margaret has a big twin-axle, two-ton truck that she drives to pull their horse trailer, which has extra room in it for living quarters. She showed me the truck and talked about its mechanical features in detailed terms I couldn't understand. Margaret said she "rodeoes" for the fun of it, although the travels and contacts help her sell quarter horses and on the road she always pays close attention to how the cattle in other areas are doing, to help her make marketing decisions on her own cattle. At the time of my visit, Virgilene was having an off year on the circuit because her horse was green, but Margaret was in the midst of one of her best seasons. A few weeks earlier, she had taken first place at the Chadron rodeo.

Margaret Hawkins is sixty-two.

THE POPULARIZED VERSION OF THE OLD FRONTIER has tended to be portrayed in much the same colors as Robert Porter's census map of 1890: overwhelmingly white, with a few reddish splotches. White, red, brown, black, yellow, and every possible shade from their combinations were the truer colors of the people—most of whom, with the exception of the Indians who were already there, had been drawn to the western frontier in pursuit of gold, silver, green grass, and greenbacks.

The annual fur trappers' rendezvous on the Green River in the 1830s were multihued, international affairs. A participant might hear not only a wide variety of Indian languages spoken, but also French, Russian, and dialects of English ranging from Scots to British to Pidgin to American. Perhaps he might meet one of the more famous mountain men, Jim Beckwourth, son of a black slave. Maybe he would hear the story from 1819 of three native islanders from Hawaii, called Owyhee at the time, who were dispatched by the North West Company to trade for furs with the Bannock and Shoshone Indians and disappeared somewhere in the mountains of what is now southwestern Idaho. (In their memory, Peter Skene Ogden named the principal river in the area for them; Owyhee County, Idaho [population 8,392; 1.1 people per square mile], an arid domain through which the Owyhee River courses, is thus the namesake of a tropical paradise.) The rendezvous system itself had been the brainchild of Manuel Lisa, a Spaniard from St. Louis.

"There are representatives from almost every race on the globe residing on the Base Ridge, and we doubt if another town in the United States can show such a cosmopolitan community," wrote a local reporter in Eureka, Nevada, in 1878, long before it became the Loneliest Town. "For a variety of nationalities, we believe that Eureka is entitled to the palm. We were particularly impressed with this fact yesterday, by noticing a group standing in front of a saloon on North Main Street. There was a native from Madagascar, an East Indian, a Spaniard, an Italian, a Chilean, and a man born on the Island of Tahiti. In close proximity was a group of Shoshones playing cards, and a Chinaman watching the game. English, French, Scotch, Irish, Slavonians, and Negroes passed during the time our attention was attracted . . . Americans were sadly in the minority."

Cosmopolitan, Eureka certainly was—in 1880 three-quarters of the adults were foreign born—but the mixture was not always as happy as the colorful Main Street vignette suggested. Ethnic divisions were sharply defined: the Welsh and Cornish were prized for their skills at deep-shaft mining, the Chinese were uniformly despised and relegated to the most menial jobs and lowest wages, and the Italians had the dirty job of providing the charcoal for the voracious ore furnaces. With nine cemeteries, Eureka preserved the distinctions even into the grave. When the Italian charcoal burners went on strike in 1879, demanding at least thirty cents a bushel, the militia was called in to prevent the work action from shutting down the smelters. After a confrontation that killed six Italians and wounded ten more, the charcoal burners went back to work. The mining companies quickly lowered the price to twenty-six cents per bushel.

Blacks were no strangers to the West. Esteban the Moor had been with Cabeza de Vaca when the Spaniard wandered across the Southwest in 1528, hopelessly lost but bringing back wild tales of the cities of gold. The Lewis and Clark expedition of 1804–1806, the United States' first probe across the continent, counted among its members Clark's slave, York, dubbed "Big Medicine" by the fascinated tribes who encountered him. There was Beckwourth the mountain man, and the Seminole Negro Scouts. Black troopers of the Ninth Cavalry served in every part of the West during the Indian conflicts that followed the Civil War; the Indians they fought called them "Buffalo Soldiers" because of the resemblance between their dark curly hair and that of the bison. The troopers were involved in both the Lincoln County and Johnson County cattle wars—surrounding but not capturing Billy the Kid in New Mexico, coming to the rescue of the beleaguered regulators in Wyoming. Of the cowboys who accompanied cattle herds north during the era of the cattle drives, an estimated one-third of them were blacks and Hispanics. Black homesteaders called Exodusters settled parts of the Plains and founded their own towns, among them Brownlee, Nebraska, in Cherry County.

A good portion of the people rushing into California following the gold strike at Sutter's Mill were from the true East: China. By the 1850s, at least 20,000 Chinese had entered the country, virtually all of them males who left their wives and families behind in their homeland and were expected to return once they had made their fortunes. They followed one ore discovery after another across the West, helped build the Central Pacific Railroad in the 1860s, and when they were laid off after the driving of the golden spike, went back to mining. By 1870, half of the miners in Idaho Territory were Chinese; a census of miners in eastern Oregon in 1879 listed 960 whites and 2,468 Chinese. Tuscarora, Nevada, now a ghost town with eight white residents, had a population of 5,000 in 1878, including the second-largest concentration of Chinese in the West.

One hundred years later, the contemporary frontier more closely conforms to the historically unfaithful stereotype of the old frontier than did the original version.

Aside from the descendants of the Seminole Negro Scouts, I didn't meet—or even see—any Afro-Americans in the sparsely settled counties. The only people from the other side of the Pacific I saw or heard of were some Japanese businessmen who own a buffalo ranch and golf resort in Saguache County, Colorado; a young Japanese executive learning how to be a cowboy at a cattle operation his company had bought in Beaverhead County, Montana; a sheepherder in Sublette County, Wyoming, who had been recruited from Mongolia under a special temporary visa because of a sheepherder and cowboy labor shortage (some South and Central American cowboys had been brought into Wyoming under the same plan); and a Korean merchant in Presidio, Texas. I stayed at a couple of motels owned by India Indians. In several counties, in New Mexico, southwest Texas, and parts of Colorado, there were sizable Hispanic populations, but not in the other parts of the contemporary frontier.

The Refuge of World Truths in Crestone-Baca, Colorado, is a kind of rendezvous of religions, although the preponderance of people there, even if they have adopted Hindu or Buddhist or native Indian names, are white Americans. The truly international modern rendezvous of the frontier West, attracting foreign tourists rather than mountain men, now convenes in the more scenic areas or at spots associated with the "Wild West." Guidebooks at Death Valley National Monument, for instance, are offered under titles like "Das Todestal" and "De La Vallée De La Mort." Billy the Kid, as famous outside the nation's borders as within them, draws people from around the world to his grave-shrine. At a dude ranch in Sweet Grass County, Montana, the owner told me he gets frequent requests from Old West clubs in Germany, who want to block out several weeks at a time and offer to bring extra costumes for the ranch's employees to ensure "authenticity."

On the whole, however, in places with fewer than two people per square mile, the multiracial, cosmopolitan flavor of the earlier frontier has been blanched over the course of a century. Many of the residents I met were second-generation Americans—descendants of northern

Europeans mostly, some Basque enclaves in Nevada and Wyoming—but to call my journey through the contemporary frontier a tour of ethnic America would be as misleading as to contend that those who participated in the saga of the nineteenth-century West all looked like John Wayne.

Even the West's original inhabitants are no longer much in evidence in these counties.

An estimated 10 million Indians lived in North America when Columbus arrived in 1492 and contact with whites began in earnest. But European diseases, against which Indians had no immunity, dramatically reduced their numbers. Far in advance of the white settlers and the armies sent on their behalf, epidemics of smallpox, measles, influenza, and other sicknesses wreaked a continent-wide cataclysm on the indigenous tribes. Even in the Far West, the last place to be inundated by the wave of white migration, some tribes had lost 90 percent of their population to such epidemics before the first wagon trains left Independence, Missouri, for Oregon.

In 1846, the Cheyenne chief Yellow Wolf arrived with his band at Bent's Fort in southern Colorado as parts of the U.S. Army were encamped there on the way to war against Mexico. Seeing the thousands of troops, with their supply wagons and 20,000 horses, mules, and oxen, some tribe members remarked that they had never before believed so many white people existed. An officer who interviewed Yellow Wolf recorded that the chief "frequently talks of the diminishing numbers of his people, and the decrease of the once abundant buffalo. He says that in a few years they will become extinct; and unless the Indians wish to pass away also, they will have to adopt the habits of the white people." Accordingly, Yellow Wolf became one of the Cheyenne "peace chiefs." In 1864, at age eighty-five, he was killed by Chivington's men in the attack on the peaceful village at Sand Creek.

Farther north, during the migrations of the Mormons, gold-bound forty-niners, and Oregon homesteaders along the Platte River, one Plains chief supposedly suggested that his people move to the East, since all the whites seemed to have left it.

In 1850, an estimated 360,000 Indians lived in the American West, including 84,000 who had earlier been removed from the Southeast to Indian Territory in what is now Oklahoma. The nation's white population at the time was more than 20 million. Ten years later, 1.4 million whites lived in the West. The 1890 census recorded 62,622,250 residents of the United States, 8.5 million of them westerners; the total Indian population was 325,464. A century later, the United States has 250 million inhabitants, 1.96 million of them Indians.

Of the 132 contemporary frontier counties, 17 have an Indian reservation or part of a reservation within their boundaries. (The reservations total 14; several of them cross county boundaries.) Many Native Americans, of course, live elsewhere, and therefore the absence of a reservation in a county doesn't necessarily mean the population is without Indians. But other than in major cities, of which the contemporary frontier has none, the main concentrations of Indians are found on reservations. And most reservations lie in counties with more than two people per square mile. The very act of creating a reservation, unless its boundaries are immense, increases the population density.

Indians outnumber whites in only two of the counties I visited: Ziebach County, South Dakota, covered from border to border by part of the Cheyenne River Sioux reservation, and San Juan County, Utah, where the northern extension of the Navajo reservation comprises about a quarter of the county.

In the course of a hundred years, the colors of Robert Porter's population-density map have assumed prophetic significance. White, with a few splotches of red, are now the dominant colors of the frontier.

WHEN I ARRIVED, AN INDIAN UPRISING WAS UNDER-way in San Juan County. The tensions from it had people on edge in the vast southeastern corner of Utah. But the weapons were ballots, not bullets; the federal government was on the scene, not with an all-male cavalry but with a woman mediator; and the only clothing indicating that a battle was raging were not uniforms or war costumes but T-shirts that said, *"Niha whol zhiizh."* For the first time in American history, an all-Indian slate of candidates was trying to unseat a white-dominated county government. *"Niha whol zhiizh"* is Navajo for "It's our turn."

Mark Maryboy, thirty-four, tall, slender, soft-spoken, was leading the political charge. He and his seven siblings had been raised in a hogan, a round-walled dwelling with a diameter of about 14 feet, on a high mesa south of Bluff. Like most of the other families in the area, his had lived without electricity or running water or telephone, using wood for heat and cooking. After he ran away from an Indian boarding school in second grade, Maryboy's parents had enrolled him in the Bluff elementary school, where he was the first Navajo to attend. Reaching the school had been a two-hour, five-mile walk each way, along the top of the sage-covered mesa, down a steep gully to the San Juan River valley, and across a rickety foot bridge that dangled over the river's roiling waters.

"My dad kept impressing on us that education was important," he said. "He wanted me to have a better life by going to college." His father, a uranium miner, had died of lung cancer caused, Maryboy believed, by conditions in the mines. A younger brother, with whom he had dreamed of joining the professional rodeo circuit, was killed in his teens in a drunk-driving accident. When Mark left for college in Salt Lake City, it was his first time out of San Juan County. Having seen firsthand the crippling conditions of the reservation—poverty, lack of modern amenities, poor health, alcoholism—he didn't plan on returning.

After graduation he went to work for Kmart, rising to become a district manager as he moved from store to store, state to state. "I'd always thought there were certain things only white people do," he remembered. "Here I was training new employees and making announcements on the public-address system." He was succeeding, making good money, but feeling increasingly that this wasn't what he was meant to do.

In 1980 he decided to return to his people, taking a job with the Utah Navajo Development Corporation, where he worked to win grants for small housing projects, water lines, educational programs, and other improvements. Six years later, after a federal lawsuit forced San Juan County to create a commissioner's district comprised predominantly of Navajos, he ran for the seat and became the state's first Indian elected official. The all-Indian slate of candidates in 1990 (running as Democrats for sheriff, assessor, clerk, treasurer, and recorder, with Mark also seeking re-election) was, he believed, the next logical step in asserting Navajo rights and trying to improve conditions.

Impoverished as the local Indians are, part of the land they inhabit, called the Aneth section, is one of the nation's top-producing oil and gas fields, generating millions of dollars a year in taxes and royalties.

Some of the money flows to tribal coffers in distant Window Rock, Arizona, the scandal-plagued governmental seat of the huge Navajo reservation, which covers 24,000 square miles of Arizona and New Mexico and a smaller slice of Utah. San Juan County and the state of Utah also receive sizable oil revenues from the Aneth fields. The problem for the Utah Navajos is that little of the oil money returns to its source.

"This is no-man's-land," Maryboy said. Oil money had financed many projects in the Arizona reservation and had been used to build roads, water pipelines, even an airport that benefited white residents of San Juan County. Meanwhile, more than 75 percent of Utah Navajo families live without running water; fewer than 5 percent have dwellings with indoor toilets, running water, electricity, and telephones.

Comprising only 3 percent of the 200,000 Navajos on the larger reservation, the Utah tribal members have little voice in decisions at Window Rock. The sense of separation is accentuated by a fact of Navajo history. In 1864, Kit Carson and the U.S. Army subjugated the tribe by entering its stronghold in Canyon de Chelly in Arizona. Rather than engaging the Navajo in battles, Carson burned their crops and dwellings, cut down their fruit orchards, killed their livestock, and waited for them to surrender. Then he led them on the Long Walk to incarceration at Bosque Redondo near Fort Sumner, New Mexico. The Utah Navajos, however, are descendants of a band who never surrendered, never were herded from their homeland, and never signed the peace treaty that allowed the others to return. They are proud of that history, but feel it contributes to the neglect they now suffer at the hands of the main reservation.

Within San Juan County, their complaints traditionally have been ignored and dismissed as someone else's responsibility. The difference is that Navajos constitute a majority of San Juan County's population (12,621 people, 1.6 per square mile), and in 1990 some of them decided it was time to put their numbers to work.

Mounting an organized campaign was a complicated task. Although Navajos outnumber whites in the county, the voting lists don't reflect it because many Navajos aren't registered. "Until a few years ago, I didn't even know we had the right to vote if we lived on the reservation," said Ruby Nakai, a college-educated Cherokee who had married into a Navajo family and was the candidate for county clerk. A registration drive had been going on for a year, but making slow progress. Radio commercials in Navajo—many of the older tribal members don't speak English—tried to encourage people to register, and volunteers were traveling across the red-rock mesas and canyons to individual hogans to sign up voters. Navajo being an oral rather than written language further complicated matters. One flyer being passed out simply showed a symbol of a Democratic ballot being put in a voting box and pictures of a water spigot, a modern house, a road-construction crew, and a fist holding dollar bills, suggesting that a vote for the ticket would help bring running water, better housing and roads, and jobs to the Navajos. Difficulties in establishing correct names and addresses and ages resulted in the county's rejection of many registration applications.

Indifference, skepticism, and a long tradition of keeping to themselves were additional obstacles. "It's hard to make them believe that the government can change things for them," said Jean Melton, the thirty-seven-year-old campaign manager. "And it's difficult coordinating this campaign. Only two of my candidates have telephones."

The divisions in the campaign were not entirely along racial lines. Factionalism within Indian reservations is often more pronounced than in Loving County, Texas, and the Navajos of San Juan County were far from monolithic in supporting the all-Indian slate. Nor did every white resident automatically support the county's established power structure. Several told me they planned to vote for Maryboy's ticket.

In these cross-cultural alliances, perhaps the most striking was Jean Melton's, who was commuting constantly from law school in Salt Lake City to help organize the Navajo effort. She is a descendant of some of the county's most prominent white Mormon families. One ancestor, Jens Nielson, had pulled a handcart across the Plains to Utah in 1856, losing a son to illness and part of his foot to frostbite on the trek. Brigham Young had dispatched him to found six Mormon communities all across southern Utah. A leader of the Hole-in-the-Rock wagon train, the arduous expedition across the slick rock and steep canyons of the Colorado Plateau to establish Bluff in 1880, Nielson became bishop of the Bluff ward for a quarter of a century and one of the original three county commissioners. His stone house in Bluff has a historical marker in the yard, and his grave, resting between those of two of his three wives, looks down on the town from a hilltop. One of

Jean's great-grandfathers, a refugee from the Mormon polygamist colonies in Mexico evacuated during Pancho Villa's raids, had helped
found the town of Blanding. He played a pivotal role in the "Posey
War," sometimes called the last Indian uprising in the West, in which
a Ute Indian escaped from the county jail in 1923 and, with some other
Indians, held off an armed posse for several days until he and another
Indian were shot and killed. The local Mormon history of San Juan
County quotes Jean's ancestor as saying, "I can't see how I helped from
hitting the old son of a '————.' He was hanging with his left leg and
lying on the right side of his horse and I was pouring the lead at him."
Her maternal grandparents had what people called the first "mixed
marriage" in the county—not between whites and Indians but between
the two principal Mormon factions, those who traced their lineage to
the Hole-in-the-Rock pioneers and those associated with the group
that arrived later from Mexico. One grandparent took part when white
cattlemen shot Navajo horses grazing on the public domain, a bitter
incident that became part of a Supreme Court case.

In general, however, the battle for power in San Juan County lined
up between white Mormons and red Navajos. Charges of racism and
corruption had been exchanged by both sides. Two Indian candidates
marching in a Fourth of July parade in Blanding said they had been
harassed by angry whites. At a particularly heated County commissioner's meeting earlier in the year, a young Navajo had stood up and
shouted, "You Mormons can't push us around any more. That might
have worked with our parents, but we're a new generation." Mark
Maryboy said he had received death threats he considered serious
enough to report them to the FBI. The federal Justice Department had
sent Silke Hansen, a mediator from its Denver office, to try to lessen
the acrimony. Virtually everywhere I went—from night meetings in
hogans lit by kerosene lanterns to offices in the courthouse, from cafés
to street corners—I kept running into Hansen as she talked with different factions. She spoke with a heavy Danish accent; without in-
quiring further, you might have thought she had been sent by the U.N.

White officials complained that their opponents were blaming them
for conditions over which the county had no responsibility and said
they resented being portrayed as racists. "We're just an easy target
because we're close to home and they [the Navajos] can vote us out,"
said Gail Johnson, the county clerk. "You can't get an objective view

of the county right now from anyone." Other residents said that since Navajos on the reservation don't pay property taxes they shouldn't be eligible for county office. Pointing to the financial scandals wracking the tribal government in Window Rock, some said that if the Indians took over the reins of the county the same thing would happen and many white residents would move out.

Mark and his group (who were also supporting a slate of reform candidates in tribal elections) contended that even if the county government doesn't have direct jurisdiction over the reservation within its borders, it could play a leading role in lobbying Window Rock and the federal agencies for assistance. They also believed that the county benefits financially from the reservation without providing much in return. As proof, they cited a study showing that over a ten-year period the reservation's Aneth oil field had generated $28 million in revenue to the county, of which only $7 million had been spent on services to the reservation; the county school district had received $87 million from reservation oil and entitlement programs, but budgeted $69 million for schools serving the reservation; and the state got $20 million in oil taxes without directing any of it back to the reservation.

"For too long," Maryboy said in a campaign speech, "San Juan County government has meant taking care of 40 percent of the population who live on 20 percent of the land open to occupancy, and who provide less than 5 percent of the county's revenue through property tax, while demanding 95 percent of the county's budget to maintain their society. The power grab has been translated into thousands of Navajos living without running water or electricity in unjustifiable poverty."

BESIDES BEING UTAH'S LARGEST COUNTY, ITS RICHest in oil and uranium deposits, and its poorest in per capita income, San Juan County is arguably also the state's most scenically diverse and spectacular. Within its 7,725 square miles (about the size of Massachusetts) are Canyonlands National Park, Lake Powell and the Glen Canyon National Recreation Area, and three national monuments— Rainbow Bridge, one of the "Seven Natural Wonders of the World"; Natural Bridges, the world's largest collection of eroded stone arches; and Hovenweep, a group of Anasazi ruins. The wild San Juan and

Colorado rivers, ochre- and rust-colored from the soft sandstone they carry, cut through the canyons before pooling into huge, man-made Lake Powell. The Manti-LaSal National Forest, snow-capped peaks with green meadows and alpine lakes, forms a mountain oasis in the middle. Such are San Juan County's neck-turning wonders that a Rand McNally map designates virtually all of its paved roads as "scenic."

But its best-known natural attraction is Monument Valley, a series of massive red buttes and pinnacles rising from a broad desert floor that straddles the Utah-Arizona border. Whether they've ever been west of the Mississippi River (or the Hudson or the Atlantic, for that matter), most people are familiar with Monument Valley. Since 1939, when director John Ford used it as the location for his movie *Stagecoach*, it has become more or less the visual shorthand image to express the words "West" and "frontier" to the world. A lot of celluloid cavalry charges have thundered across its dusty plain to rescue wagon trains surrounded by celluloid Indian war parties. A replica of Tombstone was once reconstructed there so that a celluloid Wyatt Earp could have his shoot-out at the O.K. Corral with the valley's signature buttes as a backdrop. More recently, *Young Guns II* placed a celluloid Billy the Kid and his gang in the valley, far from Lincoln County, and Michael Fox traveled through time in *Back to the Future III* for a celluloid taste of the Old West.

Turn on a television set for a week or browse through a collection of magazines and it's virtually impossible not to see Monument Valley in some advertisement: for Estée Lauder perfume, Guinness beer, IBM typewriters, new clothing fashions, and almost any make of automobile, including a new model called the Navajo. "Advertisers," the historian Walter Prescott Webb wrote in 1951, "have a very severe case of frontieritis," an affliction that obviously hasn't abated in forty years.

Popularized western history and commercialized fascination with the western frontier are selective enterprises—two truths starkly revealed by a tour of Monument Valley. Symbols and myths take on a life of their own. A lot of reality gets left out in the process. The actual Indian conflicts in the vicinity were Kit Carson's scorched-earth sweep through Canyon de Chelly in 1864, the Posey War of 1923, and the election battle of 1990—none of them likely to be appearing as a movie anytime soon in a theater near you. And advertisers may love Monument Valley as the backdrop most likely to elicit high-ticket consumer spending. But making the commercial requires a careful use of camera angles, because the inspiring scenery also includes Americans living in the most abject poverty.

I SPENT MOST OF A WEEK IN SAN JUAN COUNTY, MUCH of it following Mark Maryboy, whose quiet voice and reticent demeanor softened but could not hide the volcanic intensity he brought to his mission. Because of the redistricting, his commission seat was safe; the other Indian candidates, running for county-wide positions were long shots, he believed. (He was right. A month later, he was re-elected and the others were defeated.)

"A lot of our people are still afraid it's not yet our time," he confided. "The white people think we'll make the county go broke. But their main problem is that Indians will become self-reliant. They enjoy patronizing us. We're just symbols they can use to bring in tourists. The sad thing is they've done a good job subduing us, making us feel incapable. But I don't believe that. I think about the immigrants who came to this country poverty-stricken. I really admire them because they've made it in this nation. Hell, if they can do it, we can do it. Navajos are intelligent and competitive. The hardest thing actually is obstacles from our own people. You have to always show that it can be done. That's a constant obstacle, showing that we can do things for ourselves."

At a county commissioners' meeting I attended, the mood was the opposite of confrontational. The two white commissioners announced they had arranged for a trip to Window Rock to meet with tribal authorities about conditions on the Utah portion of the reservation; they approved an advance of travel money for some Navajos to meet with federal officials in Denver and decided that the commission should go along; when officials from the local hospital appeared for approval of more funds, the commissioners directed them to investigate whether inequities existed between Indian health services in Arizona and Utah; they sternly lectured a state game official about unreasonably enforcing hunting laws on Navajos who didn't have proper documentation with them. Whatever prompted it—the upcoming election, Maryboy's efforts over the previous four years, the presence of Silke Hansen, the federal mediator in the audience—by all accounts this was a new attitude in the courthouse.

Hoping to instill some self-confidence in his people and provide an economic boost for the southern part of the county, Mark had convinced the commission to provide funds for a Utah Navajo fair in Bluff. There were food booths, a carnival midway, a rodeo, a mud bog (specialized trucks on oversized tires drive through a man-made swamp in a race against the clock), a parade, traditional Indian dance contests, and a powwow. Several thousand people attended during the two days, including the white candidates who could no longer take re-election for granted. Mark entered the bareback bronc contest, riding the horse High and Dry to victory. "A lot of people were hoping I'd get thrown," he said after the ride. "I guess I disappointed them." Two of his brothers, who had won the Indian mud bog championship in New Mexico earlier in the summer, were defeated by a white bogger driving a truck called "Custer's Revenge."

One afternoon we drove around the part of the reservation where Mark had grown up. At the foot bridge over the San Juan, I walked halfway across, looked down into the swirling red waters and up at the flashes of lightning from an approaching storm, and beat a hasty retreat back to the shore. The light rain quickly turned the dirt roads into greasy, rutted slicks that pulled the *Conestoga* in whatever capricious direction they chose; I felt as if I had been forcibly entered in a mud bog in which victory was defined as reaching pavement, regardless of how long it took. We went past remote hogans and ancient cliff dwellings and reached the site of Mark's boyhood home: a few transplanted cottonwoods on a barren mesa, the remnants of a cinder-block house his father had been building when he died, and the round slab where the hogan once stood, a circle inconceivably small for a family of ten.

Back on the pavement, Mark directed me to a cluster of houses he had helped develop with federal grants. By most Americans' standards, it wasn't much: about a dozen tiny homes on two streets off a highway in the desert. But the streets were paved, with electricity poles rising from the curbs and water and sewer pipes underneath—things that ranked as luxuries in this part of the country. Mark's mother lived in one of the houses. The day she moved in, he turned on the lights and opened the tap in the kitchen sink. She stood there for half an hour, crying for joy as she watched the water run.

"I never thought things would ever change," he had said at the family's old homesite. His mother's tears had been proof they could.

CHAPTER 7

EL DESPOBLADO

BETWEEN EL PASO AND THE PECOS RIVER, THE CHI-huahuan desert of northern Mexico considers the idea of the Rio Grande as an international border some sort of laughably pathetic human contrivance. Disregarding the distinction, the desert annexes most of southwest Texas. It is a place of scorched-rock mountains, cactus-covered plains, and sheer canyons, sheeny khaki by the hard light of day, pastel shades of pink and rose at sunset, black as ink at night; of desert plants that jealously hoard their meager supply of moisture for a riotous, rainbow splurge of blooms once a year; of animals like the kangaroo rat, which can survive without drinking because it metabolizes water from the seeds it eats, or the speed-demon roadrunner, which lives off the body fluids of the lizards and rattle-snakes it pecks to death, and the javelina, a wild pig with bristle hair and elongated snout.

It has never been home for many people. The Spanish, who first explored the region in the sixteenth century, found neither gold, silver, good farmland, nor numerous Indians to convert or enslave. In the late 1700s, they established a few forts on the south side of the Rio Grande but soon abandoned them, because of financial difficulties in keeping the remote presidios supplied. Apaches, and later Comanches, used it as a staging ground for raids into Mexico for cattle, food, and hostages. Prior to the Civil War, the U.S. Army built its own forts and imported camels from Egypt in a failed experiment at desert adaptation; most of the camels ended up either as meals for hungry Indians or exhibits in Mexican circuses. American ranchers entered in the late 1800s and overgrazed the fragile environment within a generation. Bandits and bootleggers used the border river and the thinly populated desert as shields from the law through the early decades of this century. Currently, six contiguous Texas counties along the river, covering an area roughly three times the size of New Jersey, have a combined population of 24,996.

Geographers call it the Trans-Pecos area. Tourism promoters, directing attention to the national park at its southern tip, refer to it as the Big Bend region. The only Anglo radio station in the area, in Alpine, says it is "Texas's Last Frontier." But the Spanish had another name for it, as descriptive today as when they coined it four hundred years ago: *El Despoblado*. The place without people.

A WHITE NISSAN 4 × 4 PICKUP TRUCK, A ROLL BAR arching over its cab, a radar detector on its dashboard, a plume of dust trailing its progress, wheeled into Lajitas on the Rio Grande, an ersatz frontier town and resort that features a one-block row of reconstructed false-front businesses, a motel and inn built as a replica of an old army fort, a golf course, and a smattering of vacation homes and condos. The pickup pulled up to a small, restored adobe Spanish mission on a rocky knob overlooking the river and stopped quickly. A short, burly man with a shock of silver hair and bushy mustache hopped out, disappeared briefly in the chapel and then re-emerged, with vestments over his blue jeans, to ring a school bell he was holding. Father Melvin LaFollette, an Episcopal missionary known locally as

Father Mel (or *Padre Mel* to his Hispanic parishioners), was ready to conduct the first of his four services on this last Sunday of the Epiphany season.

"We're missing some of the sheep," he remarked as he surveyed the congregation and began with a reading from Exodus. Two women sat in the pews. Usually, he said later, as we drove in four-wheel drive along a rock-and-dust shortcut to the next gathering, six people attend the early-morning service.

Father Mel's personal road to the border had been as long and bumpy as the one we were now on. Born in Indiana sixty years earlier, he had studied literature and creative writing in college, published poems and short stories in his twenties, taught at universities, married, enrolled in divinity school at Yale in his thirties, and been assigned to Episcopal parishes in wealthy California suburbs. While pastoring and teaching for Chapman College, a "floating unversity" on an old naval vessel that sailed from foreign port to port, he got a "Dear John" letter from his wife; the divorce didn't particularly help his standing with the church hierarchy. In 1984, he volunteered to start a mission on the Rio Grande.

The quest for pagan souls ripe for conversion, like the quest for riches with which it often intertwined, provided one of the earliest rationales for the white cultures that entered the West. After facing disappointment that the fabled, golden Seven Cities of Cibola did not exist, the Spanish conquerors of Mexico (for whom the American West was their *North*) decided the frontier nonetheless was a potential growth market for the church and established their mission-presidio system. Likewise, Protestant denominations in the eastern United States saw the western tribes as savages waiting for the Divine Light and often competed vigorously for franchises. The Cree chief Broken Arm told an observer in 1848: "Mr. Rundell [a missionary] had told him what he preached was the only true road to heaven, and Mr. Hunter had told him the same thing, and so did Mr. Thebo, and as all three had said the other two were wrong, and as he did not know which was right, he thought they ought to call a council among themselves, and then he would go with them all; but until they agreed he would wait." Marcus and Narcissa Whitman, part of a missionary effort that helped touch off the homestead rush to Oregon, went west on the belief that a Nez Percé and Flathead delegation to St. Louis had plaintively pleaded for the white man's Bible. What the Indians had actually asked for was the white man's *power*, most especially guns and ammunition to fight their tribes' neighboring enemies. Instead, they were sent his religion.

Father Mel is not of this older tradition. His is technically a mission because it is not financially self-supporting, but he isn't particularly looking for heathens to Christianize. "I find people who have had some experience with Christian churches, or are church dropouts, and try to establish Christian churches the way Paul did," he said. "I go to a place that hasn't had pastoral care for years, I ask, 'Would you like me to come back?' Out here, if the church doesn't come to the people, the people have no church." When he first showed up at Boquillas del Carmen, a tiny Mexican village across the Rio Grande from Big Bend National Park, it was the first visit of any priest in six years; he later conducted forty-five baptisms "to catch them up."

In a historical sense, Father Mel is less a missionary than a modern manifestation of a different religious frontier type: a circuit-riding pastor who travels from flock to flock in a pickup instead of on a horse. His Nissan had 180,000 miles on its odometer; the closest dealer is in El Paso, more than 250 miles from his home. (As a backup for emergencies, he has a bay gelding named Holy Mount, the "only church-owned horse in the diocese, quite possibly the nation," stabled at a dude ranch.)

Other churches operate in *El Despoblado*—Methodists, Baptists, and Catholics—but Father Mel does not see them as direct competition. "I have trouble covering all my territory as it is," he said. "There's plenty of territory. The only way I can add something at this point is if I subtract from another part. I'm at the limits of getting around." A mission he once started in the border town of Presidio began with eighteen parishioners, but two of the families quarreled, others left, and some, assigned to the Border Patrol, got transferred elsewhere. "It dwindled to one or two people each Sunday for its last years of a struggling existence," he remembered. "I decided that sometimes it's just better to terminate things. Sometimes they take off, sometimes they don't."

At the second stop of the day, a retirement community north of the park, seven people attended the service; only one couple said they are Episcopalian. The third service, in early afternoon, was conducted at a crossroads near the park entrance. The "chapel" was a vacant former clothing store in a set of small buildings that includes the Study Butte Store, a gas station, and Gloria's Last Chance Liquor Store. Father Mel had scouted this particular area regularly for several years, stopping at a local restaurant to eat and chat with its owner, "an old reprobate." "I talked with him a lot," Father Mel said. "If he'd lived a little longer, I might have gotten him through the doors of the church." After presiding at the man's funeral (in the restaurant), Father Mel had been asked to start regular services. This Sunday, five people, including four from one family, showed up.

Two or three times a year he'll drive up to a place for a service and no one will be there. "The first and second time it happened, it was discouraging," he said. "Then I realized it was part of the territory, and went on to the next place. Sometimes they [church officials] start talking about how this ministry doesn't make financial sense, that it's not *cost effective*—too many miles for too few people—that it would be better to focus on the *suburbs*. I tell them the people in the cities and suburbs at least have the opportunity to go to a church if they want to. Out here, there is no opportunity unless we provide it."

We rattled off in the pickup toward the final service of the day, and he talked of the other part of his ministry, which he described as "empowerment" and which, by his excited tone, is clearly what he likes the best. He had started a summer school, principally for Hispanic children, that now had 300 students each season. He helps people with clerically mundane, but necessary things, like how to place a long-distance call or how to fill out an income tax form. His newest project was establishing a local goat-raising cooperative and specialty cheese factory, to provide a steadier income for his impoverished neighbors. "A food program I had been running didn't really solve the problem," he said. "I started looking for a way to change their economic conditions. A herd of thirty dairy goats that fed into a larger cooperative could triple, maybe quadruple the income of a family." His inspiration, he said, came from books about liberation theology, especially *The True Church and the Poor*, by a Salvadoran priest. "This is the book where I'm at," he said, patting it. "The corporate parish is not for me."

As we drove toward the river, I asked him if his move to such a sparsely settled place had changed him. "It hasn't changed me as much as it's fulfilled me," he said. "I had my own epiphany at the last diocesan convention: I'm not like these people [the other priests] anymore. I am different. My values are not the same as theirs. I suddenly saw myself as a real outsider. I ran for delegate to the national convention and came in last; they saw me differently, too. I'm not an organizational type, not a gray-flannel-suit type. I'm a poet, an adventurer. I like being involved in essential ministry instead of peripheral ministry. I would rather bring both food for the body and sacramental food for the soul to someone who's sick than to referee an argument between the St. Mary's and St. Martha's guilds over shall we paint the rectory mauve or periwinkle. I felt superfluous in a big parish. They didn't need me in their lives. Here, it's the opposite. I get discouraged all the time, wondering if I'll ever make a dent in anything. Then something will happen that gives me energy to go on—like learning that someone is ill and traveling 200 miles to give them the sacraments of healing, knowing how much it means to them and that, if I weren't here, it wouldn't have happened. And my goat project. *It's* kept me going for a year already."

At Lajitas we parked near some willows by the river, climbed into a rowboat to cross into Mexico, and then walked a quarter mile down a dusty trail to Paso Lajitas, a cluster of small adobe houses. In the middle of them is a chapel, about 8 feet by 12 feet, that he helped build in 1988. There was an altar with faded flowers on it, a dirt floor, two windows without panes, and folding chairs emblazoned on their backs with the logo of Carta Blanca, a Mexican beer. On special occasions, he said, sixty-five people had crowded into this space. Today, when he rang his bell, eleven people, most of them children, emerged from their homes and traipsed in for the service he conducted in Spanish.

The sun was starting to set and the Chisos Mountains to the west were turning pink in the glow. This would be Father Mel's last service of the day. He lived in an abandoned onion warehouse about 40 miles upriver and on the other side of the Rio Grande, in a town the Americans had renamed Redford but which the Mexicans still called *El Polvo*. Dust. By the time he returned home, he would have logged another 200 miles on his truck this Sunday, ministering to a total of twenty-five people; eleven hours, Dust to Dust.

Service over, we headed back to the rowboat. "Looks like a thin day all the way around," he said, tiredly but without dejection. As he padded down the dirt path, raising puffs with each step, his shoulders drooped from his long day and the load he carried—in one hand a mass kit containing chalice, paten, crucifix, altar breads and linens, wine and water; in the other, a valise with his raiments, school bell, and Bibles and prayer books in two languages. At this moment, he seemed even less like the missionaries of the old frontier. Instead, the image that came to my mind was from literature, not history. Father Mel was a Willie Loman, a cleric-salesman making the rounds in a territory the home office considered unprofitable. Attention should be paid to this man.

"YOU'LL EAT SOME DUST TODAY. HOPE YOU DON'T have sinus troubles."

Jerry McComb started the engine on his brown United Parcel Service truck, put a plug of tobacco in his cheeks, made sure I had fastened the safety belt that strapped me to a spartan seat perched over the right wheel well, and roared onto the highway out of Alpine, population 5,637, the fourth-largest town in all the contemporary western frontier, the principal city of the vast Big Bend region, and probably the smallest "hub" of the UPS system. His first stop was 87 miles away. We had time to get acquainted.

McComb, forty-two, a biologist by training and a rancher at heart (he also runs 50 head of cattle on seven leased sections near Alpine), has worked for UPS for eighteen years, from the time the company first opened service in southwestern Texas. "I just took this job until a better ranch job opened up," he said. "Now no job around here can touch it. It's the best job around—a godsend to me." In the early years, as one of two drivers making deliveries out of Alpine, he had the biggest territory of any UPS driver in the country: 10,500 square miles, an area a little larger than Maryland, in which he would drive more than 500 miles and make fewer than twenty deliveries a day. Now there are eight drivers dispatched each morning from Alpine; McComb's district, smaller than it once was but still larger than Connecticut, is the most remote.

"This ain't *gravy* down here for the company," he said as he drove. UPS loses money in southwest Texas (and just about every other territory I visited), a company spokesman told me later, part of the price of business in promising retailers they can send a package to customers anywhere in the country. Throughout the contemporary frontier I kept seeing their trucks. I saw them delivering machinery parts and catalog clothes at ranches in Nevada whose owners had to drive 40 miles to get their mail; at stores in towns in Montana that a mailman reached only three times a week and that long ago were dropped from bus or train service; on lonely prairie roads in the Dakotas and mountain passes in Idaho, where theirs was the only other vehicle I encountered in a day's travel. If the freight-hauling symbol of the old frontier was an ox-drawn Conestoga wagon, its bottom and front curved like a boat's keel and prow, its top a billowing sheet of white canvas stretched over arched struts, its driver a bullwhacker who urged his team on with the crack of a whip and a stream of expletives, and its average daily distance about 16 miles, the symbol today is a chocolate-colored, metal box on rubber wheels with "UPS" painted in gold on its side, a uniformed driver inside with his foot on the accelerator and hundreds of miles to cover before nightfall. The connecting thread of history is the uninhabited miles between stops, the reliance of frontier residents on this link to retail and manufacturing centers far away, and, if the modern driver's like Jerry McComb, the occasional spits of tobacco juice onto the dusty roadside.

"This is the wrong color for this part of the country," McComb said. Temperatures in the summer, particularly at lower elevations along the Rio Grande, regularly reach above 100 degrees, and the brown cab—without air conditioning, air-cushioned seat, power steering, or even a radio—becomes a mobile sweat box and isolation chamber. We were traveling on a sunny day in late February, but after only an hour on the road our doors were pulled back open to cool things off. The noise from the rush of air and the rattle of metal on rough roads was deafening. McComb usually wears earplugs, but because of my presence he had them off this day. We didn't talk, we shouted to converse.

In eighteen years he's had rear wheels fall off four times, a front wheel once. After one breakdown, he had to walk four hours crosscountry to the nearest phone, encountering a few ornery Brahma bulls and some rattlesnakes and ruining a new pair of boots on the trek. He has delivered a baby for a woman who didn't have time to make it to a hospital and rescued a motorist from a burning vehicle. He and a deer once had a minor collision, fatal to neither because McComb keeps a sharp eye out. Flash floods have forced him to wait on higher ground several times, once for two hours before he could get on with his rounds. In the border town of Presidio, his loaded truck once sank to its axles on a sand street and had to be extricated by a municipal grader. His weirdest cargo was a wounded monarch butterfly some school children in Illinois had nursed to health and then shipped to Big Bend to be released with its migrating flock.

The bulk of his deliveries this day were in Presidio—auto parts, jewelry, shoes, clothing, vitamins, processed photographs, and other items for the stores; a combination thermometer/clock for the facade of a bank; boxes of books for the high school; new movie videos for the local rental outlet (which doubles as the Justice of the Peace office); supplies for the town hall and library; a basketball goal and backboard for a private residence; a thousand dollars' worth of cantaloupe seeds for a farmer on the town's outskirts.

Everyone knew him by first name, and he knew everyone else, slipping from English to Spanish as needed. "I like this part," he said. "The driving gets a little boring, but almost all the time people are glad to see ya'." Some approached him as soon as he entered town. "Anything for me yet, Jerry?" one man asked at an intersection. "Not yet. Hang in there," he answered. It was a Border Patrol officer, waiting for a new pistol.

In Redford (aka *El Polvo*) he dropped off a repaired VCR and, after making inquiries, drove to an abandoned Catholic church to track down the father of a man he couldn't locate for a delivery. "We don't have street addresses down here," he explained. "I sometimes have to use my own set of informants." Ranchers who live on remote roads have given him the combinations on their locked gates to make sure he can get through. At one ranch outside Presidio, the wife was standing at the front door. "I think this is what you've been waitin' for," he said, handing over a box of clothes from Pennsylvania.

During the day, we stopped three times for cattle and horses to cross the road in front of us, but never for lunch. McComb said he spends extra time talking with customers—"You can't rush people on the border"—something that UPS efficiency regulations frown upon, so he takes it out of his eating time.

In late afternoon we drove 48 miles up the river to the tiny town of Candelaria with a small box for a two-room grade school with out-houses behind it. No one was there when we arrived, but he had the key to the teacherage and left the box inside, then drove the 48 miles back to Presidio. Ninety-six miles, two hours, and five gallons of gas were consumed to drop off a package from Florida that generated $2.72 in shipping revenue. "That goes under the category of *service*," he said as we headed north.

The last stop was at a remote ranch accessible only by many of what McComb called "dirt miles." It was a bone-jarring, dust-eating journey of nearly two hours, top speed 30 miles per hour, over what in many areas would not qualify as "road." The truck rattled and boomed with each jolt. Both of us were soon turning the color of the vehicle from the thick accretion of dust covering us. "This is why we don't like dirt miles and save them for the last," he shouted over the tumult. "So dishes don't break and electronics don't get tossed off the shelf. Those store people don't get too *enthused* when you hand 'em a battered box covered in dirt." The rancher wasn't home. McComb left the package in the back porch—a tiny box of bee supplies from Kentucky, another $2.50 for the company coffers.

We reached pavement after nightfall, drove another 50 miles on the highway, and reached the Alpine hub terminal at eight-thirty, having covered 338 miles in 12 hours to make 53 stops. An outbound trailer truck left as soon as McComb's shipments from local customers were loaded; an inbound truck would be arriving in the middle of the night for the next day's deliveries. After he did his ranch chores, McComb was due back at the terminal the next morning at nine o'clock to begin his rounds again. He said he'd be driving a different truck tomorrow. The one we had used was scheduled for a new engine.

JACKIE TAYLOR, STOCKY, SQUARE-SHOULDERED, blunt-talking, was finishing twenty-five years in the Border Patrol with a final assignment in Presidio, where he was agent in charge of an office responsible for 85 miles of the Rio Grande's north shore. It is a stretch of border with a long history of action.

Beginning in the early 1700s, the Mescalero Apaches, pressured from the north by their enemies, the Comanches, began invading the Big Bend area. They displaced the native Chisos Indians and for nearly two centuries harassed the isolated settlements claimed by, in chronological order, Spain, Mexico, the Republic of Texas, and the United States. During the first half of the nineteenth century the Comanches, themselves crowded by increasing white settlement on the southern Plains, got into the act. Considered the best horsemen and most warlike of American Indians, the Comanches made a series of peace treaties with the United States but they considered Texans and Mexicans a breed apart and therefore fair game for annual raids from their reservation. Each September, the full moon that farmers in the rest of the country celebrated as the Harvest Moon went by a more ominous name in *El Despoblado:* the Comanche Moon, time again to brace for a visit from guerrilla bands in search of livestock, horses, and captives.

Benjamin Leaton, an American, worked for the governments of Sonora and Chihuahua as a scalphunter, collecting a bounty for each Indian scalp he could take. Presumably they were from marauding Apaches and Comanches, although no one asked many questions. After the annexation of Texas and the Mexican-American War, he returned to the north side of the river in 1848 and built a private fort downstream from Presidio, where he went into business trading guns and ammunition with both tribes in exchange for stolen livestock. Allegiances had a way of shifting that way on the border.

The eventual subjugation of the Indians did not end the exchange of depredations, it merely changed the cast of characters. Sparsely settled on both sides, the international boundary of the Rio Grande presented a magnet for outlaws seeking sanctuary from one government or the other. Jesse Evans, one of the Southwest's most hardbitten desperadoes, terrorized the area with his gang for more than a year after escaping jail in New Mexico during the Lincoln County War. By all accounts as cold-blooded a killer as they come, Evans had instructed Billy the Kid in the finer points of outlawry (Billy once helped his mentor in an earlier jail break), then hired out as a gunman in the cattle war, on the side opposing Billy. Evans was on the lam from a murder charge (the Kid's testimony had indicted him) when he set up operations in the Big Bend. He committed murder in Fort Stockton and robbed a store in Fort Davis. He and his gang were finally captured in a shoot-out with Texas Rangers a few miles north of Presidio that killed one Ranger and one gang member.

The Mexican Revolution in the early 1900s brought another wave of turmoil to the region. Bandit revolutionaries looked upon remote Texas ranches as easy sources of guns, saddles, horses, and supplies. In one raid, at a ranch now part of the national park, three American soldiers and a seven-year-old boy were killed. In another, northwest of Presidio, a mail coach arrived in the midst of a siege; the two passengers were shot and the mailman was hanged upside down while his throat was slit. Tensions were such that Mexicans and Mexican-Americans, regardless of their loyalties, were often lynched or shot if no American could vouch for them. Hallie Stillwell, a matronly ranch wife who lived through the times, tells the story of a posse coming upon a Mexican worker who spoke and read no English. He handed them a note from his American employer: "Juan is cutting sotol for me. And when he gets done, I'll kill the son of a bitch myself." Hallie was teaching school in Presidio when Pancho Villa captured Ojinaga, a town just across the river. Her salary was $65 a month, plus $10 extra for hazard pay. "In those days," she said, "I'd face anything for ten dollars." American troops and Texas Rangers retaliated after each raid with forays of their own into Mexican villages. Peace was finally restored in 1919 with the arrival of DeHavilland airplanes that reconnoitered from the air, dropped notes of bandit locations to the cavalry on the ground, and sometimes pursued horsemen across the desert with air-to-ground machine guns.

Prohibition spawned a brisk traffic in bootleggers entering from Mexico. Law officers got little help from the ranchers. "We all knew who the bootleggers were and what they were bringing in," a former county commissioner said. "We were their customers."

Throughout much of this century, cross-border cattle and horse and goat stealing continued as a traditional means of bolstering Mexican and American herds. One late afternoon during a visit to the region several years ago, a rancher who was letting me camp on his property below the caprock palisades north of the river invited me into his home, a lonely trailer in the midst of thousands of acres of creosote bushes and thorny ocotillo. As twilight descended on the valley, he talked for hours in a grim monotone about his life: about gun battles with Mexicans who had driven their herds across the Rio Grande to graze on his land; about livestock thefts and counterthefts; about being away from his trailer for months at a time on roundups; about his wife being told during one absence that he had been killed in a border skirmish;

about his wife finally leaving him and moving back to the Panhandle, where they both originally were from; about campers and hikers unwittingly surprising drug runners and illegal immigrants and coming to injury. His monologue completed, he looked out his kitchen window at the obsidian night. "Well," he said, "I guess you'd be wanting to get to your campsite," an adobe ruin about four miles away.

Opinions differ on the modern state of crime in the region. A sign in Alpine proclaims the area has the lowest crime rate in the Southwest, but an editor of one of the local papers said many violations are kept off the official logs. During my two weeks in the region, the papers carried stories of four upcoming murder trials (two of the murders had occurred more than a year earlier; in one, a former county sheriff was accused of killing his wife), one cocaine bust, one string of burglaries (including from a Catholic church in the near–ghost town of Shafter), and a Chamber of Commerce official accused of arson and theft.

Compared to other parts of the contemporary frontier, there seemed to be more law-breaking going on. There were also a lot more law officers. The Border Patrol has forty-four people in four offices between El Paso and Del Rio, the Customs Service has an observation balloon tethered over Marfa surveying the border 60 miles away and several radar-equipped planes monitoring air traffic, a multi-county drug task force is receiving federal funds, the Drug Enforcement Administration has an office and two agents in Alpine, and several national park rangers are devoted exclusively to keeping the peace. "We probably have the highest per capita law enforcement and the least crime," one federal official said. With only three highways leading from Mexico, all with Border Patrol checkpoints on them, and little traffic on them compared to other parts of the border, he said, most of the drug smuggling takes place in other locations.

Jackie Taylor had twenty-two Border Patrol employees under his supervision in Presidio. He said that a new amnesty law, which allowed previously illegal immigrants to register as nonvoting residents and simultaneously toughened penalties for employers hiring unregistered workers, had cut illegal crossings by about 70 percent. Quite frankly, he kind of missed the higher activity of the previous years.

Prior to the new law, "wetbacks" tried every possible means to get across the river for jobs farther north. "Their determination was tremendous," Taylor said. The patrol would find them lying over car engines, squeezed between the radiator and grill, suspended under the chassis; motion detectors at river crossings would sound an alarm if someone came by; agents on a hilltop water tower would spy them with binoculars; gravel paths would be dragged smooth in early morning and then periodically checked—"cutting for sign on a drag road" it was called—and if footprints were found, agents would be dispatched on cross-country motorcycles or four-wheel drive cars to track down the immigrant.

Illegal traffic has decreased, but the possibility of violence still exists, he said: "You don't know if it's an agricultural worker or someone with a backpack full of heroin. The potential for danger is as great for us as a city policeman or highway patrol. Especially on the river. Anytime you make a bust on the river, you can count on a shoot-out."

We spent a few hours driving around his area: along a raised embankment to watch the Rio Grande, pea green, the same color as the Border Patrol vehicles; to an old railroad bridge, a favorite crossing spot; up to a hill overlooking Presidio; down some desert roads. From time to time, he would lean his head out the window and spit tobacco juice, punctuating a point he had just made with a liquid exclamation point the way Jerry McComb had—the way, in fact, seemingly every other man I met on my travels did. (An impression substantiated by statistics: the contemporary frontier has the highest per capita male use of chewing tobacco. I got used to seeing spittoons in offices, sometimes with a plastic spray shield on the wall next to them, and to men carrying a styrofoam cup stained dark brown in places where a spittoon wasn't handy. It also has the highest per capita female use of cigarettes, especially in restaurants with signs like one in Tecopa, California: "Please Don't Breathe While I'm Smoking.")

Presidio, Taylor said, is considered a "hardship station" by the Border Patrol, not so much because of danger but because of its isolation and high cost of living. After two years, an agent is given priority to rotate to another station. "A lot of wives chip at their husbands every day to get out of here," he said. "No one seems to want to live in Presidio, Texas." Likewise, teachers get bonus pay, although not for the reasons that brought Hallie Stillwell an extra ten bucks a month during Villa's days. But Taylor liked it, particularly compared to the big cities where he had once pulled duty. "It's a wonderful place to live," he said, surveying the dusty town from a hill. "I get up in the mornin', I hear chickens crowin'. I go to bed at night, I hear coyotes. It's actually one of the safer places to live. The city life? Bah, it was crazy—a rat race where only the rats win."

As we drove down a desert road, his eyes constantly scanned the ground as he talked, out of habit more than anticipation. "It's not as much fun as it used to be," he mused, "workin' a drag road from mornin' to night. It was just a hell of an enjoyable way of life. Like a deer hunt, a chase. You're matching your skill at catchin' 'em against the immigrants tryin' to outrun your ass."

Taylor looked one last time before we returned to the highway. No "sign" today. He was retiring in four months.

"Yeah," he said, lost in nostalgia. "It sure made the day go by."

WHEN BILL IVEY WAS GROWING UP IN LAJITAS, THE town's population was nine people, four of them the Ivey family. Bill's father had come to the area as a beaver trapper, then bought the adobe trading post, the oldest building at the river ford, where he went into the business of selling supplies in exchange for candelilla wax, a substance derived from boiling the desert plant of the same name for use in gum, phonograph records, cosmetics, and waterproofing bombs and bullets. The trading post was a gathering place on the border. Bill Ivey remembers boxing matches, cock fights, horse races, games of craps, dances that turned into three-day bashes, people always wearing guns on their hips as they walked around the dusty street. The 95-mile road to Alpine was all dirt. "Don't get hurt," his mother would tell him and his brother as they went out to play. "The doctor's a hundred miles away." Without electricity, the boys studied at night by the light of a kerosene lantern.

Bill is thirty-four years old. The road to Alpine was paved in the 1960s, electricity came in the 1970s, and cable television arrived in the late 1980s. "I don't know *what* to expect in the nineties," he said.

His father sold the trading post and all the land around it to a developer in 1976. The result is Lajitas on the Rio Grande, an "authentic" frontier town cum resort where a water truck drives past the replica old-time stores, the condos, motel, and restaurant a couple of times a day to keep the dust down. Seventy-five people live year-round in the town now, either retirees or resort employees, fifty more across the river in Paso Lajitas. "They took away the Lajitas I knew and replaced it with a Houston-born something," Bill said. "But I sure did like the meal I had at lunch [at the restaurant]. I like the swimming pool. I just don't like them not protecting history."

A laid-back man with long hair and well-kept beard, a taste for western art, and a college degree in economics, Bill leases the trading post from the developers. Aside from two computers in the back office, the place looks and operates much as it has from the days the U.S. Cavalry arrived in the early 1900s to quell the troubles with Pancho Villa.

Locals from both sides of the border run charge accounts for groceries, hardware items, and gasoline, though the bulk of the store's trade now comes from tourists. Soda, beer, and gasoline are the only things that are delivered by vendors; the rest Bill buys in either Alpine or at a Wal-Mart near El Paso (325 miles away) and brings back himself. He is a banker of sorts, cashing people's pay checks. As a notary he signs legal documents for title transfers and divorces. As a "minister" in the Ministry of Salvation, a write-away-for-it church in Mexico, he has performed five marriage ceremonies. A jukebox in the corner plays songs in Spanish. Underneath the tin roof of the front porch is an old pool table. Clay Henry, a dark brown billy goat penned next to the porch, is the unofficial trading post mascot, savoring cans or bottles of beer that patrons hand him to drink. "He drinks Lone Star mostly," Bill said. "He'll turn down a light beer."

Two weeks before I arrived, there had been a Valentine's Day party centered at the store—horse races, some cock fights on the other side of the river, and a *baile*, a community dance party, that started Saturday night, went on until nine o'clock the next morning and started up all over again on Sunday afternoon. The porch roof had some fresh bullet holes in it from the celebration. "My rule is: if you want to fight, do it out on the street, not in the store, not on the porch," Bill said in the perforated shade of the porch. "I guess we won't have any two-day dances for a while."

Another part of Ivey Enterprises is candelilla wax. If you eat Wrigley's gum or use Merle Norman cosmetics, chances are that one of their ingredients was sneaked across the border on a burro to the trading post. On the Mexican side, the government has a state-owned monopoly, but Bill pays a higher rate for bundles of rendered wax so Mexicans smuggle it across and sell to him. (To stay within the law on the American side, he declares his import, without a duty fee, at the Customs office in Presidio, then ships it to a refinery in Alpine, which sends it to a distributor in New York City.) At one point in the early 1980s, before the peso was devalued and the Mexican government decided that Bill's business was feeding families and therefore eased up on its crackdown on the wax smuggling, wanted posters south of the border carried his name and picture. "It's hell having a whole country mad at you," he recalled with a grin. He now has a standing order for 100,000 pounds of wax, but has trouble filling it, he said, partly because some of his Mexican suppliers have switched to smuggling marijuana to someone else. "I guess I can't blame them," he said. "It's easier money—a hundred dollars a night instead of a hundred dollars a month. Making wax is hard work."

In partnership with his father—his brother died several years ago in a crash while herding goats with a helicopter—Bill also owns 150 acres that include the ghost town of Terlingua, 13 miles north of Lajitas. During the first half of this century, cinnabar mines in the area produced most of the world's mercury. Terlingua had a store, saloon, theater, two schools, tennis and bridge clubs, an elaborate mansion for the mine owner, and a population of 2,000. By the 1940s, the ore was essentially depleted, the price of mercury had dropped, the company had gone bankrupt, and the town evaporated in the dry Texas air. Its principal fame in recent years has been as the site of annual World Championship chili cook-offs.

Bill has grandiose plans for Terlingua, including not allowing it to become a Lajitas North. He is seeking to put the whole place on the National Register of Historic Places and hopes to restore the interior of the adobe and brick buildings without changing their outside appearance. The old store has been reopened, a café operates in one building, employees of river-rafting companies live in some of the small houses, but on the whole Terlingua still looks more ghost than town. As we walked around the town and he talked of an artists' community, a mining museum, perhaps a bed-and-breakfast in the crumbling mine owner's mansion, it was as hard for me to imagine it as Bill dreamed of it as to see Terlingua as what it once was: a thriving community, larger than most current towns in the Big Bend.

If I were a member of one of the religious groups from Crestone-Baca, I would consider Bill Ivey a reincarnation. He reminded me of a historical figure from an earlier time in *El Despoblado*. Roy Bean had a trading post in the late 1800s downstream from Lajitas, near where the Pecos empties into the Rio Grande. Like Ivey, Bean had a wide range of commercial interests—a saloon, a billiard room, a pet bear named Bruno chained outside as a curiosity. In defiance of U.S. and Mexican law, he staged a world championship prize fight on a sand bar in the Rio Grande in 1896. Infatuated by newspaper accounts and pictures of the English actress Lillie Langtry, he named his town Langtry and his saloon the "Jersey Lilly." (Bill Seward's bar in Ingomar, Montana, was named for Bean's, and preserved the misspelling.) As a justice of the peace, Bean demanded that people call him Judge and declared himself the "Law West of the Pecos," which at the time he was. "I'm fining you forty-five dollars and a round of drinks for the jury, and that's my ruling," was one of his judgments. When a railroad worker fell 300 feet from a viaduct, Bean, in his role as coroner, was called to pronounce the man dead and bury the corpse. He felt the five-dollar coroner's fee didn't match his effort, so after discovering a pistol and $40 on the body, he declared, "I find this corpse guilty of carrying a concealed weapon and I fine it forty dollars." Warned by a federal judge that he was authorized to perform marriages but not the divorces he was granting, Bean's response was: "Well, I married 'em, so I figure I've got the right to rectify my errors."

Ivey isn't as colorfully cantankerous as his predecessor on the river, but some of Bean's spirit seemed to me still alive in the younger man. "When people ask me what I do for a living, I like to tell them I own a little town in Texas," he said, with Bean-like delight in the overstatement.

He surveyed Terlingua, and by the look in his eyes I could tell what he was seeing was his dream. "A tourist frontier has already started," he said. "It may wane, but it won't go bust. You won't run out of tourists. This was and is very much a pioneering area. It's a frontier. Still new. Still old."

TO REACH THE RANCH OF ROBERT AND GINA CHAM-bers from Presidio, you first have to drive to Candelaria, a hamlet of

50 souls and an equal number of miles up the Rio Grande. Until a few years ago, the final 12 miles from town to town weren't paved, enforcing a speed limit more common to bumper-to-bumper rush hour traffic. From Candelaria to the ranch is another 18 miles, much of it on a rock path the Chambers maintain with their own equipment. The Chambers' "driveway" splashes through creek fords at least five times, winds along some ridges between steep arroyos, encounters a few gates that must be opened and closed, crosses a couple of metal cattle guards, passes the home of Robert's parents, and then climbs up into the mouth of Walker Canyon, a defile in the Sierra Viejas. Robert and Gina's home, a small one-and-a-half-story structure, sits at the point of a wedge in the rock cliffs that rise 500 vertical feet on both sides of their front lawn.

With his father, Boyd Chambers, Robert leases sixty square-mile sections (38,400 acres) from an absentee landowner and raises crossbred Brahma and Angus cattle—"Enough Brahma to help 'em survive on small groceries, but enough Angus that they aren't *too* wild," Robert said. Such are the terrain and ground cover, mostly Spanish dagger, sotol, ocotillo, and other prickly plants on stony soil littered with debris from ancient volcanoes and lava flows, that the carrying capacity is one "animal unit" (a cow and calf) per hundred acres. Their herd totals 400 cattle, about the same number of cows a Vermont dairy farmer might raise on a section. "We spread 'em out real thin—like the people," Robert said. His half of the ranch is one-and-a-half times the size of Manhattan; on it are Robert, Gina, both in their late twenties, and their seven-month-old daughter, Carissa. Ten square miles for each.

They slaughter their own cattle for beef, along with an occasional hog, lamb, or goat; grow squash and tomatoes and chili peppers in their garden; get milk from their own cow. Twice a month, they make an all-day expedition to either Presidio or Marfa for groceries and other necessities. As needed, Robert will heft a butane tank into the back of his pickup, drive to town to get it filled, and drive it back, where he ties the tank, now weighing 300 pounds, to a tree, and pulls the truck out from underneath it. His father has a big gasoline tank (which they also have to transport to town to replenish) for their vehicles. The closest doctor is in Alpine, more than a hundred miles to the northeast. They do have electricity and a telephone, for which they're grateful.

(As in many parts of the contemporary frontier, the utility lines are buried underground, not for the aesthetics, although the lack of poles and wires is a pleasant byproduct for scenic vistas, but because it's cheaper for the utilities in the long run than sending a repair crew out after every big storm.) They don't receive a television signal because of their location—even if they weren't in a canyon, the nearest city with a station is El Paso, more than 150 air miles away—but they have a set and a VCR, nearly worn out from playing tapes their friends give them. One radio station, from Mexico, has a strong enough signal to reach them.

For Robert, this is the life he grew up in, changed only by the ameliorations of a better road from Candelaria downriver and the arrival of the utilities. His grandfather, a tenant on the same land, lived in this house. Robert said he'd like to own his own land, but considers it an unlikely prospect: "A rancher can't afford to buy a ranch, and someone who can afford to buy a ranch doesn't need to and usually doesn't want to." When a ranch in the area came up for sale a few years ago, it was bought by a doctor in Houston, who locked the gates and visits only periodically to enjoy the scenery and quiet.

Gina, as easy-going and unpretentiously self-confident as her husband, grew up near Midland, where Texas is flat and neighbors are always within sight. She prefers the ranch, she said, because of the solitude and "we don't have to worry about what's going on in the cities." Then she put on a jacket, disappeared out the front door and returned in a few minutes with a sprig of mountain laurel in her hand. Its sweet perfume soon filled the room. "Here," she said. "This is another reason I love it here."

The Chambers had another guest when I visited, John Littlejohn, a tall man in his seventies with a weathered face that avalanches into a bushy beard, blue eyes whose irises seem detached from looking long distances for too many years, a cavern of a smiling mouth unprotected by teeth. "I've got teeth," he joked. "I just don't bring 'em with me much. Somethin' for you young folks to look forward to."

A family friend, Littlejohn was there to help the Chambers with a cat problem. The deer population had all but disappeared on the ranch. Boyd Chambers, who had once been driven out of the goat-raising business by predators, suspected some mountain lions were responsible for the deer loss and didn't want his cattle to be next on the menu.

"I've hunted cat all my life, all my life," Littlejohn said—for jaguar in Belize, mountain lions in Mexico and the western Rockies, once even in a suburb of Denver where he was hired to capture one that had moved into a residential neighborhood. With his trained dogs, he had already been combing the ranch for two weeks, finding enough sign to estimate five cats were in the area but not coming across a fresh enough track to follow.

On a raw February morning, three of us—Robert, Littlejohn, and myself—saddled up in the corral for another day of checking. Littlejohn moved stiffly—from the chill, the last two weeks on horseback, and age. He pulled his horse next to a log to assist him in reaching the stirrups. "Something for you to look forward to," he groaned as he mounted and led us up a winding trail to a high desert plain above the house. The wind blasted and howled around our hunched shoulders. To the north of us, where the mountains are cleaved in sheer ramparts and Capote Peak disgorges a stream that cascades over the precipice to create Texas's highest waterfall, it was snowing in the higher elevations. A violent thunderstorm had struck over the ranch the night before, creating more noise and light than rain, but enough of the latter to make chances of finding a fresh cat trail slim.

Five dogs were with us, four of them older and experienced at the task, following the line of horses in single file unless Littlejohn dispatched them up a slope or into a dry stream bed with verbal orders: "Go look for him now! Go look for him! *Git* down there now! *Git* down there! Heeyah! Heeyah!" The fifth dog, a younger pup named Babe, was less obedient. She scouted out ahead and far to the side of us, occasionally sniffing out a few javelinas, some jackrabbits, and a couple of Chambers' cattle, baying loudly as she leapt to the chase. The others would raise their ears and start at the sound of her voice until Littlejohn shouted them back in line. Like a grandfather with a rambunctious grandchild he couldn't bring himself to discipline, Littlejohn seemed more pleased than vexed by Babe. "She makes life worth livin', don't she?" he exclaimed several times as the pup bounded off.

We rode for six hours, climbing and descending steep slopes on loose rock, following creek beds, crossing high plateaus. Always, spiny plants tugged and tore at our chaps. Always, the raw north wind tried to blow us across the border. The veteran dogs kept their heads down, several inches from the ground. Three or four times, their noses dropped in unison to the soil itself and they milled intently as they circled outward. Each time, a false alarm.

Like the dogs, Robert and Littlejohn kept their heads bowed, their eyes on the trail. I, on the other hand, gaped at the stark spectacle all around us. Littlejohn noticed this at one point, pulled his horse up next to mine, and I thought he might lecture me like one of his hounds. But the Babe spirit was in him. "Look at all this," he said, gesturing to the rock citadels above us and the river valley far below, where thermal springs sent wisps of steam into the gray sky. There was awe and reverence in his voice. "Just look at it. One time way back, way, way back, this land was on *fire*. You know, I've spent my whole life where there aren't any people. I get home [in western Colorado] and pretty soon I'll say to my wife: 'Think I'll go up to the camp.' And she'll say: 'You've only been here twelve hours.' "

We stopped on an elevated table, near a rim that breaks off and drops a few hundred feet toward the valley. The vista was more Mexico than Texas. Prowling with their noses scraping the ground, the dogs were in alert mode. "If we come upon a fresh track, you probably oughta grab your saddle horn," Littlejohn had advised at the start of the day. "Things can start happening real fast." For once, I forgot the scenery and followed the dogs with anxious eyes. I kept expecting them to bark and take off on a scent over the precipice, our horses galloping headlong in pursuit. The cat would have our crumpled carcasses at the bottom for lunch for the rest of the month. False alarm again. We headed back, faces to the cold wind.

We finally arrived at the ranch house in late afternoon. Gina had a dinner of warm tortillas, beans, tamales, chili, and vegetables ready for us. Littlejohn sat next to little Carissa's high chair and happily spooned food for the infant, deriving the same pleasure as he had watching Babe on the trail. Carissa would laugh and Littlejohn would laugh back, one toothless grin answering the other.

After the meal, Gina offered to help Littlejohn get his boots and spurs off. As he gratefully stretched his old legs toward her, with Carissa bouncing on his lap, he looked up at Robert and me. "Somethin' for you young fellas to look forward to."

CHAPTER **8**

DUMPING GROUND

ON THE MORNING OF MAY 19, 1953, AN ATOMIC BOMB was dropped from a tower on Yucca Flat in Nye County, Nevada, northwest of Las Vegas, and set off a blast nearly three times greater than the one that had leveled Hiroshima, Japan. The ninth in a series of eleven detonations at the Nevada Test Site that spring, when the United States was speeding to develop a hydrogen bomb before the Soviets did, its code name was Shot Harry. It soon became known as "Dirty Harry," the bomb that created the most radioactive downwind contamination of any on the American mainland.

Residents in the sparsely populated desert areas to the north and east of Yucca Flat were already well acquainted with nuclear bombs going off in their backyards. A continental test site had been deemed necessary in the late 1940s, in the midst of the Korean War and heightened world tensions, as a place where the government could develop its nuclear arsenal more quickly, less expensively, and in greater security against spying than in the Bikini atolls of the South Pacific, where previous detonations had taken place. Southern Nevada was chosen principally because the United States already owned the land, the site was remote enough to provide relative secrecy, and, as long as the wind was blowing away from Las Vegas and Los Angeles on bombing days, there weren't many people in the immediate fallout areas. It was virtually uninhabited. The "virtual uninhabitants" were scattered ranchers and miners and residents of tiny settlements, Mormons mostly, patriotic people who believed the government's assurances that they weren't in any danger.

In January 1951, two weeks after the selection of the Nevada Test Site was made public, the first bomb was dropped. Over the next eleven years, 104 more atmospheric blasts billowed into the desert skies, before testing was moved underground, where it still continues.

"We really thought it was quite a deal when they'd drop a bomb and light things up," said Keith Whipple, a rancher in the Pahranagat Valley, a series of spring-fed oases northwest of the test site. "You could count your cattle in the flash." A mushroom cloud would rise above the Pahranagat Range, turn reddish pink or orange, then grayblack. Several minutes later, the sound and shock wave would hit, sometimes breaking windows and cracking house foundations. Then the dark cloud, filled with dust and dirt sucked into the air by the detonation, would drift over, sometimes dropping its contents as it passed.

Local residents were repeatedly told they had nothing to worry about. ("You can't underestimate the importance of public relations when you are trying to dump radioactive material on people, and we worked at it strenuously," a public health official said in 1980 at a workshop of former health monitors.) But people noticed disquieting things. Horses and cattle in the path of the clouds developed sores and white spots on their hides; a deputy sheriff in Lincoln County even renamed his horse Fallout because of its new coloring. Some prospectors looking for uranium deposits found places where their Geiger counters registered high readings. They thought they had struck it rich, but when they dug down several feet the clicking stopped: there was no uranium deposit, just radioactive topsoil. Edwin Higbee, a Lincoln

County commissioner at the time, remembers that Civil Defense officials encouraged the building of fallout shelters in the event of an attack
on Los Angeles, three hours of cloud travel away, "but then they'd say
that the tests *here* were safe. They started lying right at the start. Any
cattleman knew something was crazy, but try to prove it. One government guy came by and said we had the wrong breed of cattle." A protest
letter from ranchers to Washington got the response: "That must be
the Communists trying to put out that stuff [about dangers]. You know
we'd never do anything to the people of Nevada." Prior to one test,
Keith Whipple saw an Atomic Energy Commission bus parked near
his home and was told it would be used to evacuate ranchers if fallout
got too bad in the area; when the cloud arrived, the bus took off because, Whipple speculated later, "it was too 'hot' for him."

The morning of the Dirty Harry shot was overcast. The mushroom
cloud mingled with the storm system and boiled over the mountain
range into the Pahranagat Valley. Radiation detectors began going off
their scale. Roadblocks were set up to check levels on passing cars and
direct those with high readings to be washed at local service stations.
Whipple's mother was driving a school bus to her teaching job in
Alamo, the town closest to the bomb site, when she was stopped in
the middle of a purple, putrid-smelling fog that enveloped the town.
Keith was mowing hay at the ranch, and a hot dusty wind reached
him, burning his skin and raising welts. "It felt like mosquito bites,"
he recalled. He finally ceased his work and went to town, where he
helped a friend wash down cars that had passed through the cloud.
No one advised the residents that they, too, might benefit from a
shower. Whipple's brother, Kent, who was in the school bus with his
mother, and who, like many others in the region, spent much of his
time outdoors during the years of the testing and drank milk from
their cows and ate vegetables from their garden, later developed lung
cancer (he was a nonsmoker) and died at age thirty-eight.

Four hours after the blast, after setting up a roadblock to warn
motorists headed down the road to Las Vegas to keep their windows
closed, a radiation monitor in St. George, Utah, just across the Nevada
line, noticed abnormally high readings on his detectors. He telephoned
the results to the test site, was told to take a new reading, then another,
all registering the same high dose. St. George had no radio station; at
10:15 A.M., an hour after the initial readings, the nearest station in

Cedar City, 50 miles north, was told to broadcast a request for residents of St. George to stay indoors until further notification.

Besides coming too late, the warning didn't reach everyone in St. George. Nor did it reach people in Kanab and rural Kane County, who weren't covered by the advisory anyway. But the cloud reached them.

Janet Gordon's brother, also named Kent, was herding sheep in the area, 150 miles downwind from the test site. In low areas, he found himself enveloped in a ground fog. It had a metallic taste and made his exposed skin tingle. His horse became sweaty and lethargic. That night, at the sheep camp, he vomited until morning and was wracked by diarrhea and a splitting headache—the same symptoms many other downwinders reported, the same symptoms associated with radiation poisoning. A few weeks later, his hair began falling out in patches. His horse, only six years old, died. Many of his ewes—like those of other sheep ranchers in the area—lost their wool in clumps, gave birth to premature, deformed lambs, and died. Four years later, he developed pancreatic cancer, which killed him at age twenty-six.

Proving that someone's cancer and death were the result of radioactive fallout is an impossible task. While studies have shown that radiation exposure can increase the probability of some cancers, linking it as the cause in individual cases is another matter. A number of downwinders died of cancer—six of the eight men at the sheep camp of Janet Gordon's brother, for instance; and a survey of southern Utah showed that childhood leukemia levels during the 1950s and 1960s were 250 percent higher than in the periods before and after the testing. But unexposed people contract cancer, too, and most people in the immediate fallout zone survived without obvious health consequences. "He's dead and I'm alive, and both of us were exposed," Keith Whipple said of his brother. "It would be nice to be able to blame someone, but you've just got to go on. Sometimes you don't have the best choices to choose from."

The government speedily handled damage claims for broken windows and property damage from its bombing tests, but consistently defended itself successfully against lawsuits for livestock losses and people's maladies in the wake of the atmospheric blasts. "There's no way we're gonna let you win this case," one sheepman was told during a suit for damages to his herd. "If we let you win, every woman who has a miscarriage will sue us."

Kent Whipple's widow, Jane, and their children, however, believe that the tests robbed them of a husband and father. Janet Gordon believes that Dirty Harry's fallout took her brother. I spent some time with them all—with the Whipples at their ranch near Alamo, and with Janet Gordon at, of all the unlikely places, the test site itself.

AFTER WHIPPLE DIED IN 1977, JANE STRUGGLED TO keep their twenty-section ranch going with the help of their five children, the oldest of whom was thirteen years old at the time. "Running the ranch taught them to work hard, to be responsible," she said. "We took turns getting discouraged." Eventually, the task proved too much for them. To pay off medical bills, settle debts, and send her children to college, she sold off all but the house and 500 acres.

Bret Whipple, the eldest son, was visiting home when I was there. A blond, strapping young man, intelligent, friendly, self-confident, he works for an investment company in New York City. "I like walking down Broadway," he said as he drove me around the ranch. "But I like coming back here and really feeling alive." He and his siblings were trying to figure out a way to keep the reduced ranch in business. "This ranch is what separates me from the guys in New York," he said. "It's my family's equity. It's what will provide us a future."

Bret's long-range life plan is to make good money in New York for a while, then move back to the West and go into politics, "not in vengeance," he said, "but I don't want to see what happened around here happen again. I want to be involved in making decisions instead of just taking it."

To the west, the Pahranagats towered above us like a rocky picket fence crudely built atop mounds of jumbled stone. The valley, a narrow strip of green, stretched to the south past Alamo, the last gas station for another 91 miles. On a dry, clear day, it seems that if you squint hard enough you might see the next pump. But on this morning, menacing clouds were rolling over the peaks and spilling into the valley, dumping everything they contained as they passed through. This time it was just rain, much needed. Thirty-seven years earlier, before Bret was born, the same weather pattern brought something less benign with it. Bret turned on his pickup's windshield wipers and I asked him what he thought about the atmospheric testing.

"I think about it every day," he said quietly. "It killed my father. My life has been dictated by his death."

NEARLY TWO DECADES AFTER THE DEATH OF HER brother, Janet Gordon went to see a documentary film about the Nevada tests. It included a clip from an earlier movie, hurriedly produced by the government after Dirty Harry to soothe mounting fears in the downwind region. She immediately remembered the clip, because, as a school child in Orderville, Utah, she had seen the government film when it was shown to the local PTA in its tour of the small towns. In it, a chaplain crouches down among the cactus on Yucca Flat to talk with a soldier before the blast. (Part of the testing included deploying soldiers into the bomb area after a detonation, to replicate conditions that might occur in a war theater.)

CHAPLAIN: What's the matter, son? Worried?
SOLDIER: Well, just a little bit, Father.
CHAPLAIN: Well, there's no need to be, son. Why, first you'll see a brilliant flash, feel the percussion, and then you can open your eyes and look up, and you can see the familiar mushroom cloud as it ascends into the heavens with all the colors of the rainbow. A wonderful sight to behold.

"I remembered how patriotic I felt watching that as a school child," Janet recalled. "How proud I was of being part of history being made, how neat I thought it was."

Then the modern documentary shifted to describe the immediate effects of radiation poisoning and the list of cancers associated with it. Janet and her sister looked at each other in astonishment. "That's what killed Kent!" they said in unison. His pancreatic cancer—"extremely rare in young people, especially those who don't drink," she said—had eventually swelled his stomach to the size of a basketball; then he got thinner as he couldn't digest food; his skin tightened and his eyes and mouth couldn't close. Kent had wondered whether his condition was related to his sickness after being surrounded by Dirty Harry's fallout fog, but had been assured there was no connection, and "we believed them in those days," Janet said. "First we wondered why

God was punishing us. We prayed for him to live. Then we prayed for him to die." The night before he died in 1961, his legs were bent in excruciating pain, and Janet had lain down on the bed beside him to cradle them in her arms.

In the movie theater in the late 1970s, the two images—the chaplain's reassurances in the government film and Kent's last night of agony—fused in her mind. "The anger and betrayal I felt was so intense that it lit a fire I've never been able to extinguish," she said. "They [the government] decided it was an acceptable risk. We were written off. There weren't many of us. Most of us were Mormons who accepted authority and were very patriotic. It seems an inappropriate reward for patriotism."

As with many other downwinders I talked to, what offended her most was the government's decision, revealed later in court proceedings, that advising area residents to take extra precautions during the tests might erode public support in the nation and stop the tests. ("I think they needed to conduct the tests," Keith Whipple told me. "It's just that they sneaked around and didn't tell us anything. We were just guinea pigs.")

Janet believes honesty about the fallout's potential dangers wouldn't have stopped the atmospheric testing in those Cold War times. "People would still have supported it," she said. "But safeguards would have saved lives. It was different from being *asked* to sacrifice. We weren't given any choices. We weren't told the truth. We were expected to sacrifice without being told the risks. There's something inherently immoral about a policy based on that kind of deception. The Bill of Rights is supposed to apply to two people just as much as for two hundred thousand.

"We were written off. It does a curious thing to your head that you and your children are considered expendable, not as important as others."

In 1980, she helped found Citizens Call, an advocacy group for downwinders who feel they or their family had been victimized by the tests. Her involvement led her into other issues: the fight to stop the MX missile system in the West, against new coal mines and power plants in Utah, movements to end underground testing and to close nuclear power plants, worldwide crusades for nuclear disarmament. She has been to Japan three times for commemorations of the Hiroshima and Nagasaki bombings, to the Soviet Union twice on peace missions. A few months before we met, she had been in Kazakhstan, the Central Asian steppes where the Soviets had conducted their atmospheric tests. "It was a total parallel," she said. "Not many people live there. The air even looks like southern Utah. They have the same sense of betrayal." One man she met said that after a test in 1954, his five-year-old brother came down with terrible headaches, vomiting, and diarrhea, and then died; another brother had died of cancer in his thirties.

"I don't seem to be able to let go of it and lead a normal life," she conceded. "It's taken over my life completely." Her frenzied activism had led to a divorce.

Janet told me these stories in a surreal setting. We were sitting in a Department of Energy bus that was driving through the test site as part of a tour for leaders in a coalition of groups opposed to the testing that still takes place underground.

On Frenchman Flat, a dry, alkali lake bed rimmed by mountains, stands the remnants of one of the "Doom Towns." As a way of determining the effects of atomic blasts and radiation on civilian structures and bomb shelters, elaborate towns had been built near "ground zero" and then inspected after each detonation. Houses were equipped with food-filled refrigerators, furnishings, and mannequins (Janet said some workers she knew had, as a joke, placed one couple of dummies on a bed in the act of making love); cars had been parked in garages; different designs of bank vaults had been tested to see if documents and money would survive; various configurations of bunkers, with different thicknesses of concrete, had been spaced around the desert to see which ones worked. Most of the debris had long ago been buried in craters on the site, but some relics remain in what the DOE spokeswoman on the bus called "an outdoor museum to atmospheric testing." Through the bus window we saw the shell of a concrete motel, a brick structure with bowed walls, a bridge whose girders were grotesquely twisted, a few domed bunkers, some of them collapsed, some seemingly unaffected. A sign on the desert floor warns against touching or removing scrap items.

On a hillside overlooking the site are some bleachers, where newsmen and VIPs once gathered to witness the tests. Operation Upshot-Knothole, the series of tests in the spring of 1953, had included other shots besides Dirty Harry that had gone awry. One dropped fallout on the Nevada towns of Tempiute and Ely. Another, Shot Simon, exploded with greater yield than anticipated. A drone plane flying overhead was vaporized; congressmen watching from the bleachers were rocked backward from the percussion and the windows on their buses were shattered; three miles away, sagebrush burst into flames. The fallout drifted east, registering high readings in several small towns. A rainstorm in upstate New York a day and a half later set off radiation monitors in the research labs of Rensselaer Polytechnic Institute.

"Some of the shots were pretty, little shots, fluffy and white," Janet said. "Some were dark and angry. Harry was a mean, nasty one."

Yucca Flat, another alkali bed separated from Frenchman Flat by a saddle ridge, is pocked with concavities a quarter-section large—subsidence craters created when the surface collapses after an underground test. In the early years of underground detonations, a few resulted in radioactive venting through fissures in the ground. A rancher northeast of the site had told me he was caught in two of the ventings. In one, he was working cattle and saw a dark cloud pass through a valley about 12 miles away. Then his exposed skin started "burning like you had the worst sunburn in your life," he remembered. "Your hands and face started to cook." Twice a year, he gets skin cancers scraped off his skin. "*They* say it's just sunshine."

The bus stopped at the biggest crater on the test site, and we were allowed to disembark and gape into it. The Sedan event (tests shifted from being called "shots" to "events" when they moved underground), in 1962, was part of the Plowshare program, experiments in using nuclear detonations for peaceful purposes such as freeing natural gas deposits from rock formations or moving earth for roads and canals. Sedan's bomb, buried 635 feet below the desert floor, packed a 100-kiloton wallop (the Hiroshima blast had been 13 kilotons) and lifted 12 million tons of soil and rock into the air. Its radioactive dust cloud rose more than 10,000 feet and drifted north and east, first over scattered ranches, then over Ely, more than 100 miles away, where street lights were turned on at 4:00 P.M., and finally across the rest of the country, eventually reaching the Atlantic Ocean somewhere south of Delaware, a state not much larger than the 1,350-square-mile test site. Thirty beagles, their mouths taped shut to test inhaled fallout, had been placed in wire cages 12, 30, and 40 miles from the detonation;

four died right off, six more within the next three days. The official report on the event said, "It seems reasonable to conclude that none of the offsite population in the vicinity of the Project Sedan test site received significant amounts of radiation either internally or externally."

We stared for a few silent minutes into the crater, 320 feet deep and 1,280 feet across, and then got back on the bus. We drove past a farm that the government once operated on the site to test the effects of radiation. We passed a handful of wild horses that wander across the wasteland. We toured a "Survival Town" that looked little different from the "Doom Town." And we were shown a low-level radioactive waste dump, not far from where the government is now proposing to locate the nation's first high-level repository on Yucca Mountain. In every instance, the government spokeswoman offered reassurances that the tests, the farm, the dump are conducted in the utmost safety.

"They tell you the doses are safe," Janet whispered through her teeth. "That's bullshit. There's no such thing as a safe dose. I'm a little cynical, as you can tell. They've been doing this PR since I was twelve."

She is fifty-one now, and focused as much on the future as on the past. "I believe more strongly than ever in the democratic process," she said as the bus left the test site and headed toward Las Vegas. "If you're patriotic and find a violation of democratic principles and don't try to correct it, you're part of the problem. Trying to shut this down makes me a patriotic, conscientious citizen—certainly as patriotic as anyone in the military or DOE.

"I believe that in the future people will look at what we've done in nuclear policy as evil, intolerable, with the same abhorrence as child labor and racism. Those of us who opposed it will be looked upon as patriots and pioneers."

A day after the tour, the newspapers carried two items that made me think again of Janet Gordon, the nuclear pioneer. One said Congress had approved legislation establishing a $100-million trust fund to compensate victims of atmospheric testing and uranium mining in the Southwest. Within certain tightly drawn categories, people could file claims for up to $50,000 each. It was the first time the government had formally admitted any culpability in the downwinders' fate. In 1980, the House Subcommittee on Oversight and Investigations had issued a report, *The Forgotten Guinea Pigs*, recommending that Congress "promptly compensate the victims of our mistakes." It also said: "Atmospheric testing of nuclear weapons in the 1950s and 1960s may well have been essential to secure the national defense. However, because the agency charged with developing nuclear weapons was more concerned with that goal than with its other mission of protecting the public from injury, the government totally failed to provide adequate protection for the residents of the area. There was sufficient information available from the beginning to suggest that if it was not possible to conduct the testing outside the continental United States, then the people living nearby needed protection. The necessary protection could have been provided by evacuating some of the people, but, at a minimum, the government owed the residents a duty to inform them of the precise time and place of each test and to instruct them as to what precautions should be taken. . . . The greatest irony of our atmospheric testing program is that the only victims of U.S. nuclear arms since World War II have been our own people." Ten years after the report was issued, the bill passed.

The other item was a brief story announcing that on the same day a nuclear bomb of less than 20 kilotons had been exploded a thousand feet below Yucca Flat. It was the 500th underground detonation at the test site, the 705th explosion since testing above and below surface began in January 1951. "Everything went well," a government spokesman was quoted as saying. "There were no problems. Everybody was happy with it."

A PSYCHOLOGICAL PROFILE OF THE CONTEMPORARY frontier would probably reveal an added element to the more heralded traits of fierce individualism, physical competence, and stoic fatalism. An undercurrent of paranoia is also present, like a desert river usually running just below the surface but occasionally breaking out in the open.

Some of that condition is as old as western settlement itself. Without investment capital from the East, without massive federal assistance ranging from troops protecting wagon trains to subsidies for the railroads, from enlarged homestead acts to dam and irrigation projects, the arid West could not have been developed. As many historians and sociologists have pointed out, much of the West's antipathy toward the populated East and the federal government stems from this fact, as self-evident as it is hard to swallow for people who pride themselves on relying on their own toughness and ingenuity for survival. Bernard DeVoto summarized the attitude in one sentence, "Get out and give us more money." Dependency breeds its own resentment toward those who hold the purse strings. For the West in general, and particularly for those parts with the fewest people, the knowledge that major political and financial decisions affecting their fate are made in locations far removed gives locals a constant sense of uneasiness.

More than any other Americans, residents of the contemporary frontier generally exhibit on the one hand a feeling of control over their own destinies. Doctors and other services are distant, the weather extremes are as challenging and harsh as the lives they lead, but they make do, taking pride in taking care of themselves. In politics, they're accustomed to knowing their local officials personally, as they know all of their neighbors, no matter how far away. At this level, they feel what political scientists call "empowerment" of the highest order. On the other hand, on the state level, and even more so on the national scale, their sense is just the opposite. Because of their few numbers and their remoteness from the seats of power, they feel powerless, neglected, and often picked upon. This gaping dichotomy—unique, I believe, to the sparsely settled places—only heightens their distrust and suspicion when they consider their position vis-à-vis metropolitan America. It makes them defensive and nervous.

Some of it is well justified. As the saying goes, just because you're paranoid doesn't mean someone isn't following you. Places without many people have a tendency to be chosen as sites for activities that would be rejected out of hand in populated locations. The atmospheric nuclear testing in a sparsely settled corner of Nevada was the most extreme example of this, but certainly not the only one. I came across other manifestations of it in stop after stop at counties with fewer than two people per square mile. Call it the Syndrome of Open Spaces. My list was compiled more haphazardly than methodically, but it grew like a mutant vine in my notebooks, branching into categories like waste dumps, water grabs, imprisonment, and military operations.

Waste dumps. Texas is searching for a place to bury low-level radioactive wastes, and the two finalists are Hudspeth and McMullen counties, both with fewer than two people per square mile, both fighting the selection. Another radioactive dump—for uranium mill tailings and other mining byproducts—is proposed for Kinney County, Texas, southeast of the fort that the Seminole Negro Scouts once called home. The federal Department of Energy's Idaho National Engineering Lab, an experimental facility for nuclear reactors, including the first breeder reactor to produce electricity, comprises the western quarter of Butte County, Idaho; it is also one of the nation's oldest and largest nuclear waste sites, where radioactive military wastes are stored. Loving County, Texas, is debating the merits of jobs versus possible contamination from a toxic waste dump planned near Mentone. Lake County, Oregon, is dealing with a former uranium mine that left polluted tailings and a pond whose water has traces of arsenic and radioactivity; the estimate for cleaning it up is $20 million.

The nation's first high-level nuclear dump—the "Mother of All Dumps"—is under consideration for Nye County, Nevada, parts of which have already been irradiated by the bombing tests. Adding insult to the injury, the Nevada legislature, dominated by delegations from Las Vegas and Reno, created a special county whose borders would coincide with the proposed dump's. Named after the aborted attempt to form a county near the Death Valley mines in the early 1900s, Bullfrog County would have no residents, and its "county seat" would be Carson City, hundreds of miles away; the governor would be a county commissioner. What the urban legislators hope to gain for their jurisdictions by creating Bullfrog County is a lion's share of the millions of dollars the federal government is holding out as an enticement for whatever county accepts the nuclear-waste repository. Nye County, which wants the money if it is going to have the radioactivity, has gone to court to stop Bullfrog from becoming the only county in the country with zero people per square mile and the richest per acre.

Water grabs. The greatest water theft in American history occurred after the turn of the century, when representatives of Los Angeles surreptitiously purchased some land and water rights in the Owens Valley of Inyo County. By 1913, an aqueduct was completed, stretching 223 miles from the remote valley on the other side of the Sierra Nevada crests, and water was ready to cascade down the final sluiceway into the parched San Fernando Valley. William Mulholland, the engineer and mastermind of the scheme, unfurled an American flag and addressed an exuberant crowd of 40,000 Angelenos. "There it is," he said

"Take it." Within eleven years, Owens Lake was an alkali flat, and booming Los Angeles, which soon owned 82 percent of the valley floor (it now owns more than 90 percent), was pumping more water from the underlying aquifer. Owens Valley, once a green oasis on a high desert, is now a "non-attainment area" for meeting air quality standards, mainly because of dust storms over the dry lake bed. During one windy day the town of Keeler, on the southeast corner of the alkali flat, recently registered the highest level of airborne particulate pollution ever measured in the United States, ten times higher than the federal standard of safety, three times higher than the level considered to create "significant harm to health."

Water is the West's scarcest and most precious resource. In the next century, it will be the focus of increasingly intense battles pitting cities, agribusiness, environmentalists, and the tourist industry against one another. Lacking people, money, political power, and terrain suitable for much irrigated farming, many of the counties of the contemporary frontier see themselves as future "sacrifice areas" in the upcoming water wars. Several of them—near the Fort Peck and Oahe dams on the Missouri River, and the Glen Canyon Dam on the Colorado—have already sacrificed, witnessing the inundation of their best land for the benefit (drinking water, irrigation water, flood control, hydropower) of people somewhere else. Their aquifers seem to be next on the list to be used up to sprinkle suburban lawns, fill urban bathtubs, and water some distant corporate farm's lettuce or rice crop.

The spectre of becoming the next Owens Valley haunts a number of counties I visited. The aquifer underlying Saguache County, Colorado, is being eyed for transport to Denver and other Front Range cities. Salt Lake City is looking toward sparsely settled counties in eastern Utah as a potential water supply. In the Sand Hills of Nebraska, where the Ogallala aquifer rests near the surface, residents suspect that some of the vast ranches are being purchased for future water export instead of for raising cattle. Las Vegas, running out of the water that it requires to keep its rampant growth afloat, has filed 146 applications for a total of nearly one million acre-feet of water in three surrounding counties, all of them sparsely populated. "They say there's extra water here, we say there isn't," said a commissioner in Lincoln County, population 3,775. He viewed the water applications much the way he did the high-level nuclear dump proposed for the area: through the prism of the experience with the atmospheric tests. "We've been lied to too many times," he said. "If you could trust them . . ." His voice trailed off at the very improbability of the thought. "They've got us kinda edgy."

Imprisonment. The nineteenth-century solution to the "Indian problem" had been to confine Indians in isolated pockets of the West, preferably places white people considered without value, like the Bosque Redondo of eastern New Mexico. While the contemporary frontier includes relatively few Indian reservations, the tradition of using sparsely settled areas for impounding society's unwanted was never abandoned. Inyo County, California, and Millard County, Utah, hosted internment camps for Japanese-Americans during World War II; Fort Clark and Marfa, Texas, were used as prisoner of war camps. In more modern times, when the placement of a prison is greeted with the same enthusiasm in populated areas as a toxic waste dump, several lightly settled counties I visited are welcoming the prospect on the basis that jails and prisons would create stable jobs. A highway sign east of Wells, Nevada, has this seemingly oxymoronic message: "Independence Valley. Prison Area. No Hitchhiking."

Military operations. Here's another sign you come across only in places with few people, one I saw on a gravel road in Owyhee County, Idaho: "Warning. This Road Crosses a U.S. Air Force Base Bombing Range for the Next 12 Miles. Objects May Drop From Aircraft." Military bases, being concentrations of people, generally aren't found in counties with fewer than two people per square mile. Instead, what you find are missile silos, bombing ranges, practice areas, or, in Mineral County, Nevada, an army ammunition depot that was transferred from New Jersey after an accidental explosion nearly leveled an eastern city. In the Big Bend area, ranchers complain about fighter pilots staging dog fights over their cattle herds; in southeastern Oregon and southwestern Idaho, residents are opposing a proposed expansion of low-altitude flight practices. Boise City, Oklahoma, seat of Cimarron County, has decided to make a monument to an incident there during World War II. A B-17 rehearsing night runs had mistaken the lights around the courthouse for its practice target and bombed the town. One garage was hit, but no one was injured. An old bomb is now being prepared for placement on the courthouse lawn to commemorate the event.

In the late 1970s and early 1980s, the government wanted to use vast parts of Nevada and Utah for the MX mobile missile system, sort of a thermonuclear shell and pea game in which missiles would have been carted around from remote spot to remote spot on railroad tracks to keep the Russians guessing where they were.

Cecil Garland, a sixty-five-year-old rancher in Callao, Utah, a town of fewer than a dozen people on the southwest corner of the Great Salt Lake Desert, had joined what he called an "uneasy coalition" of ranchers, miners, environmentalists, peace activists, and, eventually, the Mormon church, that successfully blocked the MX installation. The rail tracks would have been a few miles from Cecil's ranch; missile bunkers would have been even closer. "We'd have been ground zero," he said. "These places were selected because there weren't many people."

This wasn't the first time Callao had been written off. It once had the reputation of being on the worst stretch of the Pony Express route and a particularly unpleasant part of the Overland Stage road. Some famous visitors had passed through on their way farther west and recorded their impressions, none of them favorable. "Imagine a vast, waveless ocean stricken dead and turned to ashes," Mark Twain wrote of his stagecoach journey across the desert in the mid-1800s. "Imagine this solemn waste tufted with ash-dusted sage brushes; imagine the lifeless silence and solitude that belong to such a place; imagine a coach, creeping like a bug through the midst of this shoreless level, and sending up tumbled volumes of dust as if it were a bug that went by steam." Sir Richard Burton, the British explorer, had stopped at the Callao station in 1860. He appreciated its location on the transition point between the alkali flat and the gentle slopes at the base of the Deep Creek Range "where gopher holes and snipes, willows and wild roses told of life and gladdened the eye," but didn't think much of the station itself. "Nothing," he wrote, "could be fouler than the log hut." Horace Greeley, the New York editor and booster of westward settlement, had been blunter in his assessment a year earlier. "This is the most forlorn place on earth," he wrote. "If Uncle Sam should ever sell that tract for one cent per acre, he will swindle the purchaser outrageously." Had they been around a century later, no doubt all three would have heartily recommended the area for ground zero in any nuclear exchange.

Cecil came to the area in 1973 from Montana. "I was lookin' for a ranch I could afford," he remembered. "This turned out to be it. It was pretty run down." Annette Garland showed up the same year to teach at the Callao School and married Cecil within months of her arrival. When it closed in 1987 with only five students, Callao's was the last one-room school in Utah. Annette now teaches at a four-room school in Trout Creek as one of three teachers for the sixty students from kindergarten through high school; it is a "necessary existence" school serving three counties in two states, allowed to continue because the distances are too great to send the pupils anywhere else.

The Garlands' home in Callao had once been a boarding house on the early Lincoln Highway, the nation's first transcontinental road, a "highway" only in the loosest sense of the term, since when it was first promoted in the early 1900s, the western half was mud, sand, and dirt. Modern road builders decided the Pony Express and Overland Stage route across this part of Utah was the wrong way to go. To reach Callao now is to re-enact Twain's experience and be a dust-spitting bug for 50 miles of alkali road on the desert floor. The nearest gas station and town big enough to offer any retail stores are more than 90 miles away. The Garlands grow most of their food: beef, chickens, vegetables, honey, fruit. "It's a rare thing to go to town for supplies," Cecil said. Mail arrives twice a week.

Cecil, a tall man with a gray mustache, stubble beard, and gentle eyes and voice, is the kind of iconoclast I met in other remote places, as if living so far from the rest of society gives a person time and space to develop his own theories on life. "We're all misfits and outcasts who live here, people who can't fit in anywhere else and need lots of room surrounding us," he said. He is an ex-marine veteran of World War II, a vociferous proponent of the right to bear arms, but also a "rancher for peace" who has traveled to the Soviet Union to preach disarmament after the MX fight. In 1982, a satellite truck parked outside his house had linked him for a live interview on New Zealand television to talk about that country's decision to declare itself a nuclear-free zone. "There's no reason you in New Zealand should have to accept our nuclear trash," he had said, sitting in his living room and being watched by people half a world away. He can complain about federal regulations and bureaucracy as heatedly as any western rancher, considers the movement to banish cattle from public lands the work of extremists, and believes that "on an environmental scale of ten, ranchers are about a five or six and the rest of you are a three or four; why don't you all catch up with us?" But he also supports increasing the number of acres preserved as federal wilderness, a view many ranchers do not share. Once asked to speak to a local group on behalf of the Wilderness Society, he was introduced by a man who spent most of his opening remarks apologizing for bringing Cecil into their midst. "So I decided, all right, I'll let 'em have it," he remembered. "I took a pinch of snoose [snuff], put it in my mouth, and started in on 'em. Afterward, a big rancher came up and said, 'I didn't intend to pay any attention to you, but when I saw you put in that snoose and keep it in for an hour without spittin', I thought I'd better listen. But I still don't agree with you.'"

His latest battle has been with the air force, which uses parts of the desert for combat practice. Pilots, he said, locked their radar onto people's cars, tractors, and homes as mock targets. "You don't see 'em comin'," he said. "All at once is this great noise and vibration. Your sense of seeing, hearing, feeling is gone. An F-16 at treetop level is something your system is not prepared to handle. We finally got across to higher military authorities that it was a harassment. We finally convinced them, 'Hey, we *live* here. It's not the time of Fort Apache and Fort Keogh. The country's settled.' And they backed off."

About his choice of home, Cecil said, "It's a tough place to live, there's no doubt about it. That's why there aren't many people. But if you apply some intelligence and stand on your own two feet, you can do it. I guess that's the frontier philosophy."

From a distance, there's a certain logic to designating places like Callao and other sparsely settled places as sacrifice areas: if you have to dispose of deadly materials, rob a place of its water or flood its most valuable land, test bombs and aircraft, or incarcerate dangerous people *somewhere*, why not do it where it affects the least number of people? The difference between virtually uninhabited and uninhabited seems a slight one, at least from the perspective of city-dwelling decision makers. Just the same, it's equally logical for "virtual uninhabitants," who appreciate the distinction more keenly, to resent the implications.

ALPINE COUNTY, CALIFORNIA (POPULATION 1,113; 1.5
people per square mile), on the steep, tree-covered western and eastern
slopes of the Sierra Nevadas, experienced other symptoms of the Syndrome of Open Spaces. Sewage effluent from the populated tourist
mecca of South Lake Tahoe, in the adjoining county, is piped over a
Sierra pass to Alpine County, where it has already ruined one lake and
is now being treated and held in a man-made reservoir. But Alpine
County's more bizarre touches with the syndrome occurred in the
1970s, when first the Gay Liberation Front and then the right-wing
Posse Comitatus tried to take over the place.

Residents learned of what came to be called the "gay invasion"
from newspaper reports in California's big cities. After posing as fishermen and tourists to scout the area, leaders of the Gay Liberation
Front in the Bay Area announced a call for enough "Alpioneers" to
move into the county to become a majority and establish a "national
refuge for persecuted homosexuals." With adequate recruits, they
hoped to vote into office a slate of gay officials, start a gay university,
and make Alpine County a destination point for gay tourists around
the world. "We selected Alpine," one of the leaders was quoted as
saying, "because it is the only place we can have. We are social outcasts
and must go and live in a place that nobody else wants. And hardly
anyone wants Alpine."

After the first flush of national publicity, the movement claimed to
have received a thousand potential volunteers from across the country;
food was being stockpiled for the move; land negotiations were alleg-
edly under way. A fundamentalist preacher in another part of the state
said he planned to flood the county with his own missionaries to offset
the onslaught. A highway sign appeared on the main highway: "Watch
for deer—Hit a queer." One of the bars in Markleeville, the county
seat, put up a notice: "Homo hunting license sold here." When a Gay
Liberation Front advance party showed up at the courthouse in late
1970, the only others who showed up were a beagle and out-of-county
media. Whether it was because of this reception, or the ferocity of
Sierra Nevada winters and the lack of jobs in the county, the full-scale
invasion never transpired.

Eight years later, the second invasion was threatened. Six hundred acres of land near Markleeville were purchased by people associated with the Posse Comitatus, a group of fanatics linked with extremist views and various acts of violence. (One of the principals in the Alpine land purchases had been convicted of assaulting a deputy sheriff in another county during a confrontation with the United Farm Workers.) The plan for Alpine County was to bring "tax-fighting, church-going" people to the development, create a "Constitution City" with its own private schools and institutions, elect like-minded county officials, build roads "in a county where only patriots will be in charge," and "re-establish freedom with our own bank and law enforcement system." One of the leaders reportedly said "the country might shape up a bit if citizens hanged a few public officials." Given their choice, a number of local people told reporters, they would have preferred the gays. New signs went up: "Don't Be a Fool—Fight Posse Rule."

The Posse Comitatus group fielded a candidate for sheriff and registered nearly 200 new voters, who used post office boxes or vacant lots in the development as their addresses. Most of the registrants were thrown out after six people were prosecuted for vote fraud. The incumbent sheriff was re-elected on a vote of 521 to 12. Proclaiming that "the devil is absolutely ingrained in here, so strongly it's unbelievable," the leader of the posse announced that because of the publicity three other counties in the nation had invited Constitution City to their locales, and the group pulled out of town.

When I was in Markleeville, the aborted development was up for sale, and the people of Alpine County, who viewed the two attempted takeovers as bad memories they'd just as soon forget, were preparing for the kind of invasion that keeps them in business. Winter was coming. With several ski resorts within its borders, Alpine County hosts more than 3 million tourists a year.

TOURISM, NOW THE NUMBER ONE INDUSTRY IN MUCH of the West, is another manifestation of the Syndrome of Open Spaces. With three-quarters of the nation's population living in urban areas, places without people are increasingly becoming metropolitan America's playground. Once again, the locals can grow uneasy. They generally appreciate the commerce, relying as many of them do on the seasonal influx of tourist dollars, but at a certain point they realize it's the same old dependence on someone else's decisions. They're expected to flip the hamburgers, turn down the bedsheets, do the wash, perhaps dress up "western" and put on a performance, and then ride out the hard times and harsh weather while their patrons are back at high-paying jobs in the cities.

Taken to extremes—Jackson, Wyoming, and Aspen, Colorado, come to mind—the very nature of the community can be altered forever: traffic jams, sprawling development across a landscape that was the prime attraction in the first place, skyrocketing real estate prices that prevent residents from buying houses and land in their hometowns, the eventual transformation into something akin to whatever it was the tourists and second-homers had come to escape. Some people call it the Californication of the West, in honor of the people who took paradise and put up a parking lot.

That extreme has not been reached in most of the contemporary frontier, although you can see its approach in places like Lajitas on the Rio Grande, Big Timber, Montana, or the edges of some of Utah's national parks. Of the 132 counties with fewer than two people per square mile, about a quarter of them are already heavily dependent on tourists to sustain their economies. (By my count, there are nine national parks, seven national monuments, and an uncountable number of national recreation areas, forests, wilderness areas, and wildlife refuges in the counties.) People who for generations have grumbled that "You can't eat the scenery" have learned you can, however, sell it and buy groceries with the proceeds. These counties lead a dual existence, as old as the fur trade: the frenzied activity of the yearly tourist rendezvous and the stark silence of waiting for the next one. A good many other sparsely settled counties count on a healthy but nonaddictive dose of outsider traffic, either hunters or tourists in transit to more scenic spots. For others, mainly in the Plains, my *Conestoga* with Kansas license plates was the cause of curious stares; some people asked if I was lost or, more hopefully, a doctor or an oil geologist.

Long before the automobile, paved roads, jet planes, wider-spread affluence, and the emergence of a predominantly urban nation with both the time and the means to escape the crush of humanity for a lengthy vacation or get-away weekend, tourists were venturing west to marvel in rapt wonder at its landforms, immense sky, unique wildlife, and native people. Nineteenth-century dudes were usually rich people, either European nobility or members of the growing upper class in the industrial East. Many of the contemporary frontier counties had once been visited by some of the more famous ones. For instance, Prince Maximilian of Wied, accompanied by the artist Karl Bodmer, had toured the upper reaches of the Missouri River in the early 1830s. Teddy Roosevelt and the Marquis de Mores established western homes in Billings County, North Dakota, which at the time, a century ago, had more residents than it does now. Hayes County, Nebraska, and Cheyenne County, Colorado, however, hosted one of the most extravagant tourist sprees in the history of the West. Neither of them had witnessed anything like it before—or since.

In the winter of 1871–72, Grand Duke Alexis of Russia, third son of Czar Alexander II, made the first visit of a Romanoff to the United States, an event that set the entire nation atwitter. His arrival in New York sparked the biggest reception to date in the city's history; 10,000 troops and police were needed to clear a path up Broadway for his carriage, drawn by horses with gold harnesses, to make its way through the excited throngs. Washington, Philadelphia, Boston, Milwaukee, and Chicago feted the handsome, young playboy. Chicago was originally to have been the westernmost stop on the grand duke's tour. But during an earlier dinner at the White House, he had mentioned to President Grant and Lt. Gen. Phil Sheridan, commander of the army's western division, that hunting in Europe had grown stale compared to the stories Sheridan was telling of buffalo hunts and Indian wars in the West. A special addition to the grand tour was quickly arranged on the spot.

In early January, a train of new Pullmans pulled up to the siding in North Platte, Nebraska, and disgorged its entourage. This was to be no ordinary hunt on the Plains. Sheridan and the other top brass of the army were there, including Lt. Col. George Custer, chosen to be grand marshal of the event. Buffalo Bill Cody, riding his renowned buffalo-running horse, Buckskin Joe, was the scout. Two companies of infantry, two of cavalry, the Second Cavalry's regimental band, and assorted wagon masters and herders rounded out the contingent of more than five hundred. Seventy-five trained buffalo horses had been brought over from Fort McPherson. Once the wagon train of supplies was ready (it included three wagons loaded solely with champagne and other liquors), it set off for Camp Alexis, a spot on Red Willow

Creek already equipped with stove-warmed tents, some of them car-peted for the grand duke and his retinue of royal retainers, including Alexis's chef. The Sioux chief Spotted Tail, coaxed to the camp by the promise of 10,000 rations of flour, sugar, and coffee, and 1,000 pounds of tobacco, waited nearby with 1,000 members of his tribe as a special display. Alexis wanted a taste of the West; by God, the government was going to see that he got it.

After champagne toasts the first morning in camp—it was the grand duke's twenty-second birthday—the party set out on horseback for a buffalo herd grazing in the area. In deference to the royal guest, riding Buckskin Joe for the occasion and armed with a specially engraved Smith and Wesson pistol given to the grand duke at the factory in Massachusetts, no one was to shoot a buffalo until Alexis had made the first kill. This took some time. His first six shots failed to bring one down. Cody exchanged pistols with him. Six shots later, still no luck.

"Seeing that the animals were bound to make their escape without his killing one of them," Cody wrote later, "I rode up to him, gave him my old reliable 'Lucretia' [a .50-caliber Springfield rifle] and told him to urge his horse close to the buffaloes, and I would give him word when to shoot. At the same time I gave Buckskin Joe a blow with my whip, and with a few jumps the horse carried the grand duke to within about ten feet of a big buffalo bull. 'Now is your time,' said I. He fired, and down went the buffalo."

A reporter for the *Kansas City Times*, along to chronicle the spec-tacle, recorded what followed: "The Grand Duke leaped from the saddle in a transport of astonishment, turned the horse loose, threw the gun down, cut off the tail for a souvenir, and then, sitting down on the carcass, waved the dripping trophy and let out a series of howls and gurgles like the death-song of all the fog-horns and calliopes ever born. The Russians galloped up and he poured out excitement in a strange northern tongue, so steadily and so volubly that Cody reeled in his saddle. His countrymen embraced and hugged him. The gory trophy went from hand to hand till all were plastered with blood and dirt." Champagne was brought up, and each hunter was given a bottle.

During lunch in the field, a Sioux warrior named Two Lance, ap-parently offended earlier in the morning when Alexis had referred to the Indian's bow and arrows as "absurd toys," put on a demonstration to show the Russian a thing or two about hunting. Two Lance stampeded a buffalo cow toward the diners and waved his bow at the guest. As the cow thundered past, Two Lance rode up next to it, and shot an arrow that passed through the buffalo's shoulder and out the other side onto the prairie before the beast fell. With his horse still galloping, Two Lance circled and picked up the arrow on the run. Then he presented it to Alexis. "Absurd toy" indeed.

More buffalo were killed in the afternoon, with more champagne after the grand duke's second kill. ("I was in hopes that he would kill five or six more before we reached camp," Cody wrote, "especially if a basket of champagne was to be opened every time he dropped one.") That night, the Indians staged a mock battle and a war dance for the visitor's benefit. Alexis and Custer reportedly flirted with two Sioux maidens. The regimental band serenaded the entourage at taps.

On the second day, the hunt was less orderly. Bullets flew everywhere as Indians and whites rode wildly over the rough ravines of the prairie. Alexis was in buckskins, like his hosts Cody and Custer, but his Russian companions wore gold and lace uniforms. At one point in the melee, a black sergeant of Buffalo Soldiers rode up to Custer and said, "Colonel, I beg leave to report, sir, that another of them kings has done fallen off his horse." Alexis bagged six more buffalo, bringing his total to eight; the grand total for the two days was fifty-six.

The tour moved on to Denver, where a lavish ball was held in the grand duke's honor. It was the highlight of the season for the newly opulent city. The *Rocky Mountain News* reported that women of Denver's elite had collected an assortment of souvenirs from the dance: a bit of velvet plush snipped from the chair he sat in, a piece of uneaten steak snatched from his plate, a glove, to be preserved in glass, that had touched his hand. But Alexis was interested in something else. He wanted to shoot more buffalo. Sheridan speedily arranged another hunt.

The royal train stopped in Kit Carson, Colorado, and the group set out again. When they arrived at camp, Sheridan discovered that the wagon drivers had helped themselves to his whiskey barrel on the trail; they were drunk, he was enraged. During the hunt, Custer led Alexis and the others in a mock cavalry charge into the buffalo herd on Big Sandy Creek, the kind of reckless attack that would end the fair-haired colonel's career four years later on the Little Bighorn. Watching from a hill, Sheridan was nearly hit by two of the stray bullets sprayed at the herd. Disgusted and in another fit of anger, he stalked back to the camp, only to find the camp soldiers and servants polishing off the last of the grand duke's champagne and caviar. Out on the prairie, 200 buffalo were killed, a dozen of them by Alexis, who was so thrilled by it all that he grabbed Custer and kissed him.

The trip through the Plains ended with a stop in Topeka, where Custer and Alexis posed in their hunting attire for a photograph, a memento of the grand duke's vacation in the West to accompany him back to his palace in St. Petersburg, along with several hundred pounds of buffalo hump meat packed in ice and a buffalo head to mount on the wall.

Modern tourists, for whom the buffalo-less plains of Hayes and Cheyenne counties hold no fascination, take less of the West with them when they leave for home. And compared to, say, open-pit gold mining or clear-cut logging, tourism is a cleaner and, perhaps, more stable economic alternative. It sure beats trading dollars for atomic fallout and wastes. On the other hand, as those growing concerned about the tourism boom are saying, the jobs it creates are usually lower paying and at some point too many vacationers can foul the way of life they are so interested in experiencing. When the number of Americans who have rafted a river jumps from 5,000 to 35 million in one generation, it's worth wondering whether such a boom can—or should—continue unabated.

But even in its benign form, less extractive and destructive than the other symptoms of the Syndrome of Open Spaces, tourism is none-theless linked to them, as it is to the larger sweep of the West's history. Like Spotted Tail's tribe after the grand duke's visit, the residents of the open spaces, who fulfill the twin roles of assistants and colorful props, are left behind with whatever rations they received in exchange. Feeling as Two Lance must have after his bow-and-arrow display, smugly secure in the knowledge that they're better at western survival skills than the dudes they serve, they nonetheless are at the mercy of their urban patrons' whims of where to vacation next. Maybe next season the buffalo won't return, and neither will the tourists.

ONCE THE LANDS THAT NOBODY WANTED, THE WEST-ern places without many people are now the focus of fierce debates over who can use them and to what purposes. Should hardrock miners for gold, silver, uranium, and other metals be allowed to operate under a law signed in 1872 by President Ulysses Grant, which permits valuable ores on public lands to be given away to anyone who can find them and provides only the loosest forms of regulations on how mines operate? Shall open spaces be designated as wilderness areas, and what types of activities will be permitted in them? How much logging, and at what price, can take place in national forests? To what extent should cattle grazing continue—should the public domain be made "cattle free by '93" as one faction contends, or, following the theories of what is called "holistic range management," should herds be allowed to increase if it improves the range? Whose claim on the inadequate supply of water takes precedence: Indian tribes with century-old treaties, farmers, ranchers, migratory birds and wildlife, municipalities?

Who will decide these issues? Corporate executives, whose bottom line is profit, but whose businesses also create jobs? Advocacy groups on both sides of each issue? The courts? Congress? The urban majority, whose interests range from an abstract desire to preserve a remnant of America in as untouched a condition as possible to planning a two-week vacation in the Out Back with their dirt bikes, from a hope to occasionally experience the majesty of nature in its rawest form to a need for electricity and running water that their cities must import to function and grow? Or the people who live closest to the areas in question, who in some cases have been good custodians and in others have simply helped themselves to the land's bounty?

Most of the debate centers on public lands, administered by federal agencies such as the Forest Service, Park Service, Fish and Wildlife Agency, and Bureau of Land Management. The contemporary frontier contains a vast amount of public domain, although the sparsely settled places are not dominated by federal lands as much as you might initially suppose. Of the 132 counties with fewer than two people per square mile, the land in 44 of them, mostly west of the Continental Divide, is 50 percent or more federally owned; 24 of these 44 counties are more than 75 percent public lands; in 11, the federal government controls more than 90 percent of the land. On the other hand, particularly in the Plains, there are 63 contemporary frontier counties with less than 10 percent of their land under federal control; 17 of them have less than 1 percent of their area in the public domain.

Some residents of the contemporary frontier that I met explained their county's sparse population by pointing to all the federal lands, unavailable for private development, in their midst. But in truth, the correlation was just the opposite. Federal ownership is a symptom, not a cause of sparse populations. In most of the nineteenth century, the main business of the United States was disposing of public lands into private ownership and private use as quickly and completely as possible. With few exceptions—Yellowstone National Park, created in 1872, being the prime example, and national grasslands purchased from bankrupt farmers during the Dust Bowl being another—what the government owns today in the West is land that earlier settlers either disdained or found useful only so long as they didn't have to pay for it.

The passage of a century has turned the issue of public lands on its former head. In this manifestation of the Syndrome of Open Spaces, the impetus no longer leans toward encouraging more private ownership and commercial use, but toward preserving what's left of the unsettled lands, restricting their uses, even expanding the extent of public ownership. The transition, still going on, has not been a smooth one.

In the late 1970s, what came to be known as the Sagebrush Rebellion erupted over the issue of federal management of public lands. Ranchers, miners, oil and coal companies, loggers, and local officials objected to new environmental restrictions and other regulations being placed on public lands, where for generations private interests had pretty much been given free rein to do what they wished. Some contemporary frontier counties became particularly rebellious. In Utah, the commissioners of Grand County ordered bulldozers to knock down barricades and blaze roads into a canyon that the federal government had set aside for a wilderness inventory. Next door in San Juan County, a commissioner promised that violence and vandalism would greet the new restrictions; not long afterward, an ancient pictograph on a canyon wall was destroyed, a BLM office was evacuated because of a bomb scare, and federal agency employees started receiving death threats on a routine basis. In Nevada, Dean Rhoads, a state senator and rancher from sparsely settled Elko County, persuaded the legislature to declare the state (which presumably would be more accommodating to the private interests) as the owner and manager of federal lands. The election of Ronald Reagan, a self-professed Sagebrush Rebel, as president, and his appointment of like-minded people to the land-managing agencies, marked the movement's high-water mark.

A decade later, however, the tide has turned. The rebellion is clearly on the defensive, and in many places it is in retreat. The environmental laws that sparked the reaction are still in place, and even if the federal administration and its appointees are reluctant to enforce them, the courts are not. Reform is in the air for the Mining Act of 1872, a legislative relic from the times when gold and silver were the basis for the country's currency and the number of new shafts being dug was considered the principal measurement of the nation's economic health. Nevada, always considered the most wide-open state in terms of bowing to mining interests, has passed its first, if minimal, reclamation law to deal with the open pits and chemical wastes left behind by the new gold rush. Loggers are being prevented from cutting old-stand timber. In many grazing districts, ranchers are being forced to reduce their numbers of cattle on the public range. Large areas are being designated as wilderness, with stricter restrictions being placed on what can happen to the land. In eastern Nevada, Great Basin National Park—the nation's newest and Nevada's first, even though the state has the largest percentage of federal lands—has opened; Idaho, the West's last holdout in the national park department, is slowly but surely softening its traditional antagonism toward the idea.

The battle over what to do with public lands no longer breaks as evenly along East-West lines, said Dean Rhoads, one of the national leaders of the Sagebrush Rebellion, when I visited his remote ranch in Nevada's Independence Valley. Even within Nevada and other Western states, he said, "there's a growing anti-rural sentiment. They [people in *Western* cities] think we're getting a free ride" and the emerging attitude "has us scared to death about what's going on." Of Nevada's twenty-one state senators, Rhoads and one other senator are the only two who don't represent either Las Vegas (thirteen senators) or the Reno–Carson City region (six senators).

Like everyone else I met, on both sides of the battle lines, Rhoads said that tensions are at the highest level he can remember—between land managers and users, users and environmentalists, environmentalists and managers. The users claim that environmental groups have the most money and political clout, and therefore control the "bureaucrats." The environmentalists claim that the users are better funded and politically connected, and therefore control the "bureaucrats." The bureaucrats, meanwhile, find themselves in the same crossfire as their federal-employee predecessors on the frontier, even if they work for the BLM and Forest Service instead of the now-defunct Land Office.

The extreme position of one side is represented by Earth First!, a radical environmental group that advocates civil disobedience and vandalism to advance its cause. At the outer limits of the other side is Wayne Hage, a rancher/activist I met near Tonopah, Nevada, who believes that the environmental movement is simply a smokescreen for an age-old conspiracy of eastern interests seeking to dominate the West by thwarting its full economic development and that the philosophical underpinnings of environmentalism are essentially anti-Christian. Hage has devised an elaborate legal theory contending that grazing permits constitute a protected property right, not a privilege, which at least one contemporary frontier county (Catron County, New Mexico) has written into its ordinances under the guise of the Civil Rights Act.

Although increasingly in the majority, the environmentalists are far from declaring victory; the Sagebrush Rebels have not surrendered, and with powerful allies in the extractive industries and some influential politicians, they are still formidable. But the whiff of desperation hangs heaviest over the camp that clings to a frontier notion older than the Mining Act. In the nineteenth century, when the supply of open spaces seemed limitless, the value of a piece of land was simply what it could produce. Most of today's public lands were considered the least productive, and therefore worthless. Anyone who could put this marginal land to work was welcome to it. At the time virtually everyone, East and West, urban and rural, agreed on this premise. Today, however, the consensus has broken down. For most Americans, particularly those who live somewhere else, the open spaces and unused land now seem in short supply; their value is measured differently, their worth is their relative lack of use. But for many locals the old way still pertains: the worth of a piece of land is what it can produce, usually in terms of livestock feed, logs, or minerals.

Despite the tradition of several generations of frontier residents to think of them as their own, however, these are *public* lands. That's the rub. More and more, the desires of the "tenants" and the "owners," like their places of residence, are separating. What one sees as a resource to be exploited, the other sees as a treasure to be preserved. But only one holds title to the property.

I CAME ACROSS YET ANOTHER VARIATION OF THIS syndrome in the Great Plains, where the lands in question were often privately owned. As I traveled through the region, it was not uncommon for local residents, discussing the future of their county with me, to say, "Of course, there are these two *professors* from *New Jersey* who think we should just turn this place back to the buffalo." They would roll their eyes at the words "professors" and "New Jersey," as if identifying the source of the idea adequately dismissed its seriousness, but there usually was also a trace of wounded anger in their voice. Then they would shift back to some story about their parents' or grandparents' homesteading hardships.

The professors in question are Frank and Deborah Popper, one the chairman of the urban studies department and the other a doctoral student in geography at Rutgers University. Their thesis, first expressed in a magazine for planners in 1987, is that "most of the Great Plains will become what all of the United States once was—a vast land mass, largely empty and unexploited." Homesteading and trying to "privatize" the region, they wrote, had been "the largest, longest-running agricultural and environmental miscalculation in the nation's history." Based primarily on studies of census data, economic statistics, and western history, with their own observations during a vacation in Montana and the Dakotas thrown in, the Poppers believe that huge portions of the Plains are headed toward financial and social ruin. Drought and depressed farm markets; a collapse in the energy and mining sectors; the departure of businesses, doctors, amenities, and young people from small towns—all the indicators that the Poppers amassed pointed in the same direction: down. Down, in fact, to the final bust in the boom-and-bust history of the Plains. Down to the point of virtual depopulation.

"Most Plains land is simply not competitive with land elsewhere," they wrote. "The only people who want it are already on it, and most of them are increasingly unable to make a living from it."

The next step, in their view only about a generation away, will be taken by federal and state governments and nonprofit groups such as the Nature Conservancy. The few remaining Plains people will be resettled into the surviving cities, the emptied lands purchased for bottom dollar, the crops replaced with native grasses, and, in some places, wildlife such as the buffalo will be reintroduced. The future they envision is a "deprivatized" Great Plains, the "world's largest historic preservation project, the ultimate national park."

The Poppers have a vivid and evocative name for this future that would replicate the past. They call it the Buffalo Commons. Partly because of this snappy, memorable phrase, partly because the media likes nothing better than apocalyptic predictions with a scholarly imprimatur (witness the flurry of national publicity over climatologist Iben Browning's forecast that the fault line in New Madrid, Missouri, had a fifty-fifty chance of creating a Midwest-leveling earthquake in 1990), the Buffalo Commons thesis quickly leapt from the ivory-covered walls of academe and crossed over into public consciousness the way few scholarly works ever do.

Not surprisingly, it also stirred up a hornet's nest in the Great Plains. Governors, congressmen, and other elected officials have denounced it, engaging in what one observer called Popper-bashing. The Poppers have been called "deranged," and the Buffalo Commons idea has been termed a "bunch of crap," "flapdoodle," and "Popperscock" by editors of small-town weeklies. Letters have poured in to the Poppers at Rutgers, about a quarter of them favorable and the rest ranging from politely critical to downright vicious; a few, unsigned, have referred ominously to a "Zionist conspiracy" against rural America. Think tanks and state governments have launched at least four studies to refute the Poppers' findings. The uproar, of course, has only spurred more publicity.

It is the proposal to turn the area around Jordan, Montana, into the Big Open preserve, writ large. People outside the area generally consider it visionary. Local residents, who take particular umbrage at the notion that settling the Plains had been a mistake from the start —it was their grandparents and parents, sometimes even themselves, who had come and stayed—hold the opposite view. All across the Plains, the Poppers have become as well known a couple as Donald and Ivana Trump—and about as well liked.

The debate over the Buffalo Commons resulted in numerous speaking invitations for the Poppers, and I accompanied them to one in McCook, Nebraska (population 8,000), a well-scrubbed and prosperous trading center on the Republican River, the largest town within a 70-mile radius in the southwestern corner of the state, a place that bills itself as the "City Without Limits." Early on the morning of the speech, I drove them to nearby Hayes County (1,222 people, 1.7 per square mile). According to the Poppers' various indicators, Hayes County is to become part of the Buffalo Commons. As the site of Grand Duke Alexis's extravaganza—the local paper calls the county the "Land of the Last Great Buffalo Hunt"—it seemed, I thought, a place they ought to see firsthand.

We stopped on the way for a photo session. A reporter and photographer from *The New York Times* were along, and they wanted to stage a picture of the Poppers, dressed in business attire and carrying briefcases, posed atop a bale of hay against a backdrop of sweeping fields and expansive sky. In the county seat of Hayes Center (population 231), the Poppers looked over the string of storefronts, half of them vacant, that make up the two-block town center, and saw what they considered confirmation of their thesis.

Van Korell, who owns the bank in town and part of a cattle feedlot on the outskirts, let them change into more informal clothes in his home. That Hayes Center is destined for desertion was news to him, and Korell seemed bemused by the notion. Regardless of the Poppers' statistics, he sees opportunity, not decline, in the county. Since he moved there in 1972, he said, no local businesses have closed, and seven new ones have opened. Johnny Scott, owner of the town's grocery store—probably the only IGA store in the nation that consistently sells out of 25-pound bags of flour, he said—moved to town in 1976 with his wife, a Hayes Center native. "I came by covered U-Haul from Florida," he joked. "I've found where I wanted to be. I see nothing but future here. We have clean air, we have space to expand. Someone could sell a three-hundred-thousand-dollar house in California, buy a fifty-thousand-dollar house here—and just *quit*. We're a strong people. I guess to some degree I've become like those who came here a hundred years ago and struggled to survive."

The site of Camp Alexis sits on land owned by Eldon Mintling, homesteaded in 1885 by Mintling's grandfather. Eldon's wife, Geraldine, and their son, Wayne, along with five other local residents, took us on a hike to a commemorative marker near Red Willow Creek. The route out led us through a small swamp, across the creek on a fallen box elder tree, and up and down several ravines; the way back was drier, easier, and more direct. My suspicion was that Wayne, who told me the Buffalo Commons idea is "bullshit" and who was carrying a rifle, wanted his New Jersey guests to have an adventure to remember. He warned them several times to make sure and check for ticks when they got back to their motel.

The old campsite is on a small, low stretch of ground near a bend in the creek, lined by cottonwoods, the only flat piece of terrain in the immediate area. In mid-April, the hills and ravines of the surrounding prairie looked as if a tawny robe had been thrown over the humps of a herd of giant, sleeping buffalo. Meadowlarks warbled in the clear air. If the Poppers had hoped to find human faces for their bleak statistics, they were disappointed with what the Hayes County people told them. As in Hayes Center, everything they heard contradicted their theory.

Asked what he saw as the county's future, Jim Broz, a thirty-eight-year-old rancher and farmer, whose grandfather also homesteaded in the area more than a hundred years ago, said, "It looks pretty good. We lost some families in the 1980s, but the school projection for the nineties doesn't see any decrease. There will always be people like Wayne and I here. We won't leave. We've both had our chances. We could have lived in the big city."

On the walk back, he turned the tables. "What kind of problems do you have in New Jersey?" he asked the Poppers.

"Racism," was Deborah's reply.

"I suppose every place has its problems," Jim said after thinking about it awhile. "We've always had them here. I don't think it's any different from anywhere else."

Unlike the grand duke's party, we had no champagne, but back at the house Geraldine Mintling gave Deborah small jars of jam from native buffalo berries, chokecherries, and grapes, and she showed the Poppers a few old buffalo skulls.

Asked privately what she thought of the Poppers' theories, Geraldine only smiled grimly and shook her head, as if speaking her mind would make her a bad hostess. Patty Vinson, editor of the Hayes Center weekly paper and part of the tour group, said, "If we did a study on *our* terms about New Jersey, I may come up with a whole different ballgame than what they perceive."

Frank Popper had sensed the undercurrents below the veneer of hospitality. On the return drive to McCook, he told Deborah, "I don't think tonight is going to be a very good night for us. I don't get the sense people here are buying our theory." When his opening joke—"I asked for buffalo at dinner tonight and they didn't have it, but Deborah and I are trying to do something about it"—fell flat, he knew his premonition had been right.

Nearly 300 people—about twice what the organizers predicted, particularly after several letters to the local newspaper suggested that residents should boycott the event—paid three dollars apiece for a chance to hear from what the *McCook Daily Gazette* had been referring to as the "controversial couple from New Jersey." Farmers made up a large part of the crowd, judging from the pale foreheads that met sunburned faces at what, during work hours, would be their cap lines. Their wives, dressed as if for Sunday services, sat quietly by their sides in the high school auditorium. The podium was decorated with an arrangement of dried wheat, milo, and soapweed. A bleached buffalo skull rested on the stage, near a furry buffalo robe. Frank, an intense man who speaks rapidly in staccato bursts of sentences, stood at the microphone. Deborah, markedly more laid back than her husband, was at an overhead projector, ready to flash onto the screen the graphs and maps they use to accompany their presentation.

Anticipating many of the arguments they had encountered during the past few years, the Poppers had refined, modified, and scaled back their first proposal. Their original piece described the upcoming depopulation in sweeping terms and mentioned the possibility of a Plains version of the Tennessee Valley Authority to handle resettlement and land management. Now they took pains to point out they were not advocating "the rural equivalent of some awful urban-renewal project" forcing Plains residents from their homes; instead, the Buffalo Commons would form where the free market, not the government, cleared the population. "Much of the region, like McCook, is in good shape," Frank assured the crowd. "We are not talking about nuking the Plains."

Using indicators such as population loss, the level of poverty, median age, and building construction figures, they had drawn maps showing which counties, already in "land-use distress," might be most vulnerable to disappearing into the Buffalo Commons sometime early in the next century. Pictures of Hayes and other neighboring counties flashed onto the screen. Murmuring rippled through the crowd. In all, the Poppers' latest projection of likely targets totaled 109 counties, encompassing 139,000 square miles, the home of 413,000 people. It's less than a quarter of the Plains, much smaller than their earlier writings envisioned, but still a big chunk of real estate.

Frank tried to correct other "misconceptions." Buffalo, for instance, wouldn't necessarily have to be reintroduced in great numbers; national grasslands might instead be enlarged or more farmland might simply be idled from cultivation. "The Buffalo Commons is just a metaphor," he cautioned. More disclaimers: he and Deborah were not working on government grants (suspicions about their motives and funding had been a common response); they had traveled through the Plains (countering anti-outsider sentiment that often salted accusers' complaints). In a final plea to be heard but not hated, he said, "We both *like* the Plains and we *like* its people. We really do."

Despite the modifications and qualifiers, the main message was still this: large parts of the region will be deserted because of economic, climatic, and social distress. As it has several times in the past, "the Plains will reassert itself" in a final rejection of settlement. In its place, the Buffalo Commons would emerge. Barring dramatic (and what the Poppers consider unlikely) changes in governmental and agricultural policies, the process seemed inexorable. The presentation had taken an hour. When it ended, the applause was, at best, restrained.

Next came the locals' turn. A "response panel" of four leading citizens went to work. They smiled pleasantly at the Poppers as they spoke; they were civil. But their collective response, laced occasionally with personal horror stories of visits to eastern cities and contrasting paeans to rural life, was an hour-long scolding. In as nice a way as possible, they in effect told the Poppers: "You're not from here, you don't know our land, and you don't understand our people. We come from hardy stock. If we have problems, we'll handle them ourselves. So butt out." The crowd interrupted constantly with hearty applause.

Clearly agitated by the way the respondents had seemingly ignored his maps and statistics and answered instead with what he later described as "Plains patriotism," Frank attempted to get in the last word.

"We *try* to emphasize that the region has wonderful virtues, wonderful people, and a wonderful quality of life," he told the audience. The question remained, he said, "with so much going for it through booms and busts, why is it so many portions of the Plains continue to lose population, continue to lose young people? Thank you."

No one applauded. The event was over. Apparently satisfied that their point of view had been more than adequately expressed, most people left quickly. A few, however, gathered around the Poppers near the stage. Two in particular had something they wanted to get off their chests.

Paul Orman, a tall farmer from Hayes County, crowded up to Frank. Orman's tanned face, flushed even darker with emotion, was only inches from Popper's, pallid and pasty from jet lag, exhaustion, and sweat. "Don't try to come out and use our land for common property for people from New Jersey and California," Orman said heatedly. *"Don't you do that!* You'll find there's things worth fighting for. There's life, liberty, and land worth fighting for." A special deputy, one of six uniformed officers on hand as a precaution, edged closer as the evening's emcee tried to ease Orman away. "I want to stand that man up and talk to him face to face," the farmer complained as he was gently ushered down the aisle. "When you're threatened, you have to respond."

Meanwhile, Phillys Lyons, a retired school teacher and native of Hayes County, had cornered Deborah Popper. She had read the Poppers' work and written a letter to the local paper refuting them. Before the lecture, she had gathered some fellow members of WIFE (Women Involved in Farm Economics) to discuss the Buffalo Commons. "It's obvious they don't know a *damn* thing about Nebraska, and I don't like them coming in to tell us what we should be doing," she had told the group. "Don't they think we're intelligent?"

The first map the Poppers had displayed had been of the Great Plains, with abbreviations for each state. Like others in the audience, Mrs. Lyons had spied a mistake and now had found her best weapon for retaliation. Looking sweetly but triumphantly into Deborah's eyes, she said, "You've identified our state with NB, which is New Brunswick, dear. We're NE."

Driving the couple to their next speaking engagement, in Denver, I gave the Poppers my own assessment of the Buffalo Commons and why I disagree with their predictions. Their statistics and a few hasty impressions, colored, I think, by the spatial and cultural shock any city dweller initially feels from encounters with the vastness and hardness of the open spaces, had led them too far in their conclusions. They had overlooked the irreducible minimum. Places can lose a lot of people and still more or less stabilize, slowly, often painfully, adjusting to the land and economy's carrying capacity. Life at such a level can be hard—inconceivably so by metropolitan standards—but it is a far cry from falling into the abyss they envisioned. It is the difference between virtually uninhabited and uninhabited, an important distinction that perhaps only residents of sparsely settled places fully understand.

In their maps of the ten Plains states, the Poppers identified 109 counties on the road to Buffalo Commonhood. Those same states had 97 counties with fewer than two people per square mile, yet the Poppers' list included only 35 of them. If much of the Plains were headed toward depopulation, why would 62 of the counties already closest to that unpeopled condition (and most of them still losing some residents with each census) be exempt? Why would so many other places, more densely populated but now going through the contractions that the contemporary frontier experienced a generation or two ago, not be able to stabilize and adjust the way their neighbors had? Perhaps the methodology was deficient. Perhaps the whole theory.

Perhaps, as I would contend, something different is happening: A lot of counties are heading toward contemporary frontier status, the irreducible minimum, undoubtedly a scary enough prospect for places accustomed to more than only one of the services most Americans take for granted, but nothing compared to the final step in which the government or some other group becomes custodian of an essentially unpeopled Plains. Struggling, but still surviving, and proud of it; virtually depopulated from one perspective, but populated and functioning from another, if the contemporary frontier portion of the Plains isn't already the Buffalo Commons, which the Poppers agreed it isn't, then it can enlarge without becoming "the world's largest historic preservation park, the ultimate national park."

We had much of the same statistical evidence, but had reached different conclusions from it. Towns indeed are dying, although, I would point out, not many in counties already part of the contemporary frontier, where towns that weren't county seats or essential to commerce disappeared some time ago. The "team-haul" principle still applies, adjusted to modern transportation. Fewer farmers and ranchers are on the land, but the ones who leave always have ready buyers—if not their neighbors, then the Japanese or some other absentee owner who still needs someone to do the work. Buffalo, in fact, are already returning—their population doubled during the 1980s—mostly on ranches owned by foreigners or wealthy city dwellers, occasionally by former cattlemen who see a potential profit in providing breeding stock to the growing specialty market. We stopped at one such ranch west of McCook, where a part-time rancher had a small herd. He was thinking of trying to cross-breed a few buffalo with some cattle to see what would happen; Frank Popper admitted that this wasn't exactly what they had in mind for the Commons.

I also argued with their use of the term "land-use distress" for counties undergoing population loss and little construction. In my mind, land-use distress is more common to densely settled, booming locations like Phoenix or Denver. I could have added New Jersey, but I didn't want to sound like a Plains patriot. And as for the nation's "largest, longest-running environmental miscalculation," my nominee would be Southern California, not the Dakotas.

In the end, we agreed to disagree on our projections. With luck, we'll all be around in thirty years to return to Hayes County and see what's happening at Camp Alexis. Maybe one of us will bring champagne. I'm counting on the Mintlings and their neighbors to still be around to provide the buffalo berry jam.

If the whole conception of a Buffalo Commons is an example of the Syndrome of Open Spaces, so, too, is the local response to the idea. Most often, the reaction has been visceral, emotional. So intense, and so personal, Deborah Popper told me, that at one point she considered dropping the topic and doing her dissertation on the effect of nineteenth-century banking practices on the development of New Jersey's manufacturing cities. "I thought maybe I'd better find something a little less heated and where everybody involved is dead," she said. Frank, who believes they have unintentionally hit "this enormous, once-in-a-lifetime vein" that few academics strike, had convinced her otherwise.

Marty Strange, at the Center for Rural Affairs in Nebraska, said the Buffalo Commons furor has obscured rational discussion of the real challenges facing the rural Plains and their solutions. "This debate is about 'placism,' " he said. "You assign pejorative traits to places that exhibit certain demographic characteristics." The Poppers are guilty of it, Strange said, as are those who respond with epithets about New Jersey: "It's like two ethnic groups sitting around, calling each other names."

"Placism" seems to be part of many of the other debates over the future uses of the open spaces, not just in the Great Plains but throughout the sparsely settled West. Most of the plans devised for what should take place there—from creating an exotic wildlife preserve in the Big Open to keeping the public lands available for multinational mining companies—are principally advocated by people who don't live there. Residence in a place at the irreducible minimum is too often considered evidence that your views should be the last to solicit, the least to consider. Traces of arrogance can usually be detected, a smug *We know better*, an implicit assumption of someone else's expendability.

On the other side of this divide, the local response is tinged with hypersensitivity and defensiveness: *If you're so smart, how come you live where the air is filthy, the roads are clogged, and you have to lock your doors at night? If we're such untrustworthy stewards, why are our skies clear, our land untrammeled enough to be considered wilderness, and you want our clean water?* Or, as Marianne Beel, a ranch wife in the Sand Hills, told me: "It's nice not to be ignored anymore. On the other hand, we're not sure what the new attention will lead to. We were ignored for years and years. In fact, we were laughed at: 'Who would want to live *there*?' Now that they've polluted the rest of the country, they want to preserve us and tell us how to do things. Yeah, we resent it."

With the Buffalo Commons, something more is at work, as well. In calling the settlement of the Plains a mistake from the outset, the Poppers have confronted America's potent, mythological sense of its mission to conquer and inhabit a continent—every single bit of it. Because of that, the Buffalo Commons thesis left the realm of metaphor and academic discourse and entered a more rough-and-tumble world, where ideas are taken as serious proposals and where emotions are as important as fact or reason in deciding matters.

In the cycles of the history of the West, another was being relived. A century ago, a Paiute Indian by the name of Wovoka had his own vision of the future. In it, if the Indians performed a certain dance, the white men would vanish from the land and the buffalo would magically return. The Ghost Dance caught on among many of the dispirited tribes, and, whether they took it literally or as a religious metaphor, the white settlers viewed it seriously enough to demand action. In the end, in 1890, Sitting Bull was killed and a Sioux village was eliminated at Wounded Knee.

The Poppers are academics, not Indian visionaries, and, despite the fact that organizers feel the need for security officers at all their speeches, they are clearly not in the same danger as Sitting Bull. But the Buffalo Commons proposal has struck the same deep emotions in Plains settlers as the Ghost Dance—and has received the twentieth-century version of its reception.

"THEIR CULTIVATED FIELDS; THEIR CONSTRUCTED habitations; a space . . . for their subsistence . . . was undoubtedly by the laws of nature theirs," said John Quincy Adams in an oration on the Indians' claims to American land in 1802. "But what is the right of the huntsman to the forest of a thousand miles over which he has accidentally ranged in quest of prey? Shall the liberal bounties of Providence be claimed by a few hundreds? Shall the lordly savage not only disdain the virtues and enjoyments of civilization by himself, but shall he control the civilization of the world? What is the Indian title? It is mere occupancy for the purpose of hunting. It is not like our tenures; they have no idea of a title to the soil itself. It is overrun by them, rather than inhabited. It is not a true and legal possession."

Nineteenth-century American settlement was informed by views like Adams's, expressed at a time when the western boundary of the United States was still the eastern shore of the Mississippi River, a year before the Louisiana Purchase, nearly fifty years before the California gold rush and the cessation of Oregon. The same perspective pertained when Robert Porter glowingly reported that the findings of the 1890 census "completes the history of a century; a century of progress and achievement unequaled in the world's history." Exhibit A for Porter was a statistic: since the first census in 1790, nearly two million square miles of American land had been "redeemed from the wilderness and brought into the service of man."

This perspective was a judgment on the land as much as on the indigenous people. If the land wasn't used intensively, it wasn't re-deemed. It was uncivilized. Emptiness was a vessel waiting to be filled by progress. At the time, the people living there happened to be Indians; their occupancy was "*mere*"; they *overran* the land rather than inhabited it. That they were of a different color and different culture made ig-noring their title that much easier, but it was the empty land that really was at issue. Policies toward the Indian tribes oscillated across the scale of extermination, subjugation, pacification, and education— sometimes embracing all four simultaneously—and popular attitudes toward them could swing abruptly, from disdainful contempt to ro-mantic exaltation, both of which did an equal disservice to understand-ing them. But the policy and attitude toward the land remained the same: use it to the hilt, settle it to the limit. Anything less would be a rejection of Manifest Destiny, a blot on the ledger of progress.

By the end of the last century, with the Indians effectively out of the way, some of the same attitude was merely transferred to their replacements in those places not yet fully settled and therefore still "uncivilized." Beyond the frontier line, to use the Census Bureau terms, lived a "petty population . . . the solitary ranchman, trapper, or fish-erman, . . . mining parties, lumber camps, and the like." A heavy taste of condescension salted this attitude, spiced occasionally with roman-ticized, nostalgic notions that these people, like the Indians, were the unsullied embodiments of virtue. Living so far from the influences of civilization, they were either bumpkins or mythic heroes, the white equivalents of Adams's "lordly savage."

Even today, perhaps particularly more so today, when we see a place without many people the immediate response is that something is not quite right. Empty is the first word that comes to mind, but it refers only to people and the physical evidence of their presence; it sure isn't empty of much else. Not to be gaining in population is still considered a lack of progress; declining in population is still equated with failure.

The major change in the last hundred years has been a slow, but steadily building shift in what we, as a nation, want to do with the empty land. With the continent conquered, and with a burgeoning population concentrating itself more and more in crowded metropol-itan areas, the open spaces have a new value. "Redeeming" them now means the opposite of what it once did.

Nonetheless, the way decisions get made on the fate of the land is still skewed by a cultural chasm, no longer so much along racial lines as along those of life-styles and place of residence. I don't particularly care for the term, but placism is the best word to describe it. Like the "mere occupants" before them, the "virtual uninhabitants" of the contemporary frontier have gone through a century of being ignored, patronized, misunderstood, caricatured, and sometimes forced to make sacrifices without being consulted.

Though sometimes leading to opposite conclusions—open spaces as dumping ground or wilderness museum—the same perspective often still applies: the settled seeing the less settled as a place to do whatever it desires, and the dense populations seeing the sparse as, at best, romantic anachronisms, at worst, a mere annoyance in the way. Placism isn't racism. The situation of residents of the contemporary frontier in the late twentieth century isn't nearly as extreme as that of the Indians of the nineteenth. Some might call that progress. But analogies—and some ironies—are there. Like so much else in the contemporary frontier compared to its predecessor a century ago, it is an echo of history, still rumbling through the present into the future.

CHAPTER 9

OLD FRONTIER, CONTEMPORARY FRONTIER

IF YOU WANT TO PROVOKE A GOOD FIGHT AMONG HIS-
torians (both professional and amateur) of the American West these
days, just mention Frederick Jackson Turner and the frontier thesis
he set forth a century ago, when Chicago hosted a world's exposition
to celebrate the 400th anniversary of Christopher Columbus's landfall.
Turner's "The Significance of the Frontier in American History" sits at
the crux of an intense, much-publicized, and occasionally acrimonious
argument over the definition of the term "frontier," over when, even
whether, it ever "closed," and over its national significance—over what
the settling of the West tells us about American society.

The controversy took some time to build. Turner's speech was delivered as the last of five scholarly papers on a sultry July evening
during a Historical Congress convened for the exposition. The first

four treatises were titled "English Popular Uprisings in the Middle Ages," "The Social Compact and Mr. Jefferson's Adaptation of It," "The Relation of History to Politics," and "Early Lead Mining in Illinois and Wisconsin." When it was finally Turner's time to speak, the audience listened indifferently—it's hard to imagine many of them were still awake—as he expounded his theory that the frontier had shaped the nation's institutions, created a uniquely American national character, and furnished "a new field of opportunity" for pioneers hardy enough to seek it. "The true point of view in the history of this nation is not the Atlantic coast," he said, "it is the Great West."

"And now," Turner concluded, "four centuries from the discovery of America, at the end of a hundred years of life under the Constitution, the frontier has gone, and with its going has closed the first period of American history." Those words have stirred both praise and ridicule for nearly a hundred years, but in Chicago in 1893 their delivery by an obscure, young scholar from Wisconsin apparently stirred only the movement of chairs and feet as the audience headed toward the doors. No one asked any questions; newspaper and scholarly accounts of the Historical Congress paid the scantest attention to the frontier thesis. The general public was even less immediately interested in the theory, although the popular attractions at the exposition might have suggested that people already were viewing the story of American settlement with nostalgia and romanticism. The day of the speech, a replica of a Viking ship sailed into the harbor on Lake Michigan; the cabin where Sitting Bull had been killed three years earlier in the Dakotas was on display, having been torn down, shipped, and reconstructed on the Chicago fairgrounds; Buffalo Bill's Wild West Show was re-enacting Indian battles and stagecoach robberies for tourists in the grandstands. *That's* where the crowds were.

Despite the initial inattention to Turner's speech, within ten years his frontier thesis had not only swept through the halls of academe but had become the public's accepted view of the past and present. Teddy Roosevelt, on the way to the White House, had been an early convert; so had Woodrow Wilson, still a professor in New Jersey. Turner became the lion of American historiography. When he spoke it was at the top of the program and audiences sat, as one listener recalled, "in quiet rapture under the spell of words as harmonious as poetry falling on the ear in clear and resonant tones, and then [felt], as the moments go by, the heart glow, the mind expand, the fires of aspiration burn because there is added to the beauty of form and expression, thoughts pulsating with life and strength and practical wisdom and moral earnestness." Why this change? For one reason, at the time Turner was saying what people wanted to hear.

"The outstanding feature of the frontier thesis was its optimism," wrote Ray Allen Billington, a disciple and biographer of Turner. "The frontier was disappearing, but the pioneer experience had bred into Americans not only value judgments and beliefs that elevated them above lesser peoples, but a hardihood and an aggressive spirit that would allow them to protect their way of life and thought against hostile forces. Turner had pictured a Promethean struggle between man and the wilderness with man emerging triumphant. . . . Whatever the results of the closing of the frontier, Americans had been so endowed by their triumph over the wilderness that they could fashion a new civilization, embodying the best of their pioneer days, but benefiting from the new industrialism. Turner's theories were acceptable —and accepted—because they gave substance to folk myths that satisfied the need of Americans for a rose-tinted view of the future."

As popularized as it became, as influential as it was in directing American historians to use an interdisciplinary approach in their work, to study ordinary people's responses to the landscape, and to link local stories with the broader sweep of the nation's history, Turner's frontier thesis has had its share of critics. In the 1930s and 1940s, for instance, they focused on his subscription to the "agrarian myth," the Jeffersonian ideal of a United States peopled by yeomen farmers, while ignoring the rise of an industrial, urban nation.

But never have his theories been under such attack as today. Historians—mostly younger ones who came of age in the 1960s and early 1970s—are revising and demolishing virtually every portion of the frontier thesis. Patricia Limerick, probably the best known of the revisionists, points out that Turner's narrative of westward expansion ignores important characters in the story: Indians, women, Hispanics, Orientals, and blacks. He and his disciples, she argues, also tended to overlook the myriad failures—some personal, some colossal—that were part of the settlement saga; they concentrated more on the booms than the busts; their version of western history nourished the even glossier Hollywood view, all happy endings and golden sunsets while skipping over the seamier details of Manifest Destiny, the broken dreams, victimized people, and assaulted environment. She has even suggested that the term "frontier"—which she calls the "F-word"—be discarded. Another historian, Richard White, has done just that. On the premise that the notion of a frontier is an ethnocentric point of view held only by European settlers from the East, he has written a textbook history of the West without using the word.

Donald Worster, an environmental historian, has shown that the control of water in the arid West resulted in just the opposite of individual freedoms and small-scale democracy. "The hydraulic society of the West," he writes, "is . . . increasingly a coercive, monolithic, and hierarchical system, ruled by a power elite based on the ownership of capital and expertise." Frank and Deborah Popper, although not historians and not involved in directly challenging Turner's ghost, nevertheless have questioned whether the frontier ever closed at all. In fact, they foresee it expanding, not only in their proposed Buffalo Commons but in other parts of the West, as well. "We are no longer a frontier nation," they have written. "But we are still a nation with a frontier."

Many of these arguments aren't exactly new. Turner's bones have been picked at for generations, like a buffalo carcass on the Plains. What distinguishes the new revisionism, however, is its underlying moral judgment on the whole messy enterprise of making a continental nation. The emphasis has shifted from the victories to the defeats, from the conquerors to the conquered and victimized, from the larger result to the prices paid. If Turner and his early adherents can fairly be accused of tilting too much toward one extreme, the more zealous revisionists are equally guilty of overemphasizing the other.

Turner himself, who in later years was less hidebound by his own theories than many of his acolytes, would probably understand the change, even if he disagreed with it. "Each age," he wrote, "writes the history of the past anew with reference to the conditions uppermost in its own time." In an era of national self-doubt and multicultural sensitivity, so different from Turner's time except, perhaps, in its tendency toward excessiveness, the pendulum was bound to swing.

DRAWING A LINE IN HISTORY CAN BE AS ARBITRARY as drawing one on a census map. Without subscribing to many of

Turner's views, I think he had a legitimate point when he said an era was closing and a new one beginning. Perhaps 1890 didn't mark it precisely, but that year witnessed some milestones of a transition in progress.

In that year, the killing of Sitting Bull and the massacre of Big Foot's village at Wounded Knee marked the inglorious end of white warfare upon the nation's first inhabitants; a presidential decree forced the Cherokees to sell their grazing leases on the Cherokee Strip, paving the way for the first of several land rushes that eventually ended the sovereignty of the Five Tribes and led to creation of the state of Oklahoma out of the former Indian Territory. In Utah, the Mormon church traded its prescription of polygamy for the chance of statehood; with it went the use of the West as a large-scale sanctuary for nontraditional religions. And the Census Bureau, though it did so as much out of convenience as from consistency with its own methodology, decided that the notion of a west-moving frontier line no longer applied to the nation's settlement patterns.

A transition, especially one that occurs over the span of decades, differs from a clear-cut ending and beginning. After 1890, four times as much land was transferred to private hands through homesteading as had been previously. Nobody told Margaret Stafford the frontier had closed when she took out her homestead application in Garfield County in the 1920s. (She also didn't need to read historians sixty years later to learn that the pioneering life was hard, fraught with setbacks and failures.) But for the dominant white culture, as the sparse and generally shrinking population today proves, most of the land that was available in this century was the hardest to settle, with the most unforgiving climate and terrain in which to try to establish roots. By 1890, the pickings were getting slim. What one historian has called "The Great Barbecue" of the nineteenth century was essentially over.

Transitions also carry with them connections from one era to another. In his critique of the revisionist historians (he calls the movement Failure Studies), the author Larry McMurtry makes two salient points. One is that "the winning of the West was an act based on a dream of empire dreamed by people with very different mentalities and ambitions from those historians or Westerners who may now direct a critical eye, quite fairly, at the legacy of that same dream and that same act. Failure Studies, by contrast, in their effort to have the truth finally told, often fail themselves because they so rarely do justice to the quality of imagination that constitutes part of the truth. They may be accurate about the experience, but they simplify or ignore the emotions and imaginings that impelled the Western settlers despite their experience. Explorers and pioneers of all stamps needed imagination, much as athletes need carbohydrates. Fantasy provided part of the fiber that helped them survive the severities that the land put them to."

McMurtry also cautions against overdrawing the comparisons between the old West and the new: "I'm not sure the similarities really outweigh the differences. Then we had Indian wars; now we have an Indian remnant. Then we had a war with Mexico, and took a hunk of it; now we have 'troubled relations with Mexico.' Then half the continent was still unspoiled; now it isn't. It's understandable that historians would be intrigued with continuity and change, and it's interesting to pick threads of the past from the fabric of the present. Still, a Western pioneer of the nineteenth century and a Western suburbanite in the twentieth century have had profoundly different realities to contend with, and the fact that the problems of the latter stem from the behavior of the former shouldn't be allowed to blur the difference."

LIKE PINPOINTING A PRECISE TURNING POINT IN western history, defining what constitutes a frontier and what doesn't is also fraught with argument. Turner himself admitted problems with a good definition and over the years came up with several of them: "the hither edge of free land"; a "graphic line which records the expansive energies of the people behind it"; "those outlying regions which at different stages of the country's development have been but imperfectly settled, and have constituted the meeting-ground between savagery and civilization"; or "a migratory section, rather a stage of society than an area."

Walter Prescott Webb, who expanded Turner's thesis to explain Europe's four-hundred-year conquest of much of the world, encompassing what he called the "Great Frontier," wrote that "the frontier was open as long as there remained extensive areas of royal or public domain which the sovereign Powers had not yet alienated, which had not passed into private hands." Somewhere between 1890 and 1910, he said, this big boom finally petered out.

Patricia Limerick doesn't like the term "frontier" in the first place —"an unsubtle concept in a subtle world," she calls it. If a frontier closing point is necessary, she contends, it might be when the rigors of pioneering are replaced by quaintness and tourism. But, she adds, "let the car break down in the desert, or let the Indians file a lawsuit to reassert an old land claim, and the quaint appeal of nature and native can abruptly vanish. The frontier is suddenly reopened." She makes a valid argument that sparse population, by itself, does not a frontier make: "One could easily argue the opposite—that a sudden concentration of population marks the opening stage and that a population lowered through, for instance, the departure of people from a used-up mining region marks the end of the frontier and its opportunities."

For my purposes, I have referred to counties with fewer than two people per square mile as the contemporary frontier in part merely out of tradition. Arbitrary and incomplete as it was, this definition of frontier was the one the government employed until 1890, when the Census Bureau announced that an easily drawn frontier *line* no longer made sense, therefore prompting the whole notion that the frontier itself was gone. On the centennial of that census, I wanted to see for myself, so I used the same criterion.

Certainly, a place with 1.9 people per square mile is not significantly more "frontier" than one with 2.1 per square mile, or perhaps not even more "frontier" than one with three or four residents per section. Health professionals contend that counties with six people or fewer per square mile constitute a distinct "health-care frontier": a place with special medical needs and without the infrastructure or personnel to adequately attend to them. In their view, population density is a crucial factor for an important element of existence. Somewhere along the scale, as the people thin out and the miles expand, the irreducible minimum is reached in other aspects of life as well. I think it generally exists on the sparse side of the traditional census line.

Terming such places a contemporary frontier serves another useful function, one that is more suggestive than precise. It differentiates them from metropolitan America, where three-quarters of the nation's population now lives, and even from rural America, where small towns are regularly interspaced with small farms. The contemporary frontier is unlike either metropolitan or rural America, and profoundly so. In many respects, it is also unlike the nineteenth-century frontier. McMurtry was correct, but didn't go far enough. A twentieth-century western suburbanite confronts a different reality than a nineteenth-century pioneer; so, too, a contemporary frontiersman's reality differs from his predecessor's in the same, sparsely populated spot in the West. In both cases, while connections bridge the gaps, the differences often outweigh the similarities.

The contrasts (and connections) with the rest of contemporary America are as self-evident as watching a commercial for McDonald's on your satellite-connected television set and then having to drive a hundred uninterrupted miles of open road for a Big Mac. The historical dissimilarities are perhaps less expected, but equally profound.

The old frontier was seen as the locus of boundless opportunity waiting to be tapped. People went there seeking their fortunes. With a few exceptions, the contemporary frontier is viewed as an economic backwater; what few people are moving in—retirees or "quality-of-life pioneers" hoping to find a slower pace amidst nice scenery—are usually those who have already made their money. The expectation for a frontier area once was growth; it was a nearly empty place anticipating being filled. Now, it is a nearly empty place worried about becoming emptier; the prognosis most often is for decline.

A century ago, the frontier population was relatively young in age; today it is older than average. (I discovered an odd phenomenon in my travels. People in their twenties and early thirties seemed to look older than their calendar years, while senior citizens seemed to look younger than they actually were. It was as if the hard life and the weathering effects of sun and dry air prematurely aged people, but then preserved them longer. Often I would guess someone's age as about fifty and be off by ten or more years on either side.) The western frontier once was an international and cultural meeting ground, hardly a melting pot since the various nationalities and races clashed more than mingled, but it was probably more diverse in its composition than much of the rest of the nation at the time. The contemporary frontier—again with certain exceptions—is overwhelmingly white; diversity is to be found somewhere else.

The settled, "civilized" parts of America once viewed the frontier as a wilderness in need of taming and exploiting, inhabited by a savage yet quaintly noble people incapable of playing a significant role in determining the best uses of their land. Today's urban nation increasingly sees the contemporary frontier as a wilderness in need of protecting, even enlarging. (Although in a pinch—say the cities' need for water, or an energy crisis—exploiting is still one of the first options to be considered.) As before, today's frontier residents, seen by the rest of the nation as backward yet occasionally colorful, are the first ones dismissed while others debate and decide these matters.

In places once renowned for their lawlessness and extreme violence now reside people who say one of the best things about living there is that they don't have to worry about crime. Danger still lurks in the frontier—from long drives and fast cars, physically risky occupations, sudden extreme changes in the weather, and remote medical care—but not the kind that gave the "Wild West" its nickname.

As it once was, the frontier West is still the repository of many of the stereotypes associated with what defines (and sells) "America" to the rest of the world and to ourselves: plenty of open spaces, small-community values, and the rugged personality symbolized in visual shorthand by a cowboy on a horse. It is a respository of many of our national myths and dreams about who we really are and what we stand for. Ironically, this repository is now even more anomalous, even more out of sync with the preponderance of modern American life than it was when those stereotypes were formed. The contemporary frontier is also increasingly a different kind of repository: for the deadly wastes no one else wants, for the experiments no other part of the country would tolerate.

Finally, the old western frontier was the gathering spot for the rootless, restless portions of the expanding white culture. For most of the pioneers, miners, trappers, and others it was not home, it was a temporary stopping point, a place to ride some booms as long as they lasted before moving on when the inevitable busts arrived. Quite the contrary, residents of the contemporary frontier on the whole are what Wallace Stegner calls "stickers." In a nation that still equates progress with mobility, in which a strong sense of place is a quaint oddity, they are among the most rooted of Americans. Their lives are defined by the space they inhabit, while in the rest of the nation, the landscape has been redefined by the lives the people lead.

The story of the populated West beyond the 98th meridian might be titled "Technology Triumphant." In *The Great Plains*, Walter Prescott Webb drove home this point. Without advances in technology—the windmill, barbed wire, railroads, mechanical threshers, the Colt revolver, and especially irrigation systems to bring water where it wasn't otherwise adequately available—European-styled settlement would not have been possible. If anything, the modern West relies even more heavily, many would say precariously, on technology for its survival. Consider Phoenix without air conditioning. Salt Lake City without electricity from some distant coal plant. Las Vegas without airplanes. Los Angeles without water from the Owens Valley and the Colorado River. For that matter, consider almost any good-sized western city (and much of the region's agriculture) without water from someplace else. They haven't adapted to their environment. They have, for the moment at least, seemingly conquered it.

Within the contemporary frontier, however, the environment still rules. For the most part, residents there have adapted to it—admittedly more out of brute necessity than ideology, and admittedly not as completely as the Indians once did, but far more than any other part of the West. Modern technology isn't absent: cars have changed the spacing of surviving towns; satellites and telephones and computers allow people to sell cattle and real estate to people far away, to occasionally "commute" by modem, to confer with their neighbors kitchen-to-kitchen; helicopters are capable of transporting the injured and ill to the closest hospital; school buses in Wayne County, Utah, can be outfitted with small television sets so that students riding an hour and a half twice a day can watch educational programs as they travel; water pumps miles from power lines in the Big Bend may run on solar panels; and United Parcel Service might arrive every day. But these are examples of technology modifying existence, making it a little less difficult to survive in a difficult place. The land and the climate remain the major forces. The miles are still so very long, the winters so harsh and cold, the summers so hot and dry. Mere existence is still demanding and hard. The people who have remained have accepted those realities, as few others in the rest of the country have.

"It is in places like these, and through individuals like these, that the West will realize itself, if it ever does," Stegner wrote in *The American West as Living Space*. "[T]hese towns and cities still close to the earth, intimate and interdependent in their shared community, shared optimism, and shared memory. These are the seedbeds of an emergent western culture. They are likely to be there when the agribusiness fields have turned to alkali flats and the dams have silted up, when the waves of overpopulation that have been destroying the West have receded, leaving the stickers to get on with the business of adaptation."

In the last decade, twelve more counties lost enough population to fall below two people per square mile. Even more will undoubtedly join them in the next century. Forgotten, neglected, condescended toward, occasionally over-romanticized, but most often simply overlooked, the contemporary frontier is less what the West once was than it is what even larger portions of the West will become. That may be the frontier's future significance.

EPILOGUE:
A CENSUS OF
NOWHERE

IN THE SPRING OF 1990, HOWARD AND GEORGIA Kahn, ages sixty-eight and sixty-seven, respectively, both retired (she had been a school teacher), took temporary jobs with the Census Bureau to count the people in Harney County, Oregon. Like 60 percent of the county's population, the Kahns lived in the twin towns of Burns and Hines (combined population about 4,000), but because they were familiar with the southwestern corner of the huge county—they are both avid hunters and Georgia had worked eleven summers as a fire lookout in the area—they were assigned to it as enumerators.

They checked tax and school records, talked to the sheriff and other officials, looked over previous censuses and maps, and got a pretty good idea of how many people lived in the 2,000-square-mile corner (bigger than Delaware, twice the size of Rhode Island). Thirty people, it turned out. But their job was to make an on-site survey of residents and dwellings, so into the field they went.

During two months they put 7,000 miles on their Datsun truck. Most of the roads in the area are "two-tracks"—rough paths over rocky, high-desert terrain, a landscape of basaltic escarpments, dusty valleys, steep canyons, and lots of sagebrush where you drive four or five miles per hour. Their truck's four-wheel-drive came in handy more than once.

One day after a spring rain, however, the pickup mired in a soft spot of mud and they couldn't get it out. The Kahns were not unprepared for such things. They had some food and water and sleeping bags with them and spent the night under the camper shell on the pickup's bed. The next day, Howard hiked 16 miles to the nearest paved road, waited for a passing car, and hitchhiked to a place that could drive him back to extricate his vehicle. The trip took more than a day, so Georgia spent a second night in the truck. The nighttime temperature dropped into the twenties, but she didn't consider it particularly threatening or eventful. Just part of the job, part of what you should expect miles from nowhere. Howard returned, the pickup was pulled from the mud, and they went on with their business.

Near the end of their two months of enumerating, they decided to go back to a particularly remote section where earlier they had seen two horses near some empty trailers. Maybe some cowboys were there working out of a cow camp. During their travels they had already found two houses, abandoned but needing to be added to the list of dwellings, that no one had known about. And at another cow camp they had come across two cowboys nobody but their employer (in another county) had realized were there. Perhaps they'd find some more uncounted residents at the trailers in Oreano Canyon. They left on a Sunday morning. When they didn't report back in Burns on Monday, people got worried. A search and rescue effort was mounted.

Harney County covers 10,174 square miles of southeastern Oregon. If it seceded and became a state on its own, it would rank forty-first in size. Most of the sagebrush land is used for ranching, although the northern quarter of the county is forested, supporting a logging industry for which Burns and Hines are the center. The federal government controls 73 percent of the area, including national forests, grazing lands, and a huge national wildlife refuge near Harney and Malheur

lakes, two closed-basin bodies of water that are favorite spots for migrating birds and waterfowl. Other than Burns and Hines, the settlements are like Fields, in the southern end, "towns" more in name than
fact. Riley, one such place, is a combination gas station/store with a
post office on the other side of the highway; a sign outside the station
advertises "Town For Sale." Crane has the only public high school
dormitory in the contiguous states other than the one in Garfield
County, Montana. Like most other contemporary frontier counties,
Harney County lost population between 1980 and 1990, dropping from
8,314 residents to 7,060; 0.7 people per square mile.

Despite the county's vastness and sparse population, everyone
knows everyone else. In Frenchglen I saw a notice for an upcoming
Halloween party at a bar more than 60 miles away. In Burns, I met a
candidate for state representative campaigning door-to-door. She lived
in a neighboring county, but her district, the second biggest such jurisdiction in area in the Lower 48, some 28,000 square miles (about
half the size of Michigan, Illinois, or Georgia), included Harney County
and, she said, if people don't meet you face-to-face they won't vote for
you. When the search began for the Kahns, it was a personal undertaking, friends volunteering to help friends.

Rescue efforts are not uncommon. Tourists driving in the Alvord
Desert or hiking on Steens Mountain, two popular but isolated spots,
frequently get lost or hurt and require assistance. A fire in 1990, ignited
by lightning, scorched 100,000 acres of range and forest and was fought
by 2,500 people brought into the county to help the locals. Cattle and
horses perished in the inferno, but no people. Driving the highways at
night is known locally as trying to navigate "deer alley" without having
a collision. In these parts, nature has a lethal edge to it.

There were also other concerns for the missing Kahns. Harney
County shares the same paranoia felt by other sparsely settled places
—some legitimate, some of it exaggerated—about outsiders' designs
on their area. A year earlier, two strangers had been discovered and
arrested for setting up an illegal "crank" drug factory in an abandoned
building on a remote alkali flat. When I was in the county, the local
weekly paper had two front-page stories alarming the residents. One
was about a poster, with a likeness of Smokey the Bear on it, that
encouraged youngsters to spike trees to stop logging and to "help

Smokey's animal friends" by pulling up survey stakes. The other story said that a radical environmental group, opposed to grazing on public lands, was urging people to shoot cattle as a new outdoor sport.

Burns has a small hospital, suffering the same problems common to all medical services in the contemporary frontier. Doctors had been recruited with the help of a $15,000 reward for anyone who could find and convince one to locate there. (A local rancher collected the finder's fee in the spring of 1990. He said of the money: "I'll just keep ranching until it's gone.") To end a nursing shortage, the hospital had advertised in *American Hunter* and *Outdoor Life* magazines, sent direct-mail appeals to every nurse in Oregon, and even asked local churches to pray for nurses. "Whatever a frontier is, this is it," said Mary Ann Bailey, the director of nurses. She estimated that there are five trauma cases a year in which the patients would have lived or suffered less seriously if the accidents had occurred in a place where emergency services are closer. Air Life of Oregon, a helicopter and airplane ambulance service for eastern and central Oregon, was undertaking its annual membership drive. For the forty-dollar membership fee, people can be transported for free in an emergency; about half the county belongs. The local ground ambulance service has one full-time paramedic and the fire chief, who does double-duty with the ambulance, plus thirty volunteers. "What makes the difference here," Mrs. Bailey said, "is the *distance.*"

The search for the missing census takers included the use of five airplanes to cover as much of the southwestern corner of Harney County as quickly as possible. The Kahns' pickup wasn't spotted until late Wednesday morning.

The couple had reached the line shacks by a particularly rough road across some volcanic lava bluffs. Having determined to their satisfaction that no one, in fact, was inhabiting the trailers, they started back for Burns. About four miles down the road, they ran out of gas. Howard had forgotten to put an extra supply in the back. They weren't lost. They knew exactly where they were: a good 35 miles from the closest "town" and paved road to the west, a little farther than that from a settlement and pavement to the east, double those distances to the north or south. They also knew the only thing for them to do was to wait for somebody to find them.

They pushed their pickup back toward the trailers, slowly making about two or three miles before darkness descended. They left the truck and spent the night in one of the line shacks. The next morning, they pushed the truck the rest of the way. They had some crackers and cheese and sandwich makings and pancake flour with them, and some Kool-Aid and hot chocolate mix. There was a spring nearby, so they had water once the jug they had brought along was empty. Whoever had put the trailers there—nobody still knows, maybe hunters or ranch hands or the Bureau of Land Management—had left behind a deck of cards and some ten-year-old magazines. The Kahns played solitaire and rummy, read the news from the last decade, gradually went through their food supplies, and waited. With no electricity and lights, they went to bed at dusk, rose with the sun. Monday and Tuesday passed, then most of Wednesday.

They were down to pancake flour when one of the search planes landed on a flat stretch nearby. "We figured somebody'd find us," Georgia told me later. "We were warm and had water, the two things you need." She estimated they could have held out for a couple more days. As for that particular part of Harney County, she said, "We knew that there's nothing out there, but we had to prove it."

The pilot siphoned gas into their tank, charged their truck's battery, and then, back in the air, led them out. The Kahns got home by nightfall, in the midst of national publicity and incredulity that in 1990 census takers in the United States could be missing for four days.

CONTEMPORARY FRONTIER COUNTIES

COUNTY	1990 POPULATION	POPULATION DENSITY (People/square mile)
California		
Alpine	1,113	1.5
Inyo	18,281	1.8
Colorado		
Baca	4,556	1.8
Cheyenne	2,397	1.3
Dolores	1,504	1.4
Hinsdale	467	0.4
Jackson	1,605	1.0
Kiowa	1,688	1.0
Lincoln	4,529	1.8
Mineral	558	0.6
Rio Blanco	5,972	1.9
Saguache	4,619	1.5
San Juan	745	1.9
Washington	4,812	1.9

COUNTY	1990 POPULATION	POPULATION DENSITY (People/square mile)
Idaho		
Boise	3,509	1.8
Butte	2,918	1.3
Camas	727	0.7
Clark	762	0.4
Custer	4,133	0.8
Idaho	13,783	1.6
Lemhi	6,899	1.5
Owyhee	8,392	1.1
Valley	6,109	1.7
Kansas		
Wallace	1,821	1.99
Montana		
Beaverhead	8,424	1.5
Blaine	6,728	1.6
Carter	1,503	0.4
Chouteau	5,452	1.4
Daniels	2,266	1.6
Fallon	3,103	1.9
Garfield	1,589	0.4
Golden Valley	912	0.8
Granite	2,548	1.5
Judith Basin	2,282	1.2
Liberty	2,295	1.6
McCone	2,276	0.9
Madison	5,989	1.7
Meagher	1,819	0.8
Petroleum	519	0.3
Phillips	5,163	1.0
Powder River	2,090	0.6
Prairie	1,383	0.8
Sweet Grass	3,154	1.7
Treasure	874	0.9

COUNTY	1990 POPULATION	POPULATION DENSITY (People/square mile)
Valley	8,239	1.7
Wheatland	2,246	1.6
Wibaux	1,191	1.3
Nebraska		
Arthur	462	0.7
Banner	852	1.1
Blaine	675	0.9
Cherry	6,307	1.1
Garden	2,460	1.5
Grant	769	1.0
Hayes	1,222	1.7
Hooker	793	1.1
Keya Paha	1,029	1.3
Logan	878	1.5
Loup	683	1.2
McPherson	546	0.6
Sioux	1,549	0.7
Thomas	851	1.2
Wheeler	948	1.6
Nevada		
Elko	33,530	1.96
Esmeralda	1,344	0.4
Eureka	1,547	0.4
Humboldt	12,844	1.3
Lander	6,266	1.1
Lincoln	3,775	0.4
Mineral	6,475	1.7
Nye	17,781	1.0
Pershing	4,336	0.7
White Pine	9,264	1.0
New Mexico		
Catron	2,563	0.4
De Baca	2,252	1.0

COUNTY	1990 POPULATION	POPULATION DENSITY (People/square mile)
Guadalupe	4,156	1.4
Harding	987	0.5
Hidalgo	5,958	1.7
Union	4,124	1.1
North Dakota		
Billings	1,108	1.0
Slope	907	0.7
Oklahoma		
Cimarron	3,301	1.8
Oregon		
Gilliam	1,717	1.4
Grant	7,853	1.7
Harney	7,060	0.7
Lake	7,186	0.9
Wheeler	1,396	0.8
South Dakota		
Corson	4,195	1.7
Haakon	2,624	1.4
Harding	1,669	0.6
Hyde	1,696	1.97
Jackson	2,811	1.5
Jones	1,324	1.4
Mellette	2,137	1.6
Perkins	3,932	1.4
Stanley	2,453	1.7
Sully	1,589	1.6
Ziebach	2,220	1.1
Texas		
Borden	799	0.9
Brewster	8,681	1.4
Crockett	4,078	1.5

COUNTY	1990 POPULATION	POPULATION DENSITY (People/square mile)
Culberson	3,407	0.9
Edwards	2,266	1.1
Glasscock	1,447	1.6
Hudspeth	2,915	0.6
Irion	1,629	1.5
Jeff Davis	1,946	0.9
Kenedy	460	0.3
Kent	1,010	1.1
King	354	0.4
Loving	107	0.2
McMullen	817	0.7
Motley	1,532	1.5
Oldham	2,278	1.5
Presidio	6,637	1.7
Roberts	1,025	1.1
Sterling	1,438	1.6
Terrell	1,410	0.6
Utah		
Beaver	4,765	1.8
Daggett	690	1.0
Garfield	3,980	0.8
Grand	6,620	1.8
Juab	5,817	1.7
Kane	5,169	1.3
Millard	11,333	1.7
Piute	1,277	1.7
Rich	1,725	1.7
San Juan	12,621	1.6
Wayne	2,177	0.9
Wyoming		
Crook	5,294	1.9
Johnson	6,145	1.5
Niobrara	2,499	1.0
Sublette	4,843	1.0

SELECTED SOURCES

Introduction

Gannett, Henry. *International Review* 12 (January 1882).
Turner, Frederick Jackson. "The Significance of the Frontier in American History." Tucson: University of Arizona Press, 1986.
U.S. Bureau of the Census. Census Report, 1890.
U.S. Bureau of the Census. Census Report, 1990.

Chapter One: Big Dry

Alwin, John A. "Jordan Country—A Golden Anniversary Look." *Annals of the Association of American Geographers* 71 (December 1981), no. 4.
Billing, May. *Echoes of an Era.* Vols. 1, 2, and 3. Self-published, 1983 and 1989.
Bowman, Isaiah. "Jordan Country." *Geographical Review* 21 (January 1931).
Jordan, Arthur. *Jordan.* Missoula: Mountain Press Publishing Co., 1984.
McHugh, Tom. *The Time of the Buffalo.* Lincoln: University of Nebraska Press, 1972.
Schillreff, Fern, and Jessie M. Shawver. *Garfield County: The Golden Years.* Vols. 1 and 2. Self-published, n.d.

Chapter Two: Violence

Blevins, Terry W., ed. *Tri-County History: A Centennial.* Limon, Colo.: The Tri-County Centennial, 1989.

Brandon, William, ed. *The American Heritage Book of Indians*. New York: Dell, 1961.

Duncan, Dayton. *Out West: An American Journey*. New York: Viking, 1987.

Greenberg, Michael, George W. Carey, and Frank J. Popper. "Violent Death, Violent States, and American Youth." *The Public Interest*, Spring 1987.

Hoig, Stan. *The Peace Chiefs of the Cheyenne*. Norman: University of Oklahoma Press, 1982.

Kelley, Charles. *The Outlaw Trail: A History of Butch Cassidy and His Wild Bunch*. New York: Bonanza Books, 1938.

Limerick, Patricia Nelson. *The Legacy of Conquest: The Unbroken Past of the American West*. New York: W. W. Norton, 1987.

Lingenfelter, Richard E. *Death Valley and the Amargosa: A Land of Illusion*. Berkeley: University of California Press, 1986.

Mercer, A. S. *The Banditti of the Plains; Or the Cattlemen's Invasion of Wyoming in 1892 (The Crowning Infamy of the Ages)*. Norman: University of Oklahoma Press, 1954.

Smith, Helena Huntington. *The War on Powder River: The History of an Insurrection*. Lincoln: University of Nebraska Press, 1966.

Utley, Robert M. *Billy the Kid: A Short and Violent Life*. Lincoln: University of Nebraska Press, 1989.

———. *The Indian Frontier of the American West 1846–1890*. Albuquerque: University of New Mexico Press, 1984.

Wheeler, Raymond. "Southern Utah: The Trauma of Shifting Economies and Ideologies." In *Reopening the Western Frontier*, edited by Ed Marston. Washington, D.C.: Island Press, 1989.

Chapter Three: Escape

Brandon, William, ed. *The American Heritage Book of Indians*. New York: Dell, 1961.

Davidson, Sara. *Real Property*. New York: Doubleday, 1969.

Day, Samuel H., Jr., ed. *Nuclear Heartland: A Guide to the 1,000 Missile Silos of the United States*. Madison: The Progressive Foundation, 1988.

Foster, Laurence. *Negro-Indian Relationships in the Southeast*. New York: AMS Press, 1935.

McReynolds, Edwin C. *The Seminoles*. Norman: University of Oklahoma Press, 1957.

Metz, Leon G. *Pat Garrett: The Story of a Western Lawman*. Norman: University of Oklahoma Press, 1974.

Pirtle, Caleb, III, and Michael F. Cusack. *Fort Clark: The Lonely Sentinel on Texas' Western Frontier.* Austin: Eakin Press, 1985.

Porter, Kenneth Wiggins. "The Seminole Negro-Indian Scouts." *Southwestern Historical Quarterly* 55 (January 1953).

Stegner, Wallace. *The Gathering of Zion.* New York: McGraw-Hill, 1964.

———. *Mormon Country.* New York: Hawthorn Books, 1942.

Chapter Four: Boom and Bust

Bennett, James D. *Frederick Jackson Turner.* Boston: Twayne Publishers, 1975.

Blevins, Terry W., ed. *Tri-County History: A Centennial.* Limon, Colo.: The Tri-County Centennial, 1989.

DeVoto, Bernard. *Across the Wide Missouri.* Boston: Houghton Mifflin, 1947.

Eberhart, Perry. *Ghosts of the Colorado Plains.* Athens, Ohio: Swallow Press, 1986.

Gowans, Fred R. *Rocky Mountain Rendezvous.* Layton, Utah: Peregrine Smith Books, 1985.

Hudson, John C. "The Plains Country Town." In *The Great Plains: Environment and Culture,* edited by Brian W. Blouet and Frederick C. Luebke. Lincoln: University of Nebraska Press, 1978.

Hulse, James. *Forty Years in the Wilderness: Impressions of Nevada 1940–1980.* Reno: University of Nevada Press, 1986.

———. *The Nevada Adventure: A History.* Reno: University of Nevada Press, 1969.

Limerick, Patricia Nelson. *The Legacy of Conquest: The Unbroken Past of the American West.* New York: W. W. Norton, 1987.

Lingenfelter, Richard E. *Death Valley and the Amargosa: A Land of Illusion.* Berkeley: University of California Press, 1986.

Molinelli, Lambert. *Eureka and Its Resources.* Reno: University of Nevada Press, 1982.

Nelson, Paula M. *After the West Was Won: Homesteaders and Town-Builders in Western South Dakota, 1900–1917.* Iowa City: University of Iowa Press, 1986.

Paxson, Frederic L. *History of the American Frontier 1763–1893.* Boston: Houghton Mifflin, 1924.

Winzeler, Judith K., and Nancy Peppin. *Eureka, Nevada: A History of the Town.* N.p.: Nevada Humanities Committee, 1982.

Chapter Six: Rainbow of the West

DeVoto, Bernard. *Across the Wide Missouri.* Boston: Houghton Mifflin, 1947.

Durham, Philip, and Everett L. Jones. *The Negro Cowboys.* Lincoln: University of Nebraska Press, 1965.

Limerick, Patricia Nelson. *The Legacy of Conquest: The Unbroken Past of the American West.* New York: W. W. Norton, 1987.

Schlissel, Lillian. *Women's Diaries of the Westward Journey.* New York: Schocken Books, 1982.

Stratton, Joanna L. *Pioneer Women.* New York: Simon & Schuster, 1981.

Utley, Robert M. *The Indian Frontier of the American West, 1846–1890.* Albuquerque: University of New Mexico Press, 1984.

Chapter Seven: *El Despoblado*

Thompson, Cecilia. *History of Marfa and Presidio County, Texas.* Austin: Nortex Press, 1985.

Time-Life Books. *The Expressmen.* New York, 1974.

———. *The Gunfighters.* New York, 1974.

Utley, Robert M. *Billy the Kid: A Short and Violent Life.* Lincoln: University of Nebraska Press, 1989.

———. *The Indian Frontier of the American West, 1846–1890.* Albuquerque: University of New Mexico Press, 1984.

Waldman, Carl. *Atlas of the North American Indian.* New York: Facts on File Publications, 1985.

Chapter Eight: Dumping Ground

Fradkin, Philip L. *Fallout: An American Nuclear Tragedy.* Tucson: University of Arizona Press, 1989.

Hage, Wayne. *Storm Over Rangelands: Private Rights in Federal Lands.* Bellevue, Wash.: Free Enterprise Press, 1989.

McHugh, Tom. *The Time of the Buffalo.* Lincoln: University of Nebraska Press, 1972.

Popper, Frank J. "Survival of the American Frontier." *Resources for the Future,* Summer 1984.

Popper, Frank J., and Deborah Epstein Popper. "The Great Plains: From Dust to Dust." *Planning,* December 1987.

Reisner, Marc. *Cadillac Desert.* New York: Viking, 1986.

Robbins, Jim. "Tourism Trap." *Utne Reader,* July/August 1991.

Sprague, Marshall. *A Gallery of Dudes.* Lincoln: University of Nebraska Press, 1972.

Titus, A. Costandina. *Bombs in the Backyard: Atomic Testing and American Politics.* Reno: University of Nevada Press, 1986.

Wheeler, Raymond. "Boom! Boom! Boom! War on the Colorado Plateau." In *Reopening the Western Frontier,* edited by Ed Marston. Washington, D.C.: Island Press, 1989.

Chapter Nine: Old Frontier, Contemporary Frontier

Bennett, James D. *Frederick Jackson Turner.* Boston: Twayne Publishers, 1975.

Bernstein, Richard. "Unsettling the Old West." *New York Times Magazine,* March 18, 1990.

Billington, Ray Allen. *Frederick Jackson Turner: Historian, Scholar, Teacher.* New York: Oxford University Press, 1973.

Cronon, William. "Revisiting the Vanishing Frontier: The Legacy of Frederick Jackson Turner." *The Western Historical Quarterly,* April 1987.

Limerick, Patricia Nelson. *The Legacy of Conquest: The Unbroken Past of the American West.* New York: W. W. Norton, 1987.

McMurtry, Larry. "How the West Was Won or Lost." *The New Republic,* October 22, 1990.

Stegner, Wallace. *The American West as Living Space.* Ann Arbor: University of Michigan Press, 1987.

Turner, Frederick Jackson. "The Significance of the Frontier in American History." Tucson: University of Arizona Press, 1986.

Webb, Walter Prescott. *The Great Frontier.* Lincoln: University of Nebraska Press, 1951.

———. *The Great Plains.* Waltham, Mass.: Blaisdell Publishing, 1931.

Worster, Donald. *Rivers of Empire: Water, Aridity, and the Growth of the American West.* New York: Pantheon Books, 1985.

———. "New West, True West: Interpreting the Region's History." *Western Historical Quarterly,* April 18, 1987.

INDEX